AVATARS OF CONSCIOUSNESS
AWAKEN TO YOUR DIVINE
DESTINY

AVATARS OF CONSCIOUSNESS AWAKEN TO YOUR DIVINE DESTINY

The Extraordinary Truth About Consciousness, Creation & Us

Carol Romine

BALBOA.
PRESS

A DIVISION OF HAY HOUSE

Balboa Press books may be ordered through booksellers or by contacting:

Balboa Press
A Division of Hay House
1663 Liberty Drive
Bloomington, IN 47403
www.balboapress.com
1-(877) 407-4847

Because of the dynamic nature of the Internet, any web addresses or links contained in this book may have changed since publication and may no longer be valid. The views expressed in this work are solely those of the author and do not necessarily reflect the views of the publisher, and the publisher hereby disclaims any responsibility for them.

ISBN: 978-1-4525-4603-2 (sc)
ISBN: 978-1-4525-4604-9 (hc)
ISBN: 978-1-4525-4602-5 (e)

Library of Congress Control Number: 2012901200

The author of this book does not dispense medical advice or prescribe the use of any technique as a form of treatment for physical, emotional, or medical problems without the advice of a physician, either directly or indirectly. The intent of the author is only to offer information of a general nature to help you in your quest for emotional and spiritual well-being. In the event you use any of the information in this book for yourself, which is your constitutional right, the author and the publisher assume no responsibility for your actions.

Printed in the United States of America

Balboa Press rev. date: 06/12/2012

This book is lovingly and gratefully dedicated to the first light of divine conscious love that holds our beingness and guides our way.

Contents

Foreword by Angela King, AP, DOM   ix
Introduction   xiii
Terminology   xix

PART 1: CONSCIOUSNESS   1
Chapter 1:   The Quest Begins—My First Altered Conscious State   3
Chapter 2:   Misperception Brings Fear   10
Chapter 3:   A Relationship Recognized—Grace's Extended Hand   15
Chapter 4:   Seismic Activity—Tremors of Higher Consciousness   20
Chapter 5:   The Dream Changes   26
Chapter 6:   Destiny Makes Itself Known   30
Chapter 7:   Love = Conscious Connectedness to All   34
Chapter 8:   A Clash—Consciousness Shifts Sideways, Taking Reality   39
Chapter 9:   Simultaneous, Multi-State Consciousness Breaks Through   50
Chapter 10:   Paranormal—the New Normal in Quantum Reality   65
Chapter 11:   Fate vs. Free Will   75
    Fate = Predestined Possibility; Free Will = Choice
Chapter 12:   Co-Creating—Shaper of Reality and Manifested Destiny   88
Chapter 13:   Nothing About Us Is Coincidental   94

PART 2: CREATION   97
Chapter 14:   Destiny? Oh, I'd Almost Forgotten   99
Chapter 15:   Knocking at Destiny's Door   103
Chapter 16:   That's It?   116
Chapter 17:   Letting It Ride   125
Chapter 18:   Our Subconscious: Vault, Gatekeeper, and Key   127
Chapter 19:   Pulling a Thread in the Tapestry of Divine Consciousness   135
Chapter 20:   Glimpsing the Cornerstone of Awareness   141
Chapter 21:   Leaving Behind the Misperception of Separation   163
Chapter 22:   All Is Not Lost; Nothing Is Gained   180

Chapter 23: Going Back … Where? No Wonder Universe
                Gave Me a Hint   191
Chapter 24: A Threshold of Consciousness Rarely Glimpsed   194

PART 3: US   211
Chapter 25: Setting the Stage—Understanding the Nature of
                Divinity   213
Chapter 26: Divine QUA   217
                Allness Divinity, Onceness Divinity, All-at-Once
                Divinity
Chapter 27: CUSP 10,001 (Pre-Creation)   219
                The Blissful State of Divine QUA
Chapter 28: CUSP 10,000—the Original Act of Creation   223
                The Creation of Collective Human Consciousness
Chapter 29: CUSP 9,999—the Birth of Collective Human
                Consciousness   234
Chapter 30: CUSP 1,999—Our Birth as a New Soul   237
Chapter 31: Awakening to Our Remembrance   242
Chapter 32: Our True Nature of All-at-Once Consciousness   248
Chapter 33: We Long for Oneness   257
Chapter 34: We Are Light of the Same Light, Love of the Same
                Love   260
Chapter 35: The One Voice Within All of Us   264
Chapter 36: Framing Awareness   273
Chapter 37: Puzzle Piece One—Where Is My Home?   274
Chapter 38: Puzzle Piece Two—What Am I?   277
Chapter 39: Puzzle Piece Three—Who Am I?   283
Chapter 40: Puzzle Piece Four—Why Am I Here?   293
Chapter 41: Puzzle Piece Five—What Is My Destiny?   302
Chapter 42: The Ever-Unfolding You   305
Chapter 43: Be Your True Nature   308
Chapter 44: The Vibration of Love   313
                Thought and Feeling … Identical in Knowing
Chapter 45: Bridging Spirituality and Science   317
                All-at-Once Consciousness … The Unifying Concept

Epilogue   331
Afterword   341
Acknowledgments   343
About the Author   347

Foreword

The search for connection to our Source is simply a journey through our own subconscious mind. When we begin to unravel this mystery, we reveal the hidden wisdom of the ages, boundless and without form, infinite through time and space, and all within us. Carol Romine has taken this journey and expressed it through written word to help us all understand why we often feel separate and how we can again feel whole.

I had the auspicious opportunity to cross Carol's path in my practice two years ago. Carol originally came to my office seeking energy balancing to eliminate blocks that were keeping her from enjoying physical and spiritual well-being. However, Carol is an amazing mystic, and what began as any typical patient treatment soon turned into something beyond human understanding. Our work together was a gift from Source, not only in what it healed and awakened within Carol but also in how it would be used to help others on their spiritual quests.

In my practice, I use many integrative modalities to help people heal physically, emotionally, and spiritually. As an acupuncture physician, I use acupuncture and Oriental medicine to balance the body's energy system. I also incorporate classical homeopathy, nutritional supplementation, detoxification, qi gong, or guided imagery into a patient's treatment plan to create lasting health and wellness on all levels. In all that I do to help patients, I remain in awe and most inspired by the healing that occurs by using Neuro-Emotional Technique (NET).

NET is a powerful kinesiology technique that allows the patient to access his or her subconscious mind and unveil the emotional blocks that reside there. These blocks have been created from past events and continue, often unknowingly, to influence current beliefs and behaviors. These emotional blocks can be held in a person's organs, meridian systems/energy fields, or thought fields. When a person has emotional blocks stuck in the subconscious, all the positive thinking in the world will be hard pressed to overcome their power, and most often, despite the best intentions, what the person wants will not manifest. That could mean anything from perfect health, abundance, positive self-image, intimate connection with a partner, or a deep, meaningful connection to Source. I have witnessed profound healing as a result of using NET to remove these stuck emotional blocks, and I feel it is one of the most powerful kinesiology techniques ever created.

Kinesiology, or muscle testing, as it is commonly called, is used to determine the body's response to physical, energetic, conceptual, or emotional stimuli. Kinesiology is used by many practitioners, including acupuncturists, chiropractors, physical therapists, nutritionists, and energy workers. Although each of these practitioners may use kinesiology to assess the body for different reasons, the method is universally the same. To test someone using kinesiology, I will ask the patient to hold his or her arm out straight in front of his or her body. I will then ask the patient to hold his or her arm strong as I apply a slight downward pressure to the forearm. It is not an arm-wrestling contest, and there is no reason the patient cannot keep his or her arm straight and strong. However, if a certain point on the patient's body is contacted at the same time as the practitioner applies the pressure and that point corresponds either to an area of pain or an organ that is out of balance, the patient's arm will weaken instantly and drop down. It is amazing to see. My personal favorite is testing a six-foot-two body builder who thinks there is no way his arm will fall, but kinesiology knows no limits, and his arm falls like a wet noodle when the stimuli tested doesn't agree with him.

As an example, you can hold a particular food in your hand, and if your body resonates with the energy of that food, your muscle test will remain strong, even with very firm pressure. If your body's balance is disturbed by that food, the muscle test will weaken, even with the slightest pressure. The same goes for thoughts, memories, words, pictures, and people, as they are all simply another type of energetic vibration. If you think a negative thought, your muscle test will weaken. If someone says something negative to you while you're being tested, your arm will weaken if you're susceptible to his or her negativity. If you say, "My name is Joe" and your name *is* Joe, your arm will stay strong with pressure. If you say, "My name is Joe" and your name is *not* Joe, your arm will fall weak even with minimal pressure.

When I first examined Carol, I found she had several emotional blocks in her organs that needed to be cleared. That was the only thing "usual" about Carol's sessions. Quite soon into her treatment, Carol's arm would muscle test as "weak" at conception, when testing for the original event that was still affecting her body in a negative way. We then decided to test the concept of "prior to conception," and this would weaken as well. This indicated to me that her present-day issues were stemming from events that happened prior to conception or from past lives.

Carol was not surprised; as a mystic, she knew of past lives already. However, we began to experiment with kinesiology, using the concepts of NET, but creating our own process to determine the events of these past lives and how the emotions experienced during them were still blocking her in the present day. Much amazing information came forth, and it always helped Carol to understand and heal at a deep level.

As we continued, concepts came forth that were beyond human form. Carol had past lives as an angel, spirit forms, and even pure energy and consciousness. The further back Carol went in her sessions, the more profound the revelations became—revelations about connection to Source, the misperceived split, and the interrelationship of consciousness and unconsciousness.

Carol knew that Source was guiding this process and allowing us to perceive these profound glimpses, as it was her destiny to connect what unfolded in these sessions to a lifetime of divine conscious interaction and bring forth the message in this book. I was in awe but felt that I, too, was being guided to facilitate this process.

I have been humbled and forever changed by what I have experienced through Carol's sessions. I feel a closer connection to Source and have been blessed immeasurably by her journey. It is my hope that as you read this book, your questions will be answered, your fears will be allayed, your consciousness will expand, and you'll be left with a profound sense of peace, love, and connection.

—*Angela King*, **AP, DOM**
Acupuncture Physician, Doctor of Oriental Medicine
Florida—November, 2010

Introduction

Haven't we each wondered, to one extent or another, about all those great mysteries surrounding who we are, why we are here, and where we are going individually and as mankind? Hasn't nearly everyone gazed up at the sky trying to figure out how all of this really works— God, the seen universe, earth, life, our beginning, our purpose, and our future?

There are many theories, but even the most faithfully held beliefs have holes once you triangulate the tenets of that belief to your intuition and experiential reality. (Experiential reality is when we find ourselves experiencing something perceived by us to be impossible in our conventional reality world, yet, it happens, so it is not impossible at all, only incomprehensible.)

Even seeking answers from spiritual beings among us who have gained enlightenment or glimpsed ultimate truth is a road riddled with difficult material that is seemingly only intended for masters themselves to comprehend. This road often requires not only spiritual commitment but also physical sacrifice of human and worldly comforts to pursue.

There seems to be no single, surefire way to find the answers we seek—only promises that the road to awareness is either this way or that from people who certainly appear more enlightened, loving, or beatific than us.

Many adored beings—spiritual masters, teachers, saints, mystics, philosophers, and others—have brought us spiritual truth throughout the ages, and always love is the resounding core of any message. Yet human translation of those messages seems to split off into varying factions, all believing their interpretation is the only truth that opens the pathway to eternity and that they alone have favor with divinity.

At a young age, I was perplexed by all those versions of truth. To me, it was a clue that something was not quite right about any of it. If at our core we are all one, connected as divinity, then truth must be true for all. Truth cannot be true for one and not for another. It is impossible. Why, then, are there all the disparities, division, and disagreements when it comes to truth?

Truth unites, it does not divide, and truth need not be defended, as it requires nothing from us to make it true. Deep inside, this was my belief, even as a child.

This is a true story that began with a transcendent, life-altering experience that occurred when I was nine years old, which was the beginning of the unfolding of divine knowing within me. It was an unfolding centered within a consciousness enveloped in a tapestry of mysticism and human embodiment. Threads of light, love, and truth were woven throughout all conscious expressions and lifetimes, manifesting in this lifetime through a chain of events and a pathway guided by what can only be viewed as divine design.

It took nearly an entire life lived before the story could unfold. Why? Because the story is proof of the existence of all that we have longed to touch within ourselves and know about the mysteries of whom we are, our origins, our purpose, and our destiny.

This is not an autobiography but rather a series of energetic experiences revealing varied and multiple states of consciousness that eventually culminated in an astonishing period that tied together the experiences of this lifetime to *The Extraordinary Truth About Consciousness, Creation & Us.* It isn't intended to support or argue for one belief over another but rather to shatter the original misperception we all carry from the Creation of collective human consciousness (the beginning). It is that original misperception that is at the very center of all our feelings of suffering, fear, pain, confusion, and separation.

It is a profound story, one that weaves throughout consciousness and lifetimes and finds at its center a girl in this lifetime who perceives herself to be just a typical girl, with only one thing that appears unusual: her relationship with a divine presence she remembered from age four—when she nearly died.

I always thought of myself as just a girl existing on earth in a physical body, deeply connected through love to an unseen Benevolence (divinity); yet, that unseen relationship was the cornerstone of everything that would be known, awakened, and remembered within me—abilities and experiences beyond explanation in this physical world.

Every word, every event, and every awareness I write about is true. Though I had no conscious knowledge that the unusual life I was leading had been destined as part of the story, it shouldn't really have surprised me when it worked out that way, as it was a perfect way to reveal the story of us—through the experiences and consciousness of one of us as living proof of who and what we really are at the center of our beingness.

Many of us have always felt there is something about this lifetime that is special—a purpose for us being here now. There is. We all want to experience (consciously or unconsciously) the transition—the shift occurring within collective human consciousness.

The amazing moment when everything crystallized in my consciousness was definitely a picture worth a thousand words. However, this book will take significantly more words than that, for it involves so much more than just a thought, a concept, or one event. It is the story that unfolded through a lifetime of interacting with Benevolence. It is a story that relates not just to me personally but also one that embodies and reveals the story of all of us, answering questions that have befuddled us since the beginning of time—revealing the truth of who we are and the ultimate purpose of life.

In telling this story, it is my intent that you will finally know the answers to questions held deeply within yourself; you will understand who you are and your purpose in being here; you will never again suffer from feelings of spiritual separation or be afraid of where you are now, where you have been, or where you are going; and most importantly, by consciously understanding, you will pierce the veil of original misperception and begin awakening to your true nature.

The wonderful part of the story is that you are in for the most incredible of all surprises. Actually, it is the best surprise ever imaginable—not only because the age-old mysteries will be solved but also because what you embody is profoundly fantastic!

I've never been one for ruining surprises or storylines, even when friends would beg me to tell them. Why? Because some stories, some surprises, are far too wonderful to have them stolen away because we don't believe anything will really surprise us all that much.

This book is for each of you, in hopes that you may not only be as surprised as a child filled with wonderment and joy when unwrapping the present of you to yourself but also that you may find love, peace, comfort, support, understanding, and remembrance in these words, enabling you to know that now is the time for you to awaken to your divine destiny.

—Carol Romine
11-11-11

We are one consciousness ... one light,
expressing through the multi-faceted
prism of our own essence.

Terminology

What does "Avatars of Consciousness™" mean?

"Avatars of Consciousness" is a perfect description of what we are and how we consciously extend from one state of consciousness to another, from one lifetime to another, from one dream to another, and from one dimension to another in our journey of awakening. (A more detailed explanation follows in *"Chapter 38."*)

What does "All-at-Once Consciousness™" mean?

"All-at-Once Consciousness" describes the true nature of divine energy. We tend to think of ourselves as a oneness of divinity (a part of the whole of divinity) or as the allness of divinity (the entirety of divinity). In truth, we are not just a oneness of divinity nor the allness of divinity. We are divinity as each, as every, and as all onenesses simultaneously. (A more detailed explanation follows in *"Chapter 32."*)

What does "mystic" mean?

A *"mystic"* is someone who seeks direct communion with the divine through following an inner path centered on experiencing divine love through prayer, meditation, and contemplation. This quest is deeply internal, always initiated through a pure love of the divine and a thirst to experience ultimate truth ... absolute reality.

Mystics often experience transcendent states of consciousness beyond normal human perception, including personal communion (exchanging thoughts, feelings, and energetic connectedness) with the divine. A mystic can be from any culture, race, or religious background, but always at the center of any mystic's being is a devotion to the divine that is unbounded by religious doctrines or human influence. Although a mystic may demonstrate abilities perceived to be beyond normal human perception (clairvoyance, prophecy, soul-to-soul communication, energetic healing, etc.), developing these abilities is not the focus of a mystic. The mystic's only intention is experiencing spiritual union with divinity.

Always the mystic seeks to know the grace of divine love through the invisible mysteries of pure consciousness and ultimate truth. Thus, a mystic often experiences deep insights and possesses abilities that enable him or her to convey, express, or transfer the essence of divine love, divine truth, and divine energy through their words or teachings or energetic touch.

What does "higher (divine) consciousness" or "higher self" mean?

This terminology is used to describe thoughts, feelings, insight, and awareness that transcend our normal waking consciousness.

"Higher (divine) consciousness" is your own divine all-knowingness (*"higher self"*), experienced through intuitive thoughts and feelings. It is not outside of you; it is always simultaneously present and ever flowing as you. There is no difference between higher (divine) consciousness and higher self. They are identical in nature.

What do "Universe" and "seen universe" mean?

"Universe" is a collective word that refers to the essence of divine energy. It is the entirety of divinity as any thought, feeling, state of being, or form of expression. It is divine perfection; all divine knowing, and all divine love.

"Seen universe" is a term referring to the known world of matter that we physically occupy. It is our perceived or seen world.

Interchangeable terminology for "divine energy":

The terms used in this book to describe *"divine energy"* (divinity; God; Benevolence; perfection; pure or divine love; divine consciousness; Supreme Being; oneness; Creator; benevolent presence; Source; soul consciousness or divinity; allness consciousness or divinity; All-at-Once Consciousness or divinity) are all identical in nature.

As a child, I came to my belief in a benevolent presence (God) because I remembered being in the presence of pure Benevolence in a place of perfection and bliss. Whatever you believe—whether in

God, Christ, Buddha, Source, or any other divine presence or power, even your own divine beingness—it is all the same vibration at its core ... divine conscious love. So, when the words divinity, God, divine consciousness, Source, Benevolence, perfection, or any similar term is used, associate it with any interchangeable term for divine energy that is acceptable to you.

Part 1

Consciousness

We misperceive that what we consciously think is all that constitutes awareness. We perceive our own consciousness as the boundary of awareness. Actually, individual consciousness is merely the threshold of an ocean of consciousness (all awareness) within us. When drops of that ocean of awareness unfold in us as thoughts or feelings, we are living divine consciousness as both ocean and drop: All-at-Once Consciousness™.

Consciously recognizing the ocean of consciousness, our divine consciousness, no matter what form it takes or appearance it makes in our lives, is our awakening to the All-at-Once Consciousness that is our true nature.

This is the beginning, my beginning, when drops first began forming within my consciousness.

It is the story of where all those drops eventually led—to the truth about consciousness and to the truth about us. We are not just observers of the ocean of consciousness, nor are we just participants as ocean of consciousness drops; rather, we are consciousness itself.

All that separates us from our own awakening is awareness of what we already know but do not *remember*.

Chapter 1

The Quest Begins—My First Altered Conscious State

Seek truth and light will come.
Seek light and love will come.
Seek love and all will come.

Age nine. This is really the only place and the only point from which this story can begin. That is the moment that set me firmly upon the path I have walked from that point until now, though at the time I did not have full comprehension of just what a moment it was—just what a life it would unfold. I guess that's as it should be.

Before this time, I was as most children—happy and free, inquisitive, and actively investigating my little world. With me in this joint pursuit was my twin brother, Michael. He was my cohort, even at times my minion when I was the ringleader, coaxing him into great adventures and even trouble, the punishment for which he accepted without blame or finger pointing. He is a very sweet and very wonderful companion—then and all through my life. It was a relatively carefree life, one that shortly would change forever.

It was a beautiful summer day; the sky was that unmistakable blue that each of us recognizes as the perfect summer blue. There were big, billowy clouds and even smaller, fluffy ones drifting gently by, pushed by a slight breeze. The sun was shining, and warmth enveloped the spirit. It was a perfect day for playing the cloud shape game. We all play it. It involves lying on your back, facing up to the sky, and looking at clouds to recognize shapes of animals, people, etc., only to watch them transform before your very eyes into something quite different, transfixed by the possibilities ahead.

It was one of my favorite things to do when I was alone, and it was something I did alone, as others seemed to bore long before I reached maximum enjoyment of the game. I could do it for hours—as long as

3

the clouds were present, the day smelled happy, and the sounds were peaceful.

This day, in late summer of my ninth year, I had gone out to the front yard, plopped down, and begun my favorite pastime. It was nothing unusual to begin with, just drifting and pleasure in its simplest form. There were horses and knights and dogs and many things to keep me engaged in the game.

At some point in the process, a subtle shifting of my energy occurred and now all I seemed to be thinking about was God and the world, not about the animals I recognized in the clouds or thoughts about my little life in general. I was fully immersed in these random thoughts about life and God and the world and how everything works.

It is not at all unusual for me to be thinking about God. When I was four years old, I remembered God—not from being in Sunday school or Bible readings or other promptings. The remembrance was triggered when I almost died during tonsil surgery. Afterward, there was a knowing in me that I had been in a place with a benevolent presence that I would learn to call God. From that point on in my life, the deep and pure love carried in my remembrance prompted me to search for God—a search that led me many places inside of myself, for that was where the benevolent memory was anchored.

So, at age nine, in this space of a brilliant summer day, I was engaged in following the thoughts and following the questions to what I felt would be answers. The thoughts became deeper and deeper. *Who am I? Where is God? How did I come to be here? What is the reason for my being here?* More and more questions flowed through me. They were questions that years later I realized came from another part of me beyond a nine-year-old girl—questions that came from my soul.

The more I questioned, it seemed, the deeper I drifted into the sky, pulled as an energetic magnet into Universe, though I did not recognize it as Universe at the time. But I did recognize that I felt different. I felt light, transfixed in the moment, held captive in a space, drifting closer and closer to what I believed were answers to all those questions that flowed out of me. The sky turned from bright blue to deep, midnight blue as I drifted deeper into my thoughts. The deeper I drifted, the higher I went. That was a very strange feeling to a nine-year-old girl. Now I realize I was experiencing an altered state of consciousness, but back then I was feeling all and nothing at the same time. All physical realities of me fell away, and I was pure energy, pure thought, and pure love—going someplace, yet still in the same position in my yard.

At one point, the voice of Benevolence filled my mind with the thought, *Do you really want to know?* The answer came from deep within my being and was a resounding, "*Yes!*"

My desire to know became so expanded that I literally felt myself in a limitless state of being. My intent was so focused that there was nothing else in my world other than the thought and the intention to know, and that focused intention and desire, coupled with my knowing that God did, in fact, exist, coalesced in one point, one moment where everything stood perfectly still. I was no longer flying up out into the sky, into space, into this vast place. I was held in absolute stillness. That stillness was the presence of divinity, the presence of pure love, and in that stillness, the presence was answering me. There were no words. There were no pictures. There was nothing; yet, everything—all love, all knowing—was energetically flowing through me. I felt deeply aware of the benevolent presence not only around me and in me but also as me. It was a feeling of love beyond love—love so fulfilling there was nothing beyond that love that could ever be experienced. It was pure bliss.

I was not experiencing it as hopes or belief or daydreams. Especially, it was not then nor ever has been imagination; it was the still vibration of love. It was the stillness of God. All was given in that moment. Time stood still. It seemed as though I was there forever and only a moment at the same time. There was no time and no space. It was everything and nothingness at once. I felt such peace, such pure love, and such connectedness that there was nothing to capture it, to hold it in order to express it. For not one single expression nor word nor symbol was capable of holding the space contained therein. It was all expression, everything, all at once—but there was nothing at the same time. It was as though Universe was at a point between breathing in and breathing out, where there was no motion at all. There was no motion in my body, not even the sensation of breathing. I was held in absolute stillness, content beyond all expression. Love of such magnitude filled me that not one emotion or perception remained unknown. It was as though love itself carried all thoughts, for I was not only feeling absolute love, but I was also feeling absolute awareness.

In that moment, the knowing of everything was imparted to me through that perfect stillness—answers not only to all my questions but also to the allness that is the very fabric of all creation, the entirety of Universe.

And then at the precise moment that I consciously realized I was in absolute awareness, I was instantly back in my little girl body on that front lawn, and I could no longer remember that which I had fully known only a moment before. Imagine that you knew the entire contents of a book—each word, each phrase, each picture, all knowing, and all feelings expressed within the book. Then, at the very moment of absolute awareness, you have no remembrance of anything contained in that book. It's as though the book slams shut at the exact moment the entirety of its contents are known. Yet, in that fleeting moment, there is no doubt that you were fully aware of it all.

All awareness was both there and not there in the same moment. It is indescribable, really. How can I hold all knowing and then, at the very moment of that conscious realization, have no remembrance of the knowing, as though those two perceptions (knowing and not knowing) existed simultaneously? But that is exactly what happened. It was so profound an experience that my child's mind searched for a way to pull back any specific detail about what I knew I had just experienced—but nothing, not one single concept, was intelligible. My mind could not consciously grasp anything specifically revealed just a moment before, yet I knew in that moment I was in a state of complete awareness—all-knowingness.

As I struggled with the incomprehensible (that I know, yet I don't remember what I know), I was still the little girl, lying in the grass, but the clouds were now turning, as the day was disappearing into night. And it was cool, as though rain were coming. I cannot say how long in minutes or hours I was held in that still space, but in conscious time, I was there only a moment and forever at once. It was *the* single moment of my entire life. It is the moment I have followed throughout all experiences in this lifetime, in hopes of once again re-experiencing the indescribable bliss of it all—all that *love*, all that *knowing* connected through a profound sense of peace, perfection, and *belonging*.

For a long time, I remained motionless in the grass of my front yard, as I sensed any movement on my part would shatter the peace and perfection I felt. And as it should be in these types of profound experiences, as I lifted up off that grass, I felt different. I was still the same me I've always been; yet I was something else at the same time. I realized I wasn't just me anymore. I felt a presence with me. The realization came that I was not alone, nor had I ever been alone—though prior to that moment, I had never perceived this truth.

Previously, I was only capable of wondering, but now I felt a deep sense of knowing as well as purpose. I did not remember exactly what it was a knowing of, as a veil had flowed over the experience and only the details occurring up until the moment of that ecstatic bliss of all-knowing love could be grasped by my conscious mind. I was certain it all happened, because I experienced it, but I was incapable of expressing exactly what it was that I had experienced in that moment of all-knowingness, for I experienced it while in a state of consciousness that I no longer occupied. I knew I knew the answers, but I couldn't remember what they were. I felt a little disconnected from my body and from my mind for a while after, as though I was realigning with physical reality. But there is no doubt that I experienced this event and brought back a knowing. Later, as I grew and experienced, I would rely upon this knowing, as it was my steadfast companion in a world littered with words with false meaning and feelings with no sensitivity.

I stood up, walked from my yard to the street in front of my house, and began moving as though my feet and the sheer act of walking would take me home. My mind wondered at what was compelling me, because I was already in front of my house. Yet I was filled with the deepest of longings to find my way home. Most likely I would have continued walking, but it began to rain, and my physical senses returned due to my realized discomfort of being wet and cold from the rain. I don't know just how far I would have walked that day if the sun had continued to shine, but I do know that I now had a conscious awareness that home was some place other than the house I lived in on Forest Street. Now rooted deep inside of me was the need to find something, to remember something, and I believe the act of walking was activating that intention inside of me.

This feeling, this longing, became the driving force behind my life. I no longer skipped as a child through my life unaware but rather walked with a guided purpose, a more conscious awareness of myself, my surroundings, and most importantly, my thoughts and feelings. Those aspects—my mind and my feelings—shifted dramatically from that point forward. I was still a child in a physical world, but I no longer was bound by physicality alone. My feelings and my thoughts allowed me access to other states of consciousness, though I did not realize this as such for quite a while, as I had no frame in which to border this awareness. My conscious understanding had not caught up to my inner awareness. It was as though I moved to a beat, a rhythm within my soul that I had no conscious awareness that I was following. My life became an ongoing process of perceiving through my consciousness, linked to higher awareness, then pondering what I saw, what I felt, what I believed—and eventually what I knew. It wasn't then nor is it now a confusing state, as it just seems to be naturally occurring within my consciousness.

There was me, the physical being, perceiving through my eyes and feeling through my heart, but there was also another essence of me, a more spiritually aligned me, interacting with my physical consciousness. Sometimes a thought would just pop into my mind, a feeling would come over me, or a knowing would just be there. Still other times, when I could not comprehend exactly what was occurring or why, I found myself squirreling away the experience—holding it in a perfect state of limbo, along with all the thoughts and emotions of the moment, knowing the why or connectedness of it would come further down the road. Most importantly, the phrase, "Just because that's the way it is" was not a phrase easily accepted by me, as it meant no real explanation was available. Outwardly, I appeared to accept the reasons given by the reflectors of my questions—books, people, even experts—but inwardly the ponderings continued. My child's mind held the thought that if I could just connect all the dots and gain understanding, it would surely lead me home. Home was always the destination, and longing was the pathway of that intention—to somehow get back to that place of benevolent bliss I remembered.

My heartfelt belief was that experiences and perceptions of truth would eventually lead me home; of this I was certain, especially later on in my life while chasing down spiritual footprints left many lifetimes ago.

For now, though, at age nine, I had just consciously set my foot upon the path and I knew where I wanted to go—back to the place of all love and all knowingness I had just remembered, reunited with the benevolent presence I knew to be God filled with the answers to questions locked deep within my soul.

Chapter 2

Misperception Brings Fear

I am more a prisoner of myself than
walls could ever make me.

At age nine, I had experienced pure love and was securely going about the path of self and universal discovery. I was in my own world in gentle pursuit of knowing God, the Universe, and myself. It was not an all-absorbed pursuit but rather one that was kept hidden by the presence of a child experiencing fun, wonderment, and peace. It only skipped through my mind during quiet times of reflection, interaction with benevolent beings, or at certain events.

One of those events occurred in my fourteenth year. My father was working and would arrive home in about a half an hour—long before my mother, who worked in Chicago and relied on train schedules and travel time, as we lived in a small town approximately an hour away. I'd decided to lie down on the couch and await my father's arrival before beginning dinner. It was a peaceful, lovely day. The front door was open (no locked doors back then—no need; there was no thought of crime nor fear of it), and I heard the neighbor mowing his lawn and smelled freshly mown grass. The back of my head rested on the couch's armrest, and directly behind me was the dining room that connected to the kitchen, where there was a staircase leading down to the basement. My eyes drifted to the clock, which read 4:00. I was not sleepy, but I found the clock sounds, the day's smell, and the peace flowing through me causes me to drift into what I believed was sleep. It was no sleep like I'd ever experienced before, however.

My eyes appeared to be open, as I could clearly see the clock in front of me on the wall. But strangely, I could also see all around me—the open front door to my right and the dining room directly behind me with an archway to the left, leading into the kitchen. It's as though my eyes are above me seeing everything. I was in this state for only a minute when I realized I heard footsteps coming up the basement stairs. But they were not my father's footsteps. I knew this because my father is an amputee and his natural footfalls have a stepping, clicking, stepping rhythm caused by the prosthesis. The thought flooded my mind that someone I didn't know had entered the house and was now climbing the stairs toward me. I felt tremendous fear. Next the thought popped into my head to just jump up, run to the stairway door, and lock it, as the door was already closed. My confidence was not very strong, but I was young and athletic and thought I could at least get the door locked, keeping the upstairs part of the house safe from violation, before I ran out the front door for help. I believed it to be a viable plan, as I recognized that the footfalls were very slow and deliberate and did not seem at all hurried. It was almost as though the person intended me to hear.

My plan was formed, and I leaped into action. Weird. I just jumped up off the couch, but my body did not move, not one inch. There was no movement at all. Okay, it was just a dream. Right? But why, then, did I feel fully conscious, fully awake? I'd never had a dream such as this. I tried once more to move and realized that I was completely frozen. At the same moment, I also realized this was no dream. There was definitely someone coming (actually, now I sensed two people, two presences coming), and I could not wake up; I could not move. Panic and fear now manifested into screaming as loudly as I could for help. Surely the neighbor, who had stopped mowing (as I no longer heard the lawn mower) would hear my screams and rescue me. My voice would carry through the open front door to where he stood in his yard across the street. I was screaming as loudly as I could, yet my terrified body emitted no sound, no screams; only a slight, almost inaudible whimper escapes my mouth. I could not move, and I could not scream; fear beyond reason surrounded me.

My full attention turned to my options. I realized there were none except to fight with all my spirit, with all my will. Tears were flowing down my face. I felt the wetness on my cheeks, and I realized my eyes could cry, my heart could race, my mind could think; but that was all that can be done in this state. What's happening? I had no former point of reference for what I was experiencing. Yes, throughout my life I had visitors—angels in my room at night, prophetic dreams, and knew things without knowing why or how. But this—what was this?

As all these thoughts were rushing through my mind. I was somehow believing if I could just figure this out, I would know what to do to prevent whatever happened next and save myself from untold harm. Then I realized the footfalls had stopped as the person had reached the top of the stairs. I heard the door opening—there was the squeak of the doorknob turning—renewing my terror. My next awareness was that there were now two entities standing at my head directly behind where I was lying on the couch. One was shorter and appeared as an energy field with no definition; and the taller being appeared as a man, clothed, but the vibration emanating was spiritual, not human.

At this very moment I was experiencing such conflicting thoughts and emotional reactions, I was not sure what to believe. On one hand, I was feeling absolute terror about the entire experience, while at the same time, I was feeling only love and benevolence from these spiritual beings—nothing at all threatening in their energy or their intention. Why, then, was my mind filled with terror, even when there was no threat—nothing to fear? Eventually, fear completely took over, negating all other feelings, and I continued fighting the entire experience in my mind, questioning how any of it could be real or happening, as I was wide awake yet not awake at the same time.

The only thought that prevailed was that I had lost my mind. My father would find me dead or with my sanity gone. I was saddened by this thought, as my family had some rough times due to my father's illness and my death would land a devastating blow to my mother. I realized I didn't want to die—not so much for me but for the pain it would cause my family. Many thoughts were racing through my mind, causing me to focus on a way in which to move through this event, remaining sane and alive. I was only fourteen, for God's sake—that's too young to go crazy for no reason.

I was sending out mental cries for help to God or anyone who would save me from what I was on the edge of experiencing. What happened next was not at all what I expected—what I had prepared to endure. The man-like spiritual being extended his hand and gently and lovingly touched my forehead. I heard words coming from him—but no voice, no sound, carried these words. His words were carried as an energetic thought that filled my mind. They were six little words that stole my breath: "Not yet; she's not ready yet." His hand fell away, and the spirit-form energies receded via the same route they came, footsteps now retreating down the basement stairs.

Upon their leaving, my first thoughts were: *Oh, my God, what did "not yet" mean? They must be coming back again—sometime in the future.* All I focused my attention on was that phrase, "Not yet, she's not ready yet." My mind leapt to the conclusion that the meaning of this phrase was that there would be continuing fork tests for doneness by unseen forces throughout my life. It was truly the most traumatic event of my young life, yet I couldn't even quantify it with a statement that it was real. It was not real in the sense of the physical world or one that people would normally recognize or accept as real. But without a doubt, it happened. It was real, for it happened when I was awake, which at this point in my life was the gauge of reality. (Later that marker would definitely shift as the true nature of divine consciousness and reality unfolded in my conscious awareness.)

As I looked at the clock, I realized twenty minutes had passed, though it only felt like a moment. Where was I for twenty minutes? How was that even possible?

Within a minute or so of their departure, I felt released from the trance-like state that held me, and I was able to move and sit up fully. Immediately, my fear was receding, and I realized that I was not nearly as afraid in my waking, mobile state.

This was a monumental event in my life—in my spiritual awakening—with the truth behind the experience eluding me for many years. My inability to isolate my emotional reactions until I understood them created a misperception about the entire event. That misperception caused fear to live inside of me in a way I had never before experienced—fear of spiritual contact. My fear was not based on anything that happened, as this spiritual contact was benevolent and kind; there was nothing at all to fear.

So, if there was nothing to fear in the immediate situation, then why was I feeling fear? Something inside of me was triggered by this experience, but there was no basis for it in reality. Though I didn't yet know it, this was the strongest subconscious reaction to any situation

I'd ever experienced in my life. It was the first time that a deep, subconscious fear had made itself consciously known to me through my reaction, although the reason for that reaction would remain unknown for many years. (It was a reason related to my role in this lifetime as a mystic that was bound up in conflicting emotions, locked deeply within my subconscious.)

But for now, at age fourteen, fear of spiritual contact had imprisoned me, creating walls and chaining me to this moment in a way that would prevent me from knowing peace in all moments, making me a prisoner of myself.

Immediately, I lost any interest in questing in spiritual realms, and my mind slammed the door closed to experiencing anything at all paranormal.

Later, I would learn that there are no doors in Universe, so nothing was ever really closed. Universe was just subtly at work on other planes of consciousness.

I was still right where I'd always been, traveling along a path designed by a power much greater than the little me could fathom.

Chapter 3

A Relationship Recognized—
Grace's Extended Hand

As the years continued to unfold, I assumed all the unusual interactions with Universe were over, as nothing really earth shattering occurred. In fact, lots of things happened, but I had basically fallen asleep at the wheel—lulled there by my inability to understand my own spirituality and my relationship with Benevolence.

All of that changed when I was eighteen and the benevolent hand of Grace reached across reality and awakened a new perspective within me, one I would live the rest of my life acknowledging more consciously.

Between those years of fourteen and eighteen, though no momentous spiritual events occurred, there were plenty of subtleties at work. Dreams, feelings, and thoughts about people or events proved accurate, and slowly and strongly my connection with my feelings, my thoughts, and my intuition grew. Somewhere along the way, I realized that a lot of my feelings or thoughts were real—not that it was apparent at the time. It came later, when I consciously recognized that I had "seen" or "known" it beforehand. I learned, like stretching a muscle, that if I lived my life and did not consciously block that other state of awareness, something quite remarkable happened. It was as if there was a perceptive observer co-existing as me.

The most insightful times were when I experienced conflicting energies simultaneously. A person could be saying something with their words, yet my feelings spoke to me of something entirely different. It began very simply, with a thought or a feeling inside of me that uttered, *There's more to this story.*

But I'd never want to intentionally hurt anyone's feelings, so I kept quiet about that other perspective, sensing it was not shown me in order to dispute words or events but rather to hone a perception and learn respect for the path that everyone walks. I only shared it if compelled to do so. Ninety-nine percent of the time, I just interacted in a traditional way, while another part of me energetically sensed other, more subtle things, and that sense grew in depth and perception as I aged and trusted.

By age eighteen, I had become good at recognizing my perceptions, creating a bridge inside of me between two sets of feelings and thoughts. One set was mirrored through physical eyes and limited thoughts while the other, quite different set originated from an unknown place within me. My intuition became the bridge between those two perceptions, and the intuitive bridge was gaining in strength within me. Even though my perceptions were accurate, I did not yet follow my intuition as though it were my guide. Instead, I viewed these perceptions as superfluous information rather than insights that needed to be followed or that might prove crucial to my survival.

I was about to learn just how inaccurate my attitude toward my perceptions had been, and the strength of my intuitive bridge had never been more tested than by what I was about to experience.

There are many moments in all of our lives that can instantly transform us because they are so enlightening. They coalesce a group of experiences into a pinpoint of awareness that awakens us to people, situations, ourselves, or even our destiny. Once that moment arrives and awareness dawns, it is our choice to act upon it and use it to launch ourselves in another direction, bringing us closer to an understanding or even our purpose.

A moment like this happened to me when I found myself a newlywed at age eighteen. I was just recently married and seated in a car next to my husband on the way to meet his family and friends in rural Indiana.

It was late at night, and the narrow, two-lane road was the type with which many of us who grow up in rural areas are familiar. It switched from gravel to pavement to dirt, with many stretches of isolation and darkness. For many miles there was nothing but the sound of the wheels on the road transitioning from gravel to dirt and so on, creating a hypnotic state while seated next to a man with whom I was just beginning a new life.

One moment I was a young, peaceful bride, with no thoughts at all of anything but marriage and all the dreams it held of what we would experience together. It was a rare moment of complete contentment, such as I did not often feel. It was as though my entire world would be perfect now that I had a partner to share it with—and one with whom I would build a life.

The next moment a feeling had come over me of such dread, such terror, that I could not speak, nor could I reason the why of it. Logic inside of my head said, "Nothing is wrong," yet a voice deep within me was echoing the thought, *You are in grave danger.* Grave danger? It is a lovely, cool evening. There was no rain, no fog, and no traffic—not a single other car within miles. Yet the feeling persisted, growing stronger until the strangest thing occurred. At the same moment I had the thought of danger, the feeling of an energetic hand, firm and strong, ran up my back from the bottom of my spine all the way to the back of my head. I was completely covered in goose bumps, and the hair on the back of my neck was raised as I felt that hand even now resting on the back of my head; yet, in glancing over at my husband, his hand was still firmly where it had been all along—on the steering wheel.

I could not understand. Had he touched me and quickly removed his hand? No, that couldn't be right, as both my husband's hands were on the steering wheel; yet I still felt that strong hand, even now, on the back of my head. All these thoughts flooded my mind in a matter of a few seconds, when I realized I was also processing on other levels, levels that now told me to stop—stop the car. The words grave danger were gone, replaced by, *"Stop. Stop the car now!"* I kept hearing these words over and over in my mind until I realized that I was not just hearing these words in my mind, but I had been screaming them without any realization of just when I had started screaming—just when those words began flowing out of my voice.

Not all that surprisingly, my husband had already started slamming on brakes. Who wouldn't when someone begins hysterically screaming in the middle of serenity itself? I found myself in a very still place as we came to a stop, my eyes glued to the front of the car, but why I kept staring ahead I couldn't fathom. I was immune to the part of the experience where my husband was now speaking quite loudly, turned directly toward me, expressing how upset he was that my screaming had startled him from a tranquil state. He was yelling words like, "What the hell is the matter with you? Are you crazy?" I realized that I couldn't answer him because I really didn't know why I had screamed, only the feeling deep within me, deep within my knowing, that stopping the car was all that was important. I couldn't look at him—not because I was trying to avoid him and his anger but because I couldn't seem to take my eyes from the front of the car, even with all his accusations demanding my attention.

Within a minute or so, my calm stare drew him to where I was focused, awaiting my perception to clarify the scene before me. I had been thinking about how, just before my screamed words shattered the peace, we had been traveling at a high rate of speed down a dark dirt road with no signs of danger. And now, all that disturbed the prior peace was the dust of the road swirling in front of our car's headlights, dust that was settling, bringing an eerily quiet, otherworldly sense of stillness.

The goose bumps began to rise on my arms as the scene now before us fully unfolded in conscious realization. We had been traveling down an old country road—unfamiliar to either of us—and at the very place in the road where we had come to a stop, the headlights of our car were shining directly below the movement of a passing train on a railroad track with neither crossing gates nor lights. Instantly, we both realized that if we had not stopped when we did, our car would have crashed into the undetected passing train at a speed that would have killed us both. The train was not visible in our headlights while we were driving because the road was pitched at such an angle that our headlights were shining underneath the passing train, creating the illusion of a clear road ahead.

In that moment, many things happened. My then husband freaked out completely—not about our lives being saved by a knowing beyond explanation but because he couldn't fathom anyone like me, and basically, he didn't want to even try. At the same time, I mentally flipped back to the day of my wedding. Upon awakening the morning of my wedding, I was so physically ill I couldn't stand, and even after seeing a doctor, I sat in a chair through my entire wedding ceremony. Earlier that day my mom told me it was a sign for me not to go through with the wedding, which I dismissed at the time.

But tonight, my husband's reaction was validating my mother's warning that my wedding-day illness may well have been a sign to call off the wedding, as I was now seriously wondering about the possibility that this was not the right man for me at all.

As my thoughts shifted from the past into the present moment, overwhelming love and gratitude broke through my heart and my conscious mind as realization poured through me that my sense of well-being and protection was not provided by another person, such as my husband, but through the benevolent relationship that had enveloped me my entire life. Though it had just now made itself physically known to me, the strong hand of Grace had been my constant companion, bringing love, comfort, protection, and insight—insights given through intuition and knowing that until this very moment I'd never been capable of comprehending. I realized all my unusual experiences and perceptions were not accidents or happenstance. They were well-intentioned by Benevolence to awaken me to my inner knowing so I would trust and embrace my relationship with myself and Universe beyond anything reflected in the physical world or another person.

In that moment, I understood my profound connection with Universe. Not only was I never alone, but a beautiful, benevolent energy was also always interacting with me. All along it had been my choice to recognize it, trust it, and allow interaction that would only deepen and strengthen that connection consciously.

It was a pivotal time in my life, one where I consciously chose to trust and act upon what I *sensed* rather than what I *saw;* and in doing so, the scale inside of me forever tipped. No longer would I view what my senses told me as merely scenery or window dressing in my life. From that day forward, I viewed my intuition and my senses as a reflection of my symbiotic relationship with divinity (Benevolence), ongoing my entire life.

This was the moment that solidly aligned me with my knowing, as well as an implicit trust of the benevolent power moving through my life. And although I didn't realize how important a role this relationship was to play, at age eighteen, I knew that I would forever lean toward the knowing I could not see or touch rather than the physical reality I was living.

Chapter 4

Seismic Activity—
Tremors of Higher Consciousness

Within only a year of my wedding, it was clear divorce was imminent, and my parents offered their support and a place to live. Emotionally devastating experiences offer invaluable insights if used as reflection ponds for the true causes behind the experience rather than finger pointing or just pushing forward, daring cause and effect to repeat the lesson once more. Hours spent in solitude and quiet reflection brought an unexpected gift—a connection to myself never before experienced. It was a connection where I learned to really enjoy my own company and even make friends with myself through honestly viewing my motivations and intent rather than telling myself little white lies about who I really was or what I really wanted. We don't lie to friends, but we lie incessantly to ourselves, even about silly things.

This honest connection to myself held firm within me through the struggles of growing out of my teens and into my twenties. It was a time I enjoyed very much, especially when my twin brother unexpectedly moved back to the area and we ended up sharing an apartment. We have always enjoyed a very close bond and each other's company, which is probably normal with twins.

Michael, my brother, is the opposite of me. He very much enjoys going out, partying, and being in the company of many people. I, on the other hand, enjoy more intimate settings with only a few people or my own company, reading books on history, or learning photography.

One night, on our twenty-first birthday, my brother was out celebrating with friends, while I had gone to dinner earlier and ended up home and asleep long before midnight.

One minute I was soundly asleep in my bed and the next, I was launching myself awake, into a sitting position, while screaming Michael's name so loudly that the intensity of the scream reverberated in the stillness of the room. Never in my life had I awakened from sleep so absolutely terrified. Without waiting for my heartbeat to slow or my mind to fully adjust, I threw off the bedcovers and rushed to my brother's room. All I could focus on was whether my brother was safe. My heart was pounding as I turned on his bedroom light and discovered that he was not yet home.

In returning to my bedroom, I noticed it was just after 1:30 and thoughts fill my mind as to what caused me to literally launch myself awake, screaming my brother's name. My intuition told me something was terribly wrong, and I remained awake the rest of the night, praying for my brother's safety and checking out my bedroom window, which faced the parking lot, every half hour or so for his car.

Just before daybreak, I got dressed and walked outside to find my brother asleep in his car, awkwardly sprawled across his front seat. His car was parked helter-skelter across two spaces, down from where he usually parked; that's why I couldn't see his car from my window.

As I softly knocked on his driver side window, I was filled with dread, thinking he might be hurt. His eyes fluttered open, and he seemed a little dazed, but he rolled down the window to speak with me while he continued to pull himself from sleep.

He appeared unharmed, and I was feeling a little foolish for my reaction, but I shared with him that I awakened from sleep screaming and had been up all night worried about him. I was curious as to why he was sleeping in his car when it was so cold outside. Why didn't he come inside? Why was he parked so haphazardly? Though I didn't realize it, I was not sharing much about what I experienced, but rather I was bombarding him with questions.

My brother waited until I was done speaking, as I can talk fast when excited, while his nature is the epitome of peace and calm. Finally, he called me Nina—a shortened version of my family nickname Carolena—and asked me to step back away from the door so he could get out of his car.

As he stood and closed his car door, he began to speak about his night. "I was having a beer after work, with the guys, when Mark decided that we should all go to Chicago for dinner. Only Mark and I ended up going, and we found a great restaurant with tons of good food and really fun people. When the restaurant was closing, we decided it was time to head home. But after I dropped Mark off, I was having a difficult time staying awake. I thought about pulling over to sleep, but my car isn't reliable when it's cold and I was afraid of getting stranded. Instead, I had the radio blasting. I was periodically rolling down my window so the cold air would hit my face or I was slapping myself every once in a while to stay awake. But nothing was working. I kept falling asleep and jerking awake."

My brother took a long breath and looked me in the eyes as he continued, "I must have dozed off for a minute, Nina, because the next thing I heard was your voice screaming my name. It was so loud, it was like you were sitting right next to me in the front seat. Your scream woke me up just in time for me to jerk the steering wheel to the left and miss hitting a tree head on."

By this time, I was stunned speechless as he began walking me around to the right front side of his car where there was excessive damage not noticeable to me while standing at his driver's side door. I began feeling sick as the full weight of what he had told me impacted my emotions. I began crying, and I was shaking as I told him, "Michael, I woke up at 1:30 screaming your name and thought something horrible had happened to you." All the fear and stress over the past many hours poured through me, released in those tears. I was feeling tremendous relief that he was okay, as I now realized there was definitely something wrong all along.

It was very apparent by Michael's expression that he was shocked by what I had just said, and as he reached to give me an emotional hug, he whispered in disbelief, "Nina, you saved my life. It's so weird. I don't understand, but the clock on the dashboard read 1:30 when your scream, your voice, woke me up."

We were both struck silent by our thoughts as we continued to view the serious damage to his car, simultaneously realizing that something quite extraordinary had saved Michael's life. He was going so fast at the time of impact that if he had hit that tree head on, he most likely would have been killed.

I was feeling shock, relief, and astonishment—but mostly, I was feeling overwhelming gratitude that my brother was alive, as I loved him very much.

It was an amazing experience. We were both "unconscious," yet able to communicate in real time through our consciousnesses, altering the outcome of an immediate event (hitting the tree head on) that was unfolding. Extraordinarily, Michael and I were both consciously sharing this event as though no space existed between us. My brother was consciously experiencing the approaching event while asleep behind the wheel of his car and I was consciously sharing the approaching event he was experiencing while I was home, asleep in my bed.

What this said about us, as beings, was completely lost on me at the time, as I was definitely more caught up in the drama of the experience rather than the insight revealed.

During extreme situations such as these, we get rare glimpses of what is really going on below the surface of our awareness. These events are energy spikes of higher consciousness that penetrate our normal conscious awareness.

We perceive these events to be rare, weird, and unnatural occurrences. In actuality, we have many subtle higher consciousness spikes that occur in our lives every day, but we aren't aware of them consciously until they are linked to a monumental anomaly—one where the intensity of the experience makes a huge blip on the radar screen of our awareness. The magnitude of an event brings it into our awareness, much like experiencing a major seismic event. But once we have experienced a significant seismic event, if we allow ourselves, we become much more sensitive to the subtleties of the smaller seismic anomalies occurring long before an incident like this takes place.

For instance, until you experience a major earthquake, you aren't always aware that you've been feeling little tremors for some time because you're unfamiliar with the signs of seismic activity. The major spikes make you aware of not only the event unfolding but also of all the little spikes that have been occurring all along that went unnoticed. This awakens you to their presence and can lead to major leaps in awareness.

Often we take these major spikes (events) and share them as uncanny stories, missing the main purpose of the experience. That's normal. How else do we eventually awaken from a deep sleep unless we are elbowed a little throughout the dream? These events are nudges that can awaken us to so much more than just paranormal events, as that's the least of it.

Think of these events as when unconscious awareness spills over into conscious reality. The awareness is always going on under the surface, spiking into consciousness as energetic subtleties, but until the spike is huge, it doesn't break through our conscious awareness. We just move along, oblivious to all the subtle interactions occurring throughout our lives.

At the time of this seismic higher consciousness event with my brother, I only perceived it as just one more inexplicable experience. And if I had kept on thinking of it in only those terms, a very powerful example of our beingness would have been lost on me.

This experience is verification that consciousness can simultaneously communicate in nonlocal space, whether asleep at home or asleep behind the wheel of a car. Through our individual consciousness, we are simultaneously connected to each other, to everyone, as though no space exists.

Although each of us (my brother and I) were in a sleep state in different locations, our higher conscious minds were linked as though we were sharing the same time and space—as though no distance separated us. My higher consciousness, linked to my sleeping physical consciousness, was aware of my brother approaching that tree, and as I screamed his name out loud in warning, his higher consciousness, linked to his sleeping physical consciousness, heard my scream. My scream simultaneously awakened both of us from sleep, giving him time to avoid hitting the tree head on.

It was an extraordinary experience, not just as a seismic higher consciousness event but because of what it reveals about us and our consciousness. Clearly we possess the phenomenal ability to perceive, connect, and interact with all consciousness. Never again should we feel isolated within our own beingness, as we are never isolated from anything or anyone.

These types of profound experiences not only confirm our connectedness, but they also reflect the true reason for our connectedness. They do not happen because we are merely connected. They happen because all of us are one indivisible divine conscious beingness.

Though it may be difficult to comprehend at this point in the story, there are no separate consciousnesses at all—just the appearance of separation created through our individual human perception—a perception that tells us many things that are not true.

Although these experiences, these seismic events, have no foundation within our conventional reality, when viewed as overflow of our ever-aware higher (divine) consciousness, we begin to perceive them as reflections of the true reality of each of us—reflections of the boundlessness of our consciousness.

But that is a truth we cannot perceive without sometimes experiencing seismic events of awareness, and sometimes we must experience many, many events before we can sense the vibrations, the seismic activity, always occurring within us—the tremors of higher consciousness awakening within our conscious awareness.

Chapter 5

The Dream Changes

For every dream that touches the sky,
a thousand more never find wings.

Life had been good for me these past few years—even wonderful. Yet, there was a restlessness within me that I couldn't reconcile with my life, as I was a person easily entertained who sought laughter and fun and found it in even the simplest of things. It always felt as though restlessness was guiding me toward an unknown destination, a place different than the life envisioned, but with no hints of where it might be.

At age twenty-six, my restlessness perplexed me, as there was nothing whatsoever wrong in my life. For the past couple of years, I had been in a relationship and in love with a man who made life feel magical. We enjoyed a beautiful and fun-loving relationship and were deeply connected on many levels. Though we had a strong emotional and spiritual bond, we did not share spiritual beliefs. He did not believe as I and sometimes even teased me, but I took no offense, as I knew he meant no harm.

Even while with him, I felt this same restlessness but thought I was crazy because I couldn't imagine anything more wonderful than a life with him; he was my dream. I was in love with a wonderful man who was in love with me, yet I could not deny that something else was tapping on a different door inside of me.

I answered that door the day my father died.

My father was an amputee very early in life due to a rare disease that gave him arteries of a man much older. By his fiftieth birthday, he was being hospitalized at Veterans Hospital outside of Chicago for kidney failure, and treatment was not working.

During the time he was in the hospital, I had been experiencing fluctuating periods of heightened waking conscious awareness as well as bouts of insomnia. I did not sleep at night during this time but rather I rested with my eyes closed and drifted, consciously aware of my inability to sleep fully. I couldn't imagine how someone could go months with little or no real sleep, yet it was happening to me. On a deeper level, I probably sensed my father was not going to live, and the emotional turmoil was reflected in my inability to sleep.

On this particular day, my fiancé, Raoul, a Parisian-born restaurateur, was planning to drop me at the hospital so I could meet up with my family and visit my father. I was feeling very quiet and thoughtful while Raoul was hurrying through his prep work so he had enough time to make a round trip to the hospital before he reopened for dinner. I found his easy nature and natural optimism especially soothing on this day, and as we are driving to the hospital, we very much enjoyed comfortable conversation and each other's company, as was typical in our relationship.

Just before arriving at the hospital, I leaned back in my seat and closed my eyes to pray for my father. Immediately I experienced what can only be called a vision. I shared with Raoul that I had just seen a vision of my sister and twin brother standing at the hospital entrance behind a high wall of hedges, smoking and waiting to tell me my father had just died. Where they were standing was out of sight until you reached the front door, and only then were they visible if you turned your head to the right, as they were standing back from the entrance, completely hidden by a wall of thick, tall hedges.

Although Raoul had planned to drop me off at the front entrance so he could hurry back to his restaurant in time for dinner service, I asked him to park the car and walk with me to the front because of the vision I'd seen. Initially, Raoul dismissed my vision as any sort of premonition, believing it instead to be a dream from briefly falling asleep. I assured him it wasn't a dream, as I'd experienced these types of visions before and they always manifested as seen. He was very gentle with me as he told me he was certain my father was fine. There was concern in Raoul's eyes as he took my hand and squeezed it lovingly. He urged me to only visit with my father for a short time and then to go home and get some rest. From Raoul's perspective, I was just emotionally exhausted from lack of sleep and the stress of my father's illness, as he was not a believer in the paranormal.

At first, it hurt me that he didn't believe what I had seen, but then I realized that it was not his nature, and though he was kind and tried to understand, it just wasn't his reality. I smiled in response to something funny he said, squeezed his hand in return, and leaned over so we could kiss good-bye. I was thankful that his humor made me momentarily forget my pain, but as I watched him drive away, I could not help but think about other visions, praying that this time it would be different—this time the vision won't manifest.

When I reached the entrance door, I turned to the right, and I was not surprised to see my brother and sister—both smoking cigarettes, eyes red from tears and filled with grief—standing just as I had seen in my vision. They rushed to me, hugged me, and delivered the news my father had just died.

Immediately, many thoughts of my father and life and death filled my head. His life was short, as he died only a few days past his fiftieth birthday, and he fought hard to live. A thought popped into my head: *Will I die before I live the life I am intended to live?*

With this thought, realization instantly dawned that my restlessness had nothing whatsoever to do with my physical life, as I was in love and life was truly wonderful. This restlessness was coming from another part of me—a part I did not consciously acknowledge or pursue. My restlessness stemmed from my hidden desire to more fully experience my spiritual nature, the part of me more real than any physical life I could ever live. Finally, on one of the most emotionally devastating days of my life, I realized this particular desire had been living within me for years, but it was not something I had ever consciously recognized.

At that very moment, I realized the man I loved and who loved me had no real concept of my spiritual essence. How could he? It was something I'd kept hidden most of the time, as I sensed it would interfere in our relationship. I knew we were true companions, but I now also knew that where I needed to go would be uncomfortable for him and was a spiritual journey he would resist.

It was a shattering day. My father had died, and most likely my fiancé, my love, would be lost to me as well because I realized the something else calling to me—my restlessness—now had a voice. The restlessness was my spiritual essence longing to awaken more fully within my conscious reality so I would live my true life—a life experienced through my spiritual nature rather than through the more conventional way I had convinced myself to live.

That day, when my father died, was the day I claimed my spiritual nature as my true path, as I recognized it as the inner voice calling to me from my earliest memory. Deep within I knew that voice would eventually lead me to the life I was intended to live.

But breaking from my conventional life was not easy, and for many years, the restlessness was easier for me to endure than embracing a life not governed by traditional structure—a life where true love would be lost to an unknown fate. It was a scary prospect to fully embrace a realm I sensed would manifest the life I was supposed to live, armed only with faith and intuition as my guide.

Throughout the transition years from one life to the other, there were desperate attempts to pigeonhole myself through conventional jobs or relationships or circumstances in order to convince myself that I could make peace with the restlessness that seemed to be pushing me to a different destiny.

For those in-between years, my resistance to consciously and wholeheartedly embracing my spiritual path—reflected through the choices I made—played havoc with my emotional life.

Then one day, Universe opened up my path through a series of unexpected events, and I found myself in Florida. What a wonderfully unexpected occurrence!

Florida is where my real life—my spiritual life—began. All spiritual interaction was energetically shifted from back burner to the front and was now the main focus of my life.

Florida is where my life answered the calling of my soul. It is where I flipped on my spiritual light switch and began living my truest life.

But as sometimes happens, there can be a gap between the time the light switches on and our eyes adjust enough to be able to clearly see the world revealed before us.

Chapter 6

Destiny Makes Itself Known

Florida—what a paradise – bright, sunny, and warm; no need for heavy clothes. I was in my element, as I'm a beach girl at heart. Give me a bright day, warm sand, cool water, and the smell of coconut oil in the breeze and I'm in heaven. It was on a day like this that I got my first hint that maybe my soul or divinity had a certain destiny in store for me.

So far I had been experiencing many spiritual awakenings. The first time I meditated with a group of people, I experienced transfiguration (a blinding spiritual light followed by a person transfiguring into a spiritual presence). Then, shortly thereafter, I also began experiencing the kundalini (an energy associated with higher conscious awakenings in self awareness). There were many phenomenal experiences, and many times, while meditating, there was interaction with benevolent energies or beings, such as angels and spiritual masters working with humanity. All of this, as well as my clairsentience (a term describing an ability to vividly feel or sense things), just came forth naturally and effortlessly.

It was a time filled with wonderment. I was a child in a spiritual candy store, with a varied and wide assortment of delights. It was all very uplifting and interesting for anyone who likes unwrapping mysteries, as there is no mystery greater than the spiritual nature of one's self.

As guided by higher consciousness, I did not read many spiritual books, but I very much wanted to, as I was interested in spiritual concepts. Although I wondered about the reasons, I followed this impression from Universe and only read what I felt I was led to read. How would I know? Sometimes books would just fall off the shelf. Yep, that must be something I need to read. Hopefully it isn't expensive. Other times I would run my hand or my mind across the shelves and know from the vibration if a book was calling to me. In this way, I learned to develop a pure relationship with my own inner guidance, trusting inner knowing to shape my truth.

My sense of knowing, which formed my spiritual truths, did not ever come from anything studied. Rather it was just a natural unfoldment of a deep connectedness to Universe, to Benevolence, that began when I was nine years old. When it came to spiritual matters, Benevolence intended for me to develop and trust my connection to Universe and myself—my knowing—rather than anything impressed upon my mind by books, teachings, or other people. And that is exactly what happened. Without this trust, I would have been confused, resisted, or denied what I experienced in other states of consciousness, and I would have never been consciously focused or intuitively secure enough to perceive what I was really being shown through the experience.

So, on one beautiful day in Florida, I was relaxing on a beach reading a section in a book I'd been drawn to read. But on this day, while sunning on this beach, I had no idea why I'd been intuitively directed to this particular chapter. As a matter of fact, I'd thought about just closing the book and then giving it away. But I had been impressed by Universe to read it, so I assumed there was a reason, and I kept on reading. Finally, the last part of the chapter was about someone who experienced phenomenal spiritual awakenings from an acupuncturist placing needles in their third eye while doing chakra[1] balancing. Wow! Now that part was really interesting and resonated within me, and I immediately recognized it as the part Universe intended me to read.

The weather was warm, and the sun was making me sleepy, so I set the book down and closed my eyes, planning to nap and enjoy the beauty of the afternoon. Almost immediately the following energetic thought flashed into my mind, *Someday an acupuncturist will open up your destiny.*

An energetic thought or thought-voice is what sometimes occurs when interacting with higher (divine) consciousness. The nature of

---

1 Chakras are commonly considered to be seven energy centers (vortexes) within the subtle energetic field of the human embodiment, located along the midline of the body from the base of the spine to the top of the head. It is thought that chakras function as energetic networks to keep all aspects of the body (physical, mental, emotional, and spiritual) in balance.

higher conscious communication is through thoughts, feelings, and a sense of knowing. For instance, when a thought such as, *Someday an acupuncturist will open up your destiny* comes into my mind, the thought carries an energetic frequency, much like a tone of voice, that resonates as a benevolent higher conscious vibration. It is very important to consciously realize higher conscious interaction is occurring and distinguish it from mind noise, because the more you recognize and work with higher consciousness, the stronger the conscious connection grows and the more fluidly higher (divine) consciousness unfolds in your waking awareness.

After a lifetime of interacting with higher consciousness and various spiritual vibrations, there is absolutely no doubt that the thought, "Someday an acupuncturist will open up your destiny" was a higher conscious thought. The most difficult aspect of learning to interact with your higher consciousness is that it communicates as a very subtle whisper of knowing that greatly resembles your own mind-voice. But if you learn to listen for higher consciousness and allow yourself to experience it long enough to perceive the subtle difference, there is no greater voice than that *One Voice* within all of us.

It was extremely rare for me to receive a specific message about myself—let alone this kind of a message, which I really, really liked. Maybe in finding my destiny, the longing inside of me would be fulfilled. Yippee! was all I could think because it not only sounded fun but also interesting. If Universe had presented me with a contract, I would have signed it in ink right then and there.

Now I understood why Universe directed me to this particular chapter of the book; it was to lay a foundation for conveying this awareness to me. I absolutely loved the idea of knowing my destiny. Wow, I never even thought about having a specific destiny, so I was definitely on board this train!

Since I could see no point in delaying my destiny for even one day longer—now that I knew I had one—I planned to immediately begin searching for this acupuncturist. Universe instantly responded to my intention with the energetic thought, *You must not seek this person out, as it will all open naturally and in the proper time.*

To me, this benevolent instruction meant that I must not intentionally try to force this event open through energetic pursuit but trust that it would unfold when appropriate. Though I certainly didn't enjoy the thought of waiting, I had no doubt that it would eventually happen.

What I didn't know at the time, and something I was to learn, was that a big part of the process of trusting what we know to be true is our ability to hold on to that trust throughout the process, even if it doesn't manifest when or as expected.

But for now, the seed was planted on the beach that day and stored away inside of me that someday an acupuncturist will open up my destiny.

Chapter 7

Love = Conscious Connectedness to All

Many experiences while interacting with spiritual vibrations in other planes of consciousness (dimensions) awakened my understanding of the true relationship and connection we have to each other. It is not a fleeting connection but rather one deeply rooted in our heart (through love) that we are able to access through our consciousness, if we are open and willing.

In the winter of my second year in Florida, I went home for Christmas and was happy to find my grandmother, Nana, had recently moved in with my mom, which meant I could enjoy her company for the entire time I was home. And we did enjoy each other very much for those few short days.

As my car was pulling away from the house, on my way to catch a plane back to Florida, a strong feeling came over me to stop the car, turn around completely in my seat, and smile and wave to my grandmother. She was standing in the front yard watching me leave, and we each waved, smiled brightly, and were very happy, though our eyes were beginning to tear. When I turned back around and was driving away, an unexpected energetic thought flowed into my mind from Universe: *It will be the last time you will see her.* It was horrible, and I kept thinking that it couldn't be right. She looked fine and healthy; yet, less than seven months later, she was gone.

Her death was a painful experience because even though my conscious mind was aware of the spiritual truth that we are never separated and nothing of love is ever lost, I had not yet learned to live it. Knowing truth in your mind and consciously living truth through your heart is not the same thing. My reaction to my grandmother's death revealed this disparity within me.

One night, a short time after her death, a very unusual interaction with my grandmother occurred in another dimension. Initially, I thought it was a dream, but I soon realized it was not a dream state at all but another dimension (plane of consciousness), one that I had previously experienced while in a deep meditative state. At the time I first experienced this other conscious dimension, higher conscious thoughts revealed that this particular dimension is one where souls linger in limbo until they are ready to transition to another state of consciousness. It's sort of an energetic way station where we harmonize our vibrational frequencies from one plane of consciousness to another. This dimension is very unusual and cannot be mistaken for a dream, as it is very otherworldly—sort of grainy, like diffused, misty light, and absolutely everything in this dimension is cast in a blue-grey hue, a bluish light.

When I greeted my grandmother while experiencing this unusual plane of consciousness, I shared with her that I was there to help her to the light. We exchanged no words. All communication was done as though our hearts, and our minds were linked. We just knew what we each were thinking and feeling.

Sensing my grandmother's hesitation, as she seemed a little disoriented, I reassured her that everything would be all right and there was nothing to fear. I remained quietly by her side until I felt her discomfort dissolve. Then, as we stood together enjoying each other's company, I asked her to place her hand on my arm as it was time to leave. Immediately, Nana wrapped her arm through mine—a gesture she did many times in life when we would walk together—and her love and trust flowed through me. I affectionately patted her arm with my left hand, leaving my hand to rest on her arm as I consciously turned us toward our intended destination.

Almost instantly, I was back in my bedroom, now consciously awake in my bed with full realization that I had just been with my grandmother in another dimension of consciousness. It was an amazing experience, and it brought me great joy to have been able to interact with her in such a conscious and loving manner, especially since I felt like we never really got to say our good-byes.

A few days later, I was sitting up in bed reading when a bolt of energy struck my chest. (It felt similar to a very strong static electric shock you get in winter from touching metal after walking across carpet.) At the very same instant the electric vibration hit my heart, I heard my grandmother's voice in the room exclaim, "Hi, honey!"

Her entire essence was carried in that vibrational touch, and it was flowing through me as an energetic knowing. Not only could I feel her joy and well-being, but all the love we shared was also pouring through me—an energetic waterfall of love. The sense of love and peace was so powerful that there was no room in the memory of her for grief, pain, or separation. Only love, joy, and connectedness existed. There were no words—there was no need. Love carried all knowing, as though the vibration of love was an energetic conduit transferring thoughts and feelings between us. Instantly, my feelings of loss and longing were transformed into peace and knowing that my grandmother's love is always with me and love will forever connect us—a knowing that remains the same even now, all these years later.

To me this experience and others are amazing proof that our consciousness is nonlocal, able to penetrate and travel anywhere— to any person, place, or experience. Our consciousness allows us unbounded access to everything—all people, all places, all dimensions, all timeframes (past, present, and future), and most importantly, all knowledge. Absolutely everything.

Later I would realize that our consciousness never really "goes" anywhere. Consciousness is always simultaneously everywhere at once, as there is no time or space or distance that ever separates our consciousness from any other consciousness. But this is not a realization we normally perceive in conventional, matter-based experiences, as this awareness is more reflective of the quantum nature of consciousness, the true nature of us and everything.

Sometimes we unexpectedly encounter the quantum nature of consciousness without being able to comprehend what we are experiencing. Our consciousness seems to slip into a quantum stream where profound and impossible things occur. When this type of experience happens, it can save a life (as reflected in the experience I had at age twenty-one with my brother) or assist in a transition from one dimensional reality to another (as in this experience with my grandmother).

Because we do not understand what we are experiencing, we often choose to dismiss or deny these type of experiences rather than delve into how they are possible in matter-based reality. But once we are able to glimpse the source that makes these anomalies possible, we realize the true nature of consciousness, ourselves, and everything is love.

Love is not just a word at all. It is the ultimate energetic vibration that consciously connects all of us throughout eternity, regardless of distance, time, space, or matter. And although these words were ones that I had accepted within my mind as spiritual truth, I was unable to perceive their true meaning until I had experienced this spiritual truth as energetic knowing moving through my heart.

This experience with Nana was the bridge between my knowing a truth in my mind and living a truth through my heart. In a moment of clarity, I realized that every truth must be lived from the heart, consciously, in order to experience the full embodiment of love.

The more we seek to experience love and allow love to flow through us unimpeded, the more we consciously awaken to the limitlessness of our essence and begin living the spiritual truths that we embody.

An erroneous thought is that we give our love to someone and expect it returned. In reality, *love is never given or received; it is only experienced.* What we give is our intention to experience love for ourselves and for others—but experiencing love is entirely up to each person. The sooner we realize love is not ours to possess but only to experience, the sooner we will relinquish our need to control our love and the love of others and just get on with experiencing love for the sake of the experience.

Love just is. It is not created by our feeling it. The vibration of love is always present and breaks through consciously when we are no longer blocking it through our feelings of fear, need, desire, etc.

For anyone seeking to experience the oneness of Benevolence, there is really only one path that ever need be followed … love. Love is the shortcut to enlightenment. You can sit all day and night in conscious contemplation with the intent to be enlightened, but until you realize that love = conscious connectedness to all, you will only be working on the "consciousness" part of the equation. If you would simultaneously work on the "love" part of the equation, you would arrive at enlightenment much faster.

Why? Because all conscious contemplation basically leads to one spiritual truth: love is all, and all is love. No enlightened state can ever be fully awakened without consciously holding the vibration of love. Period.

Seek truth and light will come, seek light and love will come, seek love and all will come. These were not just words but higher (divine) consciousness lighting up my pathway of enlightenment.

My way is to seek spiritual truth, which brings en*light*ened conscious awareness. Then en*light*ened awareness leads to experiencing love. Once the vibration of love began to consciously awaken within me, the knowing came that we are always all, even when expressing as one.

Why? Because there is only one absolute at the core of each of us—at the core of all of us … the divine conscious vibration of love.

Chapter 8

A Clash—Consciousness Shifts Sideways, Taking Reality

It is not prudent to limit your potential
to the circumference of your view.

Understanding aspects of our connectedness to each other and the true nature of our consciousness can occur when interacting with other consciousnesses (souls) through dreams, visions, telepathy, or intuitive awareness.

But sometimes we experience something so physically extraordinary that the truth of our beingness bursts through into our own conscious reality. These times in my personal life have contributed significantly to my understanding that there is a lot more to us than just our physical matter or present conscious reality.

We are born and grow into maturity in a world shaped by our perceptions, all of which revolve around a physical world of matter governed by accepted laws of physics—our conventional reality. But what if, every once in a while, something overlaps our conscious perception that cannot be explained by or even defies conventional reality? Does that mean we did not experience it? Not necessarily.

I experienced one such event when I was nineteen years old and living in Illinois. It first awakened me to the fact that something beyond conventional reality was physically possible to experience while in waking consciousness. The type of overlapping consciousness I experienced was what I can only describe as a time shift.

It was a winter morning, in heavy rush hour traffic, and I was driving on a four-lane road with the two eastbound and two westbound lanes divided only by a double yellow line. Traffic was moving steadily at around fifty mph, with no more than a few car lengths separating any of the vehicles. Traveling parallel with me in the lane to my right, there was a Corvette positioned right alongside of me that was just beginning to accelerate. While I had no conscious sense of danger, I felt that familiar sensation of an energetic hand running up my spine to the back of my head, and my arms were covered in goose bumps, while there was a simultaneous feeling something like a gentle hand had lifted my foot off the accelerator, immediately slowing down my car. But I didn't have time to even wonder about these impressions, because at the very next moment, everything shifted and I was instantly in a slowed-down version of reality, a reality where there was no sound and everything seemed to click in frames of slower conscious time.

First Click: The Corvette just ahead of me by a matter of inches and to my right starts to skid, with the front of the car going left and the rear moving right. *Click*: The Corvette continues to skid at a perpendicular angle, crossing directly in front of my car, avoiding impact by only inches. *Click*: The Corvette continues across not only my lane but also the other two lanes of traffic, traveling in the opposite direction. *Click*: The Corvette clears all three travel lanes without hitting anything but is heading for a telephone pole and a deep ditch. *Click*: The Corvette stops just short of hitting the pole, off the road, missing the ditch completely.

Final Click: Everything snaps back to normal time/speed and sound returns.

As normal reality returned, I was very aware that I'd just been in some sort of slowed-down version of reality that saved not only myself but also many other drivers from being involved in a serious—if not fatal—multi-car accident. There was no way in this type of steady, heavy-flowing traffic that a car could have safely skidded across three travel lanes without being hit by several vehicles and setting off a chain reaction of collisions. This was a feat that would have been an absolute physical impossibility in "real" time.

My heart accepted that divine intervention was involved, but that did not prevent my mind from reflecting on this event many times as the years progressed. I could not stop wondering about what in conventional reality allows for time shifts to even be possible.

Nothing in this experience, however, had prepared me for an even more profound event that would occur within a couple of years of my moving to Florida—an experience that would unravel my concept of reality and propel my thoughts, for the first time, toward consciousness as being significantly involved.

It was a beautiful, clear summer morning, typical of Florida weather, and I was enjoying the warm breeze flowing through the open windows while driving to work.

At the time, I was working for a large contractor in south Florida, and my supervisor had already reprimanded me for being a few minutes late two days earlier, so this particular morning I was focused on arriving at work on or before 8:00 a.m. This was not an easy task, even when I left early, as rush hour traffic on I-95 southbound was unpredictable and more often than not extremely heavy.

Today heavy construction traffic on I-95 had caused usually long delays. Once again, it was going to be a race to make it to work on time, but upon exiting I-95 onto Oakland Park Boulevard, I was surprised to find westbound traffic was extremely light. Oakland Park Boulevard is a major thoroughfare, heavily traveled and typically congested at this time of morning. There were three lanes westbound as well as three lanes eastbound, separated by a median strip with open sections that allowed cars to make turns to and from intersecting streets. I was traveling at well over forty-five miles an hour in the center of the three westbound lanes, exercising caution while trying to make up time. I was feeling it was a stroke of good fortune that traffic was this light, as there was now enough time to stop at a drive-thru a few blocks ahead for a much-needed cup of coffee. At the moment, my only issue was whether I had enough money for even a small cup of coffee, as my wallet was empty. All I had was loose change in various compartments of the car, and I was rummaging through them to gather as many coins as possible on my lap in hopes I have the required $1.50 needed to deliver the coffee I could almost taste. There was coffee at work, but it paled in comparison.

As I was driving, picking up coins and depositing them on my lap, I clearly sensed a familiar angelic vibration convey the following energetic thought, *Do not look down, my dear, it is not safe.* At the time my eyes were looking ahead, and all I saw was clear road in front of me. Certainly nothing appeared dangerous or unsafe. But I slowed down just slightly in deference to the warning, with every intention of looking down for the final $.30 required. I weighed the scene, the warning, and the need to find just $.30 more. This warning seemed irrational, for my eyes told me something entirely different, as the road was dry and clear. You would think by now that when these specific types of warning thoughts from higher (divine) consciousness appear in my mind that I would instantly heed them, as they have never proven wrong. But I can be a slow learner, especially when my senses tell me the opposite of the benevolent thoughts; and my senses, my eyes, just then told me the road was safe and clear. So, what did I do? Yep. I looked down to pick up several more coins, keeping count in my mind, and as I deposited the final few coins on my lap, I was feeling happy I'd reached my desired goal of $1.50.

The very next moment, as I looked up, I was shocked by what I saw. There was a large beige Cadillac completely stopped, resting perpendicular to the road, blocking the entire left lane ahead of me. Though that's certainly a dangerous situation and one that would require great attention and deceleration in speed, it wasn't why I received the angelic warning. In addition to the Cadillac blocking the entire left lane, there was also a very large, white utility truck blocking the entire right lane as well as over half of the center lane— the lane in which I was traveling. The Cadillac and utility truck were resting face-to-face across the lanes as though they had been involved in some sort of mishap, but I didn't really have enough time to mentally process exactly why or how it occurred. The situation was so completely unexpected and extreme that I instantly realized I was in serious trouble. No action I took would give me enough time to avoid a collision, as there was neither room to negotiate nor time to stop. In only a matter of moments, I was going to hit both vehicles, most likely seriously injuring or killing not only myself but also anyone else inside the other vehicles.

I was so stunned by the scene before me that I didn't even consider slamming on the brakes. All I had time to do was grab the wheel with both hands, close my eyes, and utter a prayer, completely surrendering to the knowing that only God can save me. All I was thinking about was how that beautiful, protective voice had been guiding me my entire life and what a fool I was for not listening. I was sad that my obtuseness was going to hurt other people, and I sent prayers for their safety.

At any moment, I expected to hear the crash of metal and feel the physical pain of impact. Instead, all my senses were aware of an otherworldly feeling. Sound disappeared, and at the same time, I sensed a shift in my awareness, as though something inside me had moved sideways. There was the sensation of slight pressure and resistance around my body, sort of like how you feel when you are suspended beneath water in the stillness of the deep end of a pool.

Though I don't want to witness the impact, these sensations were so unusual; I couldn't help but open my eyes. But what I saw when I opened my eyes so completely confounded my mind that I was not at all able to fully process or comprehend it.

I was now on the other side of the vehicles blocking the road without any impact having occurred.

Instantly everything snapped back to normal time and sound returned, carrying with it the awareness of car horns blaring.

My first thought was, *Oh, my God, they must have gotten the vehicles out of the way before I reached them.* (This seemed physically impossible given the amount of time before impact, but it was the only feasible reason I could find for not hitting anything.)

But when I glanced in my rearview mirror, I realized the vehicles had not moved so much as an inch and were still sitting in their exact same positions. Being so close, as I was just clear of the vehicles by only a matter of a few feet, I could plainly see that there was not even enough room for a motorcycle, let alone my car, to safely clear the gap between the Cadillac and the utility truck. My mind could not comprehend what had just happened—*somehow* my car and I had physically passed right through those vehicles, with no impact or harm occurring.

Immediately, I began replaying the entire event in my mind, trying to mentally grasp anything that would logically explain what had just occurred. I remember approaching the two stationary vehicles, grabbing the steering wheel, closing my eyes, and saying a prayer just before impact. With my eyes closed, I felt unusual sensations, a loss of sound, and my awareness shifting, as though my mind slid sideways. When I opened my eyes, I realized I was in a slowed-down dimension, similar to the one experienced at age nineteen. There was a strange quality about time and space, as though

I was encapsulated in a stillness within a wave of energy—as though only the sensation of time shifting (in and then back out again) existed. As the shift occurred, time felt retarded from its normal flow, with space entwined with time, and sound entirely ceased. There was nothing but the stillness and the sensation of slow motion.

Then, the very moment I consciously realized that I was on the other side of the vehicles—the other side of this potentially horrific event—everything instantly snapped back to real time.

All the arguments going on in my mind—with logic—did not alter the fact that I had just physically ended up on the other side of those vehicles without hitting any part of them. There were no smashed vehicles, no injuries, no death—not even a scratch; and no logical explanation either, even though I searched frantically through my mind trying to find one.

While processing all of my thoughts, rationally searching for answers, I was thinking about turning around and driving back to the scene and interacting with the drivers of the other vehicles in hopes of better understanding what had just happened. The gentle angel presence immediately conveyed the energetic thought, *Keep going, my dear, for all is well and what has occurred is not to be explained.*

Of course, I no longer cared about getting coffee. Instead, I drove directly to my office parking space, turned off the car, and tried to gather my senses and stop shaking before I entered the building.

Although at age nineteen I'd already experienced a time shift that prevented me from being physically involved in a multi-car accident, I had never been privy to anything as physically impossible and energetically profound as what I'd just experienced. Amazingly, I had just consciously experienced a time and energetic shift where not only my physical body but also my car's physical matter had just safely passed through other solid, physical matter—which was nothing less than miraculous.

How is this type of experience possible? It wasn't just about space-time reality slowing down (time shift) but also about physical matter shifting into energy.

In thinking about it, the only aspect that could make it even remotely possible was consciousness. Why did I think it was related to consciousness? Because a few times over the previous year or so

I'd experienced very deep meditations where I had opened my eyes and seen the physical matter of my body appearing as vibrating molecules—pure energy. The molecular matter of my physical body, my cells, had shifted into pure energy. No doubt this was caused by my raised consciousness, which increased the vibrational rate of the energetic field of my body. There is definitely a correlation between consciousness and the energetic/vibrational rate of matter. The higher the consciousness, the faster molecules vibrate, and the less dense matter can appear.

Therefore, can a raised consciousness (increased vibrational frequency) affect the vibrational rate of matter so that it accelerates to a point where solid matter energetically shifts into pure energy? Yes, through a state of higher consciousness that is certainly possible.

Could it also be possible to consciously raise the vibrational rate of matter and intentionally shift from physical matter into pure energy while in normal waking consciousness? Once again, the answer is yes. But our normal waking consciousness must be *simultaneously* perceiving and expressing from a higher, more lucid state of consciousness in order for us to be able to consciously initiate and sustain this type of energetic shift.

At the time of this occurrence, while driving on Oakland Park Boulevard, I'd only been able to raise my consciousness to a point where I was able to experience and observe this type of event, assuming that the power of divine intervention had orchestrated the energetic shift that saved my life. Later on this experience would serve as the catalyst for intriguing thoughts about the possibility that we can not only witness when matter shifts into energy but also orchestrate that shift by simultaneously holding conscious intention while being in a state of pure consciousness. I couldn't help but wonder if we might be labeling these type of inexplicable experiences as "divine intervention" because of our inability to fully comprehend the true omnipotent nature of consciousness.

For me, this experience while driving in Florida was an overlap of consciousness—a clash between conventional reality and experiential reality, because at the time of this event I could not logically reconcile the reality I experienced (experiential reality) to that of normally accepted (conventional) reality.

How can something be physically present (a human body; a car) yet not physically present in the same instant (dense physical matter vs. vibrational energy) (form vs. essence)?

There was no clash in my mind as far as knowing the seemingly impossible had occurred, but rather the clash was in trying to assign known logic and conventional reality to this experience.

In one reality, conventional reality, solid physical matter (my car and my physical body) passing through other solid physical matter (a Cadillac and a utility truck) is impossible, according to traditional laws of physics.

In the other reality, experiential reality, solid physical matter was able to pass through other solid physical matter because one set of matter (my car and I) was accelerated to a state of pure energy, shifting physical matter into vibrational energy able to fluidly pass through another set of solid physical matter (the other two vehicles).

Two dots were definitely connected for me on that day:

Dot 1 (experienced in meditation): My physical body's molecular structure appeared to be altered and shifted into pure energy due to an acceleration in the vibrational field of my body, caused by raised consciousness during meditation.

Dot 2 (experienced while driving): Divine intervention had accelerated the vibrational rate of my car's physical matter and my body's molecules, causing them to shift into pure energy and safely pass through other solid matter.

Connection: Consciousness *affects* matter.

Connecting these dots shifted my consciousness and my focus dramatically. I left both of the "time shift" experiences (Illinois and Florida) in the "divine intervention" category, but I pulled them out of the "paranormal" pile (where the inexplicable was always tossed) because I perceived a connection to consciousness. Both experiences, though still inexplicable, were now glimpses (and even proof) of another unperceived reality we are all simultaneously living. My awareness expanded as I realized that a more subtle vibrational reality very much existed within the fabric of our normal reality. These experiences are not paranormal in the sense that they are outside the boundaries of our world; they are just paranormal in that they are not normally perceived nor readily explained.

This was the first time I'd ever consciously perceived a direct relationship between consciousness, vibration, energy, matter, space, and time.

Now, for the first time in my life, I was squarely focused on consciousness as the source that made the reality of what I had just experienced not only logically and physically possible but also the key component that orchestrated the energetic shift from physical matter to energy that allowed my life to be saved.

In reflecting back on this experience, I wondered if I perceived this event as slowed down because I was viewing it from a shifted frequency that was very accelerated. Then one day, while listening to someone talking on the radio about Einstein's Theory of Special Relativity, I realized that it sounded very much like a description of what I had experienced. The gist of one of the components of Einstein's Theory of Special Relativity, as I understood it, is that time slows down for you when you're going extremely fast, and you can end up in a future point relative to what you were experiencing. Time certainly felt slowed down, and I did very much end up in a future point (on the other side of those vehicles). My experience very much seemed to be an example of this particular aspect of Einstein's Theory of Special Relativity. And it certainly makes for very interesting thoughts and possibilities, as it ties scientific theory to the reality of what I had experienced.

Many times throughout my life, higher conscious thoughts not immediately logical to me were either dismissed by me or set off to the side and ignored. Often these thoughts involved concepts that were so inconceivable to me at the time that I not only ignored them—I balked at them.

For instance, once when I was young and I was frustrated that I couldn't wear my new dress on a dinner date because the strap lines from my sunbathing experience would be visible, I received a thought from Universe that someday there would be bathing suits that would let you get a suntan right through the material! I laughed myself to tears on that one. But the laugh is on me, as these types of bathing suits now exist.

Even though this is a rather silly example, it showcases how we typically handle subtle attempts by higher (divine) consciousness to enlighten us to a new perspective or truth—with disbelief, ridicule, dismissal, or even fear.

At the time of this consciousness-shifting experience (my car and I energetically passing right through solid matter) a thought did come into my mind that it would someday be possible for me to consciously intend to shift from physical matter to pure energy. I would not just be observing through higher conscious awareness, but I, vibrating as a higher consciousness state, would be able to shift frequency and even maintain that frequency. After years of seeing physical manifestations in our world of concepts previously given to me through higher consciousness (some of them fun and others involving technology that would save lives), I did not automatically dismiss this higher conscious concept as impossible just because I could not conceive of it happening.

It fascinates me to think about how much further along in my unfoldment, my conscious awakening, I would be if years before I'd had a more panoramic outlook in place whereby unusual, incomprehensible events or thoughts had not automatically been dismissed by me as impossible. But rather than feel regret at my more limited perspective, I believe it much more positive to view it from the standpoint that all those opportunities helped to awaken me to what I had been ignoring.

Now I choose to keep an open mind about possibilities, hoping all the years experienced have taught me that it is not prudent to limit your potential to the circumference of your view. That doesn't mean to accept everything as fact, especially what you may intuitively believe to be simple imaginings or mind noise, but it does mean that you shouldn't automatically push aside what may well be higher conscious awareness flowing through your waking conscious mind.

To me, the difficult part of any unusual experiential reality is holding on to my knowing of what happened in the face of logic or acceptable, conventional reality. It is challenging to hold fast to what you know you experienced, because your natural reaction is to immediately discard or ignore what you can't rationalize by choosing to move on as though it didn't happen. No one likes to feel challenged by an experience such as this because it means there will be energy expended in not only trying to figure it out but also in trying to explain it. There is no doubt that something in our world makes these things possible, because I have personally experienced them. But what?

I've long ago accepted that a more subtle vibrational reality co-exists in our world, and the higher conscious insights I've gained over the past couple of years not only explain how it is possible but also that it really isn't a clash in consciousness at all but a reflection of the true nature of our world and ourselves. (Hint: All-at-Once Consciousness is very much involved.)

But back then, recognizing my life had very much been saved by divine intervention, I was enthralled by the possibilities of how Universe, consciousness, dimensions, matter, reality, and space-time entwine. And I couldn't help but wonder, *Why am I experiencing the impossible?*

The easiest answer is that it just wasn't my time to die or Benevolence had a purpose for me that had not yet been fulfilled. But what if the reason is also because my purpose is somehow linked to all these rather unusual experiences?

For me, at the time I experienced this energetic shift related to matter, space, and time, I couldn't help but wonder about how we are bound to the physicality of our lives—and whether we are really more unbounded to physicality than we realize.

An unknown conscious power initiated the acceleration of my vibrational frequency and that of my car to allow us to safely pass through stationary solid matter. Was it only a case of divine intervention or had a consciousness within me, of which I was unaware, been able to manipulate the space-time continuum by accelerating the vibrational rate of matter?

Could this mean that there is more than one consciousness at work within us at the same time?

Most definitely—as I was about to personally learn.

Chapter 9

Simultaneous, Multi-State Consciousness Breaks Through

*Our consciousness is the only thing
that allows us to experience
absolute transcendence.*

While working for the same construction company, I had been actively pursuing more conscious connectedness with the divine through meditation and prayer. During the day, I worked a traditional job, but after work, my only interest was pursuing spiritual enlightenment.

Enlightenment was viewed by me as the way in which to return to that benevolent place of perfection and oneness I experienced at age nine that I knew and remembered as my home.

The path that I followed to find my way home (my intention) was through meditation and prayer (reflection), while unfolding higher consciousness and working with it to understand spiritual truth in relation to my own nature and that of the divine (perception and attention). This was the beginning stage of my learning the importance of intention, reflection, perception, and attention.

Although I never had any conscious awareness that I was a mystic, the inner path of mysticism naturally unfolded as love, truth, and beauty flowed through me while pursuing spiritual enlightenment.

There were many insights delivered from higher (divine) consciousness during this time that very much assisted me in gaining spiritual awareness. One of these insights occurred one night while I was experiencing a very deep meditative state.

At some point in the meditation, I began experiencing a vision. In the vision there were four people, including myself, standing in a very large arena, with great distance separating all of us. A very old man was standing directly across from me; to my left there was a younger man in a white robe and to my right, directly across from the man in the robe, was a Roman soldier. I feared something soon to be released into the arena would cause my death, so I began constructing a barrier out of bits of materials that seemed to just be manifesting as I needed them. The old man across from me was mimicking my actions and also building a barrier to insulate himself from harm.

As I glanced toward the robed young man to my left, I saw him just standing with arms outstretched, raised above his shoulders, looking toward the soldier. Immediately, I dismissed him from my mind as foolish for not protecting himself. Meanwhile, the soldier had unsheathed his sword and readied himself in a protective stance. After briefly surveying these three other people and the situation, I turned my full attention to frantically completing my protective barrier, as I believed it provided me alone the chance to be saved.

Just as I finished my barricade, I became aware of the sound of gates ratcheting open, but my eyes did not travel to what I was hearing. Instead my eyes were drawn to the man in the robe, as though his presence captured me and was energetically pulling me into his vibration. All distance collapsed, and only the ebb and flow of love now separated us. As he turned and faced me fully for the first time, I realized he was the Christ and I was held mesmerized by the full beauty of his essence. His face was radiant, and as his gaze fell upon me, never had I felt such love while in a state of meditation.

As he spoke to me, there were no words, only the pure vibration of love emanating from his eyes, filling my mind with the energetic thought, "*You must learn to flow with no resistance.*"

These words continued to vibrate through every level of my beingness as I came out of my meditative state, and I instantly realized the barriers around me were symbolic of not only my not flowing but also of me creating self-imposed walls out of my fear, walls that do not protect but rather wall me off from my own awareness, further impeding my ability to flow with no resistance.

In reflecting upon this message, I became consciously aware of not only how I resisted the flow of my physical life but also how strongly I resisted my spiritual unfoldment. I realized a deeper, completely unperceived resistance had been occurring. The profundity of this message was the multiple meanings carried in those eight simple words, "You must learn to flow with no resistance." Resistance not only pertained to my physical life or spiritual unfoldment but also to my natural state of awareness (higher consciousness). Higher consciousness is always present, yet I resist it, and in that resistance, I'm not flowing in harmony with the full potential of my beingness.

This insight was to prove pivotal in awakening me to just how resistant I was to flowing with higher consciousness. During further reflection, I perceived there were three steps in learning to flow with no resistance to higher consciousness. *Step 1* was that I must first recognize higher consciousness as ongoing in my life. *Step 2* was that I must trust my relationship with higher consciousness (higher self). And *Step 3* was that I must act or flow with no resistance to my higher consciousness, even when faced with human, conscious perceptions that can cause fear, doubt, or confusion.

And as always happens when thoughts such as these appear in consciousness, an experience was about to occur that would consciously amplify just how resistant I was to going with the flow of higher consciousness when that flow involved something I consciously viewed as illogical.

One night during this period of time, I awoke and found myself standing by the side of my bed with my arms raised and palms facing out, sensing I had just been interacting with someone—though the details were unclear.

As I was standing there, it felt as though I was in a twilight state, an in-between state of consciousness. How better to describe it? It felt as if I was there, yet I wasn't. I pondered this feeling for a few moments, and then I thought, *Well, as long as I'm up I might as well go to the bathroom.* I had the conscious intention of walking to my bathroom. Immediately, higher consciousness, through the angelic presence from my childhood, responded with the energetic thought, *Do not move, my dear. You are not back yet.*

Huh?

My mind was filled with questions: *Back yet? What does that mean? Back from where? I don't understand; aren't I standing right here?*

Sometimes higher conscious perceptions make no sense to the rational mind. On this night, I saw no foundation for this warning, as I was standing in a warm, safe bedroom. What could possibly happen if I moved? It sounded ridiculous. Though I perceived no reason to follow this warning, I did recognize the angelic vibration that has saved me from harm many times and even saved my life on more than one occasion. But tonight, I wasn't listening. (How many of you are covering your eyes or feeling exasperated with me? You're not alone. I exasperate myself.)

All I wanted to do was go back to bed, as I was tired; but first I needed to use the bathroom. So, I trusted my own senses, discounted the warning thought, and consciously intended to take my first step toward the bathroom.

What I then experienced I could not even fathom. As I consciously intended to take a step, I saw a foot, transparent and ghostlike in appearance, separate from my physical body and move as though I had began to walk, to take a step. But this foot was not of flesh and bone but rather an energetic foot, which passed right through the carpet and padding and into the floor below. My state of awareness allowed me to see the floor material underneath the carpeting, which was not visible to the human eye.

My ghostlike foot was now suspended halfway above and halfway below the physical floor, caused by my intention to step. The front half of my foot was pointed downward and resting below the physical floor while the back half of the foot was resting above the physical floor. Huh? What the heck is happening?

In the next moment, I realized I was experiencing this event while in a more lucid state of consciousness, as I was instantly comprehending various facets of the event as it was now unfolding. My physical body was standing motionless next to my bed, but there was also an energetic, transparent-looking body that perfectly matched my physical body, to which the ghostlike foot was attached. When I took that first step, I could clearly see that my energetic foot had separated away from its matching physical foot, as though I was stepping out of my own physical body. There was also a third transparent-looking body that now appeared to be in the process of returning and merging back into the other two embodiments (physical and energetic) standing there. I perceived that the transparent body "standing" by my bed that matched my physical body was, in fact, my etheric body, and that the other energetic body, the returning body, was my astral body.

These perceptions flooded my awareness, and I then realized the reason for the angelic warning. My conscious intention of taking a step had caused my etheric foot to be out of alignment with not only my physical foot but also with my returning astral foot/body. When the returning astral body began to merge back with the physical body and etheric body, the etheric foot was not only misaligned but also partially imbedded in a physical object (the floor). This caused an energetic collision between my etheric foot, astral foot, and physical foot.

As all those conscious bodies impacted, there was a smack of energy, and I immediately fell to the floor, no longer in a state of lucid consciousness. Now I was in normal waking consciousness, experiencing tremendous pain in my foot.

I was so completely shocked by this event that I cried out loud, "Why did this happen? I don't understand. I thought I was protected." Gently and calmly came the responding angelic thought-voice, *You are protected, my dear, but when you flow one with Universe, you must learn to listen; it may mean your life.*

Thoughts filled my mind: *Listen? Listen to what? That didn't seem like a message; it sounded absurd. Do not move, you are not back yet.*

Then, as the last of these thoughts left my mind, a knowing came over me, and I felt energetically lifted above the experience, able to calmly reflect on all that had just happened. In this moment, I begin perceiving through higher consciousness, clearly understanding that if I had not moved, as instructed, the entirety of the returning astral body would have seamlessly merged with both my physical and etheric body, with no impact occurring.

My inability to trust higher consciousness and simply flow with no resistance had altered the realignment that would have naturally occurred had I not consciously moved my energetic foot out of alignment by intending to take a step.

As my thoughts continued, I realized I had been experiencing awareness through my higher consciousness, not through normal waking consciousness. Although my physical body consciousness (normal waking consciousness) was still present, it had receded. Waking consciousness was now in a dormant, sleep state, no longer the dominant consciousness.

In thinking back, I realized that as I stood by that bed, I felt aware; yet, it was a very different feeling of awareness because I was "awake" yet perceiving through a different state of consciousness than I normally recognized. I was actually perceiving through higher consciousness while normal, physical body consciousness was at rest, in a sleep state.

It was a phenomenal realization. We simultaneously hold different states of consciousness, and one or more of those states of consciousness is at the forefront of our awareness in direct relation to what we are experiencing.

Amazement filled me as I realized I had just physically and consciously experienced a simultaneous, multi-state consciousness never before perceived by me.

Next, I consciously realized there were more than just three or four consciousnesses simultaneously existing within me. Knowing flowed through me that we have an energetic conscious body for each of the planes of consciousness (dimensional vibrations). There is physical body consciousness that is related to our human physical form and normal waking consciousness. But our physical form does not bind our consciousness, and we have other conscious bodies that can energetically access other planes of consciousness while simultaneously experiencing human embodiment.

Our etheric body consciousness holds the energetic space of our beingness while we are experiencing physical body consciousness as well as other subtle realms—vibrational planes (dimensions) of consciousness. The etheric body is an energetic, vibrational twin to our physical form and acts as a seamless conduit between physical, waking consciousness and vibrational, energetic consciousness(es). The etheric body maintains consciousness while the physical body is sleeping, and it is basically the energetic gatekeeper of the physical form while our other conscious energetic bodies are projecting into other planes of consciousness (dimensional realities).

There is also a conscious body that projects and travels through what is known as the astral plane when we are sleeping, dreaming, or experiencing out-of-body. This conscious body is our astral body consciousness, and it also replicates our physical body—but it, like our etheric body, is also energetic and ghostlike in appearance. Our astral body travels through other planes of consciousness as we are sleeping, and this was the returning body that I saw energetically impact my etheric foot/body and my physical foot/body.

These subtle conscious bodies simultaneously co-exist within us, and we utilize then to access the subtle realms—the realms that are purely energetic or vibrational where the physical body cannot go; the dimensions where consciousness alone can travel.

In this moment, I realized that our consciousness is the only thing that allows us to experience absolute transcendence.

While all of this awareness was flowing through me, I remembered something that happened when I was a teenager. Once, in the middle of the night, I had awakened and saw my sister's ghostlike body standing in my bedroom, appearing to be talking to me, while she was physically asleep in the next bedroom. Immediately, I jumped out of bed, ran to her room, and woke her up, as it was a little scary to see a transparent (ghostlike) form of my sister standing in my room with her mouth moving as though she were speaking with me. When I woke her up, my sister told me she had just been dreaming about me but couldn't remember the dream.

Until this experience, I didn't realize that I was seeing the astral projection (astral body consciousness) through which my sister was experiencing while dreaming. For years I wondered what ghostlike form I had seen, as my sister was very much alive, so it couldn't have been her ghost. Now, I realized it was her astral body.

The relationship of interconnected, simultaneous multi-state consciousness is why we sometimes just know things without knowing why. Our conscious energetic bodies know all of what is experienced while in various states of consciousness, and that awareness is simultaneously broadcast within all aspects of our own beingness, all consciousness. But until we are fully conscious—conscious on all levels of awareness—our normal waking awareness is only able to perceive limited aspects of those broadcasts. And those perceptions are carried into our waking conscious mind as feelings, thoughts, knowings, symbols, or impressions—all hints of something else quite phenomenal occurring within us. In my current state of conscious awareness, I realized this explained many aspects of my experiences and why certain things are possible.

Out of all our conscious bodies (physical, emotional, mental, spiritual, etheric, astral, etc.), only the physical conscious body appears solid. All other conscious bodies are energetic—made up of less dense, subtler vibrational energy. Also, I sensed there were other conscious bodies besides these, but I was not able to clearly perceive their role. For instance, it seemed as though I was sensing an overlapping consciousness to the spiritual body consciousness, identical in nature, like a dual spiritual consciousness, but it was so very subtle, it only carried a hint, a whisper of being there.

Though each of these conscious body states simultaneously exist and all overlap, in our waking conscious state, we are typically only conscious of our physical body, our emotional body (emotions), and our mental body (thoughts). And even though we are conscious while awake, we are not fully aware of everything occurring, as there are many things occurring that are perceived by our subconscious/ higher consciousness that do not register within our waking conscious awareness.

Quite extraordinarily, I had just experienced the inner workings of these subtle conscious bodies. Our physical body consciousness is not the only "consciousness" present during our sleep state. In my current state of higher conscious awareness, I was able to perceive that at the point where we fall asleep, normal waking consciousness subtly shifts, and etheric body consciousness becomes more dominant. This simultaneous, multi-state consciousness allows us to continue sleeping, physically resting our bodies and our waking consciousness, while our energetic consciousness(es) move through other dimensions (planes of consciousness), which we interpret as dreams, astral travel, etc. Also, our higher consciousness is always fully present in any and all states of consciousness.

The concept that another consciousness is fully present while we are sleeping explains many things—especially how we can be "asleep" yet "aware" simultaneously. For example, once in the middle of the night, when I was sleeping, I suddenly became consciously aware that there was a huge brown spider on the headboard directly behind and above my sleeping head. This so alarmed me that I immediately woke up. At first I dismissed this as some type of dream, but the feeling was so strong that I got up, groped my way in the dark over to the wall switch, and turned on the bedroom light. Then, when I turned and looked back at my bed, there on the headboard was the exact spider I had seen while in my sleep state. Seeing that spider with physical eyes while sleeping was impossible, not only because the room was pitch-black but also because the spider was behind my sleeping body. Physical eyes don't see in the dark and aren't in the back of our heads, so seeing anything in that room with my physical eyes was not even a remote possibility. But perceiving something in a darkened room while sleeping is possible when you realize that another consciousness, a more lucid higher consciousness, is fully aware of our body and our environment while we are sleeping. Actually, our higher consciousness is aware all of the time. Our higher consciousness holds the space of consciousness while our physical body and normal waking consciousness sleep. This is why we sometimes awaken with a sense of danger without consciously understanding why. Our higher consciousness warns us by stirring us awake while our physical body sleeps.

Then my thoughts drifted back to the situation in which I now found myself—in my bedroom, with an injured foot. I realized that at some point while sleeping, I had "awakened" in multiple states of consciousness while awaiting my astral body's return and realignment with my other conscious bodies (physical and energetic).

I was able to perceive these simultaneous, energetic conscious bodies interconnected with my human physical embodiment, and I became aware of several things. Each of these various conscious bodies corresponds to a plane of consciousness to which they are in harmony (physical conscious body to earth plane consciousness; astral conscious body to astral plane of consciousness, etc.). And all of the conscious bodies (both physical and vibrational) interlock and interface with the etheric conscious body, as it is the energetic gatekeeper that allows these conscious bodies to maintain their various forms and move in and out of various states of consciousness while simultaneously entwined as physical embodiment.

Now I realized that I was warned not to move because conscious movement would throw the etheric body out of alignment with the physical body, as well as the returning astral body. "Do not move, you are not back yet" was a combination statement about two things: my conscious intent of taking a step (do not move); while my astral body was away (you are not back yet).

Normally any movement our physical body makes while our astral body is projecting in a dream, etc., would cause no problem because consciousness is mirrored between the physical and the etheric. But my conscious intent to move, to take a step, had thrown a wrench in the natural energetic flow between all the various conscious bodies by overriding the natural intention of remaining still. The etheric body had no choice but to move in accordance with my conscious intention, causing the etheric foot to shift out of alignment/sync with the physical foot to which it is consciously linked through the symbiotic relationship between the etheric body and physical body.

In other words, when we sleep, there is a symbiotic conscious relationship between our physical body and our etheric body where movements of the physical body are mirrored in the etheric body. For instance, if my hands had moved unconsciously through the air while sleeping, nothing would have collided or been thrown out of sync, as movements the physical body makes while sleeping are instantly mirrored in the etheric body. This is just a natural relationship between the physical body that is sleeping and the etheric body.

When I consciously intended to take a step, I was not in normal waking consciousness because my waking consciousness as well as my physical body was in a sleep state. At the time I intended to step, I was actually perceiving through higher consciousness connected to etheric body consciousness. So, when I intended that step, my etheric body consciousness had to respond, and my etheric foot (not my physical foot) moved to take a step.

If I had not injected my new conscious intention to take a step, the etheric body would have remained motionless and the returning astral body would have perfectly merged back into alignment with all other conscious bodies.

That is why the warning not to move was issued.

This experience profoundly affected me from that day forward because I realized I had been allowed to glimpse the power behind the curtain of our awareness: simultaneous, multi-state consciousness.

This event was vastly different than anything I'd ever before experienced. It was light-years beyond experiencing thoughts, feelings, impressions, and visions, as it was the first time I had ever physically witnessed and experienced simultaneous, multi-state consciousness through energetic conscious bodies we utilize while experiencing other realms of consciousness (sleep, etc.).

Nothing I thought or understood about consciousness compared to the possibilities I now perceived, as I realized that everything we are, know, and experience is about consciousness. This experience catapulted me into consciously intending to become aware of all consciousness within me.

Then my thoughts shifted back to the physical me, lying in pain on my bedroom floor (I had forgotten all about me while unfolding this higher conscious awareness), and I knew that it was divinely intended for me to experience this event. I realized that had I listened to the angelic thought-voice warning and remained motionless, I would have experienced those subtle conscious bodies fluidly and naturally reuniting with my physical embodiment, and I would have consciously perceived the message higher (divine) consciousness was revealing: multi-state consciousness—various subtle energetic bodies simultaneously existing within me.

Even though I was in tremendous pain, I realized what a blessing it was for me to be able to experience this type of awareness. I also realized there was absolutely no need for me to have experienced a broken foot. That was all my doing by not listening—by resisting the flow of higher conscious awareness.

My next thought was to ask Benevolence for help, as I did not want to have a broken foot (I now perceived this foot had, in fact, been broken when energetic reunion occurred between those misaligned subtle conscious bodies). Universe immediately responded to my prayer with an energetic thought that, yes, my foot was broken by this event, but even now, it was in the process of being mended—though not by normal means, so I should not go to a doctor.

Okay. It was already starting to swell, and the pain was tremendous, but I try to be a good student of Universe (hah!—I'm definitely flunking out on this one), so I did not go to the hospital.

Instead I took mega doses of aspirin, eventually went back to sleep and even found my way to work later that morning.

Hobbling into work, trying to keep weight off my foot, a coworker asked what had happened. At my response, her face became stricken (oh, I didn't even tell her the part about breaking my foot while sort of out of body—I sensed that would send her over the edge). She told me that if my foot was broken and it was not set properly, I could get gangrene and my foot might need to be amputated. *What?* I had an immediate collapse of the beautiful thought field—the belief I was holding about Universe healing my foot. I could not hop to my car fast enough, racing down the road to a doctor that was recommended. It's funny now, because I know what comes next, but at the time I was not listening to anyone or anything but my very own fear-filled Carol voice yelling, "Get going, idiot; you could lose your foot!"

I was now in the doctor's office, in a chair, awaiting an x-ray so the doctor could confirm the foot was, in fact, broken. All the varying shades of color and the tremendous swelling weren't enough, as they had to know exactly where the break was in order to set it properly.

An office assistant placed me in a quiet room in a massive, comfortable chair. Though I was still in pain, I was now confident that I was in good hands.

Once more, I felt the angelic presence as an energetic thought flowed into my mind: *My dear, they will take seven x-rays before one turns out, as we are working on your foot and they will not understand what they are seeing.*

Hum … Now that's interesting. What did "will not understand what they are seeing" mean?

Now that I was in a doctor's office, confident my foot would be saved, these thoughts from Universe captured my curiosity, so I decided to just sit back and see what happened.

True to Universe, the first x-ray was taken and all that was visible was an outline of my foot, with the entirety of my foot just a fuzzy grey mass. The doctor and staff were perplexed, as not only have they never seen an x-ray turn out this way but they had just taken an x-ray a short time earlier, which turned out perfectly. This went on for five more x-rays, with the exact same result. All that was visible in any of the x-rays was the outline of my foot, with the mass of the foot just a grey, fuzzy blur.

Completely frustrated by the situation, the staff was in the process of calling around, trying to arrange another place to send me for an x-ray, when I received a final energetic thought from my familiar angelic presence: *Ask them to take one more x-ray. It will turn out. There is no longer a break; and my dear, it would have been healed completely had you not taken this action. You must learn to listen—to trust.*

I jokingly thought to myself, "Easy enough for spiritual beings without physical feet that can be amputated to say."

The next x-ray turned out, and the entirety of my foot was clearly visible. The doctor was ecstatic, for it meant his expensive machine was not broken. He marched in with x-ray in hand to give me the news: "You have an old, previous fracture, right across the middle section of your foot that seems to have been re-stressed."

Startled by his diagnosis, I blurted out, "I've never, ever broken anything in my life accept my big toe." The doctor, who was probably a little frustrated from the malfunctioning x-ray experience, irritably responded, "Impossible. This foot has definitely been broken years previously, as clearly evidenced in this x-ray, young woman." As he exclaimed this opinion, the doctor was jabbing the x-ray with his finger for emphasis, and pointing to what he believes is a "previous" fracture line in my foot.

I couldn't help but look at the x-ray, as the doctor was very insistent, and I saw a very thin line to which the doctor was referring. Amazingly, that thin break line was delineating the exact place where my etheric foot was embedded in the floor when impact occurred between those reuniting energetic bodies.

As I stared at the x-ray, a feeling of gratitude swept through me as I realized that, true to their word, Universe had healed my broken foot. All I could do was smile. This doctor must have thought me dopey. I didn't care. I had an entire Universe that I adored at that moment. Living life with Benevolence as my conscious companion is very inspirational and fulfilling. At that moment, I realized how much I loved my life. I especially loved how patiently and lovingly Universe interacted with me, and even though I didn't at all enjoy breaking my foot, maybe I could learn to listen and trust more fully and eventually learn to flow with no resistance.

This experience revealed some very phenomenal aspects of consciousness that are not usually apparent.

First, there is more than one consciousness simultaneously existing, interacting, and interconnected as our beingness, which means we are able to hold multiple states of consciousness at the same time.

Second, these multi-state consciousnesses overlap our human conscious embodiment as subtle energetic bodies that are simultaneously "aware" of all conscious states.

Third, there are times (such as when we are asleep, unconscious, dreaming, or in a deep meditative state) when our physical body's waking consciousness recedes and other more subtle conscious bodies flow forward, maintaining conscious awareness.

Fourth, higher (divine) consciousness is always simultaneously present and fully aware at any state of conscious beingness.

Fifth, intention (thought) can affect matter (form). Through intention, conscious bodies can be affected and react as we consciously intend (as with my etheric foot moving because of my conscious intention to step).

The most phenomenal part of the experience is recognizing that as we more consciously awaken and engage with our own ever-present higher consciousness, the more we are able to *consciously* experience simultaneous, multi-state consciousness.

But just how do we begin experiencing higher conscious interaction in our everyday, waking conscious lives? First, it happens by recognizing that higher (divine) consciousness is always broadcasting through all aspects of our beingness; and to receive the broadcast, we must consciously tune in so we can begin to fine-tune the reception. Then, we must choose to not just store away higher conscious insights as they come into our waking conscious awareness, but we must learn to utilize these insights to shift our consciousness, and transform the way we are living our life.

Imagine that higher conscious thoughts and feelings are seeds of insight planted in the garden of our beingness through our own intuition and knowing. But in order for higher consciousness to sprout through waking conscious awareness and grow into a solid bridge of conscious knowing, we must live higher consciousness through our hearts. In this way, we not only know higher conscious insights but we also live higher conscious lives. Then we are truly flowing with no resistance to our own higher (divine) conscious nature.

This experience planted a garden of seeds within my waking consciousness, capturing my attention, while focusing my intention to be more fully conscious, for I very much recognized the unlimited possibilities of consciousness not only within me but also within all humanity.

We are always both participant and observer in our own life. Learning how to simultaneously hold, express, and experience higher conscious awareness (observer) while in individual human consciousness (participant) creates a living bridge of divine energy.

Then one day we find, quite remarkably, that our higher consciousness (higher self) and our waking consciousness are interacting as one and the same consciousness, and that is a phenomenal awakening!

Chapter 10

Paranormal—the New Normal in Quantum Reality

Dictionary definition of word "paranormal":
"Beyond the range of normal experience
or scientific explanation."
Houghton Mifflin Company,
The American Heritage Dictionary, Third Edition.
(New York: Bantam Doubleday Dell, 1994): p. 602.

The first time I interacted with a consciousness that was not physically alive on earth, I could not reconcile my experience to anything accepted in the known world and had no option but to label the experience as paranormal. Once that happened, I just automatically tossed all of these types of experiences into the paranormal category.

But one day, while listening to a scientist on the radio discussing quantum physics, a big aha light came on. It wasn't anything specific he said about quantum physics but rather how scientists, even Einstein, saw anomalies in physics they could not reconcile to our world. Although my experiences certainly transcended the laws of nature or involved things that existed beyond the visible world, it struck me that my experiences weren't paranormal at all but somehow related to the quantum world typically only observed by scientists. And if scientists know this world exists, then what I was experiencing was not paranormal at all—just not yet fully understood. Bingo!

It's as though we've all been hypnotized, through the act of participating in waking reality, into believing we are just mortal, dense, physical matter. Once we sense we are something else, we begin searching for the deeper truth of us (soul searching). As we begin to perceive and experience our true nature, the glimpses that unfold within our conscious awareness are at times so confounding that it is normal to relegate them to the realm of paranormal rather than believing it is our true nature, because the basis for what we are experiencing is not to be found within conventional, physical reality.

Once we come to believe and embrace the profound nature of our beingness because it resonates as truth within us, we often find ourselves standing outside the boundaries of the acceptable norm.

If we experience what is not yet fully explainable, those experiences become exceptions to the rule rather than proof the accepted rule is not yet an accurate reflection of what is really occurring in both worlds: the classical world and the quantum world.

We as participants in collective consciousness have the ability to shatter rules and transform acceptable standards—but that doesn't happen without us stepping beyond the borders currently defined and revealing new awareness.

Many things were once considered impossible because they were incomprehensible or viewed outside the laws of nature: Sailing across the ocean and not falling off the edge of the known world. Flying in an airplane. Walking on the moon. Precognition. Interacting telepathically with another person. Yet one or many of us have experienced these very things.

Most importantly, we shouldn't ever define ourselves by where we fall on the yardstick of accepted norm as established by the collective, because the collective didn't establish the norm. They merely flowed into it after someone else established a new point of acceptable perception—the new normal.

As our collective consciousness shifts, so moves the gauge of acceptable reality. Even forty years ago you would never have seen shows on television related to personal paranormal stories: near death experiences, encounters with ghosts, etc. Now as never before more and more people are openly sharing their paranormal experiences, as these type of experiences have become more acceptable to the collective. But even so, until these experiences are explained to the satisfaction of science, they will still be viewed as paranormal—outside of normal reality.

Since awareness begins within individuals and spills over into the collective, we should never automatically assume we're wrong just because others don't share our views or awareness. When faced with perceiving something outside of the norm, it would be prudent to not automatically dismiss or devalue what may actually be a higher conscious moment simply because we fall victim to our own preconceived notion of acceptable reality. We may actually be standing at the forefront of an awareness not yet mirrored in the collective. Recognizing these moments can not only shatter individual misperception and awaken us more fully but also eventually shift the entire collective forward in conscious awareness.

It will soon be time to recalibrate reality, consciousness, and normal, as paranormal will most likely be established as the new normal when we are perceiving quantum reality. But we cannot do this until we understand how it is possible. We always need to consciously understand in order to shift awareness.

The challenge we face in this visible world is to never automatically consider an experience impossible merely because it is not readily explainable. There are hundreds of things I have personally experienced that go beyond the calibration of normal reality, but I knew it was real when it was happening, and the awareness gained and accuracy of the information conveyed could not be denied.

According to our perceived conventional reality or even our traditional laws of classical physics, people cannot be energetically connected while separated by time and space (telepathy), nor can people experience future events while in present time (precognition). Yet, this occurs.

Profound experiences with multiple and various states of consciousness may be outside of traditional science's domain, but it is a place where many of us live a part or even much of our lives—lives lived in a physical plane of consciousness, interacting with a vibrational (spiritual) energy or power.

When we experience paranormal or metaphysical phenomena, we are not necessarily looking to science to verify or validate our experiences because we know what we experience is real and trust our knowing. To many of us, whether scientific principles can be applied or not, these kinds of energetic realities are most certainly occurring. My life and many, many other people's lives are proof.

Even as a child, I was the little detective, pondering the whys and hows of nearly everything. There wasn't ever any room in my life or my mind for fantasy, as you can't unravel the mysteries of anything if the mix includes a potpourri of muddled-up imaginings and dishonest perceptions. To be a good steward of your consciousness, you cannot be floating adrift, untethered in a stream of convoluted reality but must be consciously anchored to innate knowing, trusting the flow of higher conscious perception. And when flowing with higher conscious perception, you can't always perceive the reason or the intention for the experience, but most definitely intention is always involved. There is always a connected purpose.

I've personally experienced the powerful affect of these intended higher conscious experiences in not only my life but also in the lives of others. Not only does higher (divine) conscious interaction bring comfort, support, upliftment, or a new perspective, but it can also sometimes dramatically shift the direction our life is moving, affecting our current reality and even ultimately our destiny.

Some of my most poignant higher conscious interactions have been with the consciousness of souls that have moved on from this world. These interactions proved to not only be spiritually uplifting and insightful but also personally fulfilling.

Experiences like those with my grandmother confirmed to me that something of us exists beyond this world. But naysayers could argue this experience was caused by my grief or inability to let go and was only a figment of my imagination reflected in a dream. Of course, this is not true at all; but still, it was experienced while in a sleep-like state—and that state of mind can easily be used to wield the sword of disbelief.

The most consciousness-altering experiences for me have been those events experienced while completely awake, not necessarily the ones experienced in dreams. Although I believe my dreams, there is something about being wide awake when you experience something profound that helps amplify the experience throughout your entire beingness.

And being awake while experiencing conscious contact involving a spiritual being that is a complete stranger to you, yet personally known to the party with whom spiritual contact is initiated in order to deliver messages of love and spiritual support, extends beyond what anyone can call coincidence or imagination. It reaches in and transforms hearts, lives, and reality, although it would certainly be typically viewed as paranormal—even to the one experiencing it.

Jonathan—Mission of Love

While in meditation, I sometimes experience very active interaction with higher (divine) consciousness, including vibrational contact with spiritual masters, angels, and other benevolent beings. Never did I seek interaction while in meditation, as my goal was only to let my thoughts go and seek feelings of love and peace. Lots of those feelings (love and peace) came, but sometimes other things came as well.

One night I was meditating with a group of people, as I typically did several nights during the week. This particular evening, someone who had never before meditated was present. He was the adult son of one of the women who regularly attended. I'd only seen him a few times in passing and really knew nothing about him, but I had the distinct impression he was not at all interested in meditation or spirituality. I was a little surprised to find him seated directly to my left as our meditation began.

On this evening, near the end of my mediation, I became consciously aware of a young boy. One minute I was completely immersed in feeling love and the next, the spirit of a little boy was present. There was a sense that this spiritual child was accompanied by another presence, angelic in nature, and after a minute or so, I began asking Universe why I was seeing this child—why was he here?

Immediately, the child turned his full attention to me, as he had previously been entirely focused on the man sitting to my left, and this child began speaking with me through his energetic thoughts. He told me his name was Jonathan and he was six years old when he and his mother were killed in a car accident over ten years before. He was a lovely little boy, bathed in light and love, but I was perplexed as to why he was here, now, speaking with me. Jonathan responded to my thoughts, energetically conveying that the man sitting next to me was his father and that he had permission to come here and give his father an important message. Jonathan then asked me to deliver the following message to his father: "You must learn to bend like a tree, lest ye shall break in the wind." What strange wording for a child's message.

A struggle immediately began inside of me, as I knew this spiritual being, this child, expected me to pass this message along. First of all, I knew nothing about this type of tragedy occurring with this woman's son. She was a woman I knew fairly well, so I was wondering if I had correctly received Jonathan's message. And second, it was very unusual for me to be asked to deliver this type of message—one from a long-deceased child to his father. This situation would definitely require delicacy.

When the meditation ended, I shared that there was a spiritual being, a child, present who was asking me to carry a message to the man to my left. I then asked the man for permission to speak the message out loud, which he gave. Gently, I shared my experience, including the physical description of the child and words and feelings he was bringing to his father.

Immediately, I could see emotions welling up in the man; yet, the man, the man's mother, and his mother's friend remained quiet, just furtively glancing at one another. I did not quite know what to think, as there seemed to be some type of non-verbal communication going on between the three of them.

Finally the mother of the man spoke up, "You have no way of knowing and this isn't something we ever speak about, but everything that Jonathan said to you is true. Ten years ago, my son's wife and his six-year-old son (my grandchild), named Jonathan, were killed in a car accident. Your physical description of him as well as his name is accurate."

Chills were running up and down my body—a form of energetic confirmation of the truth of these words.

The man to my left was still sitting quietly and had not yet spoken a word, and at first I was concerned that the spiritual contact had upset him—that I had somehow hurt or offended him. But then I perceived that his silence was due to the overwhelming feelings of love energetically passing between he and his child. Though entirely unexpected, this man completely accepted that his child was present in this room, and he had opened his heart, his entire beingness to this experience. By doing so, this man, this father, had created an energetic highway whereby all of his child's love and peace could flow into him—and likewise this man's love was flowing back to his child. The entire room was filled with the vibration of love—and as an observer, I was moved to tears by the overwhelming purity of what I felt exchanged between that father and son. The feeling touched me deeply, and the beauty of the moment seemed to be suspended in time, shared from one heart and consciousness to another. It was a profound demonstration of the power of love—the power of conscious connectedness.

This radiant vibration continued for a few minutes and then Jonathan sent me the energetic thought that it was time for him to leave, but before he did so, he wanted me to verbally tell his father that he loved him very much and then to ask his father if he understood the meaning of his message. As I spoke Jonathan's words, both the man and his mother verbally responded, "yes" that they understood Jonathan's message.

Jonathan's energy then receded, along with the other silent spiritual presence, but quite amazingly, I felt the love of this child remain with his father. In that moment, I realized love always remains with us, for even now, after Jonathan's spirit had withdrawn, I could still feel the love that enveloped Jonathan's father. Love just is—but our ability to feel it is limited by our beliefs, pain, or awareness. Once we break down our barriers of disbelief, walls of pain, and pockets of misperception, we can feel what is always present: love.

This event, experienced when I was in a state of contemplative consciousness (meditation) and waking consciousness, revealed truths about our relationship with spirit forms (Jonathan) in other conscious states (the light/heaven/peace), and that our connectedness is always present, even if we are not consciously aware of it.

This child impressed upon me the importance of the message he was bringing to his father and that it was an act of spiritual assistance or intervention in his father's life. Jonathan was not resting between states of consciousness like Nana. He was in the light (at peace) and returned here to assist his father, who was rigidly moving through his life, headed for extreme suffering due to the confining grip that grief had on his heart and spirit—even after all those years.

It was one of the most touching moments of my life, not just because the spirit of a child was able to consciously and energetically communicate with his father and impact his father's life by easing his grief, but because I was privy to experiencing the pure power of love moving unobstructed from one conscious being to another. The vibration of love is so sweet and clear that it overcomes any other thought or feeling. It makes you want for nothing more. It is the same love I feel every time I interact with Universe, angels, and Benevolence in any form or energy.

The energy of that man changed completely. He entered the room that night beaten and suffering, and he left peaceful and filled with the love of his child. Tears come to my eyes in just the remembering of the moment—that is how powerful an experience it was for me. I can only imagine the emotions experienced by the father and the grandmother.

On that night, all of us peeked below the fabric of waking consciousness, our visible world, and truly experienced the vibration that runs throughout everything ... love.

I or anyone in the room that night would be hard-pressed to call this experience paranormal, as it seemed all perfectly natural and normal. It was made normal by the knowing that it was real and not springing from imagination or anything of the mind. This experience was all about consciousness and love.

This man, this father, when faced with something paranormal or outside acceptable reality, chose to open his heart, accepting that this experience was real—that his deceased child was definitely communicating with him. All of us could see that this was a man not comfortable with being in meditation or very open to this type of experience. It must have been very personally challenging for him to go into a meditation and begin experiencing a message being channeled by a stranger from his beloved child. He must have found himself at a crossroads—stuck between conventional, accepted reality and an experiential reality that was completely foreign to him. (No doubt, this must have been one of his seismic higher consciousness events.)

It must have been a situation that momentarily confounded his mind; yet, he made the conscious decision to at least hear a message from a spiritual child. (At this point I don't think he yet realized this spiritual child was his son.) But the pivotal point that created the shift inside of him, emotionally and spiritually, was after he heard the entirety of this child's message. Intuitively, I sensed something break loose within this man. It was his heart surrendering to the moment, a heart that only a moment before was hardened to life and walled off from emotions by his young son's tragic death. I felt the very moment his heart broke loose of its self-imposed prison, as previously there was no energetic pathway at all between this man and this spiritual boy. There was only a sad man sitting in his energy and a spiritual child encapsulated in love and light. The shift occurred when the man accepted that this was, in fact, his long-lost child who had been taken in death many years prior, removed so tragically from his life. When this man opened his heart, his awareness, that this event was real— even though there was no foundation for it in normal reality—the channel of love burst open, flooding this man, this child, and the room with love. It was love beyond what we normally feel. All the love bottled up in this man—and all of his pain—was released in that moment. It was beautiful to experience.

And though this experience may not yet be normal reality in the established collective world in which we live, it is certainly a very acceptable reality to any of us who long to know our loved ones are still energetically connected to us—and especially to any of those among us who have personally experienced this undeniable reality.

What made this man come to meditation that evening? He might have thought it was his mother, who finally caved him into at least trying to learn to meditate in order to find peace. But I know it was something entirely different—his mother was only the catalyst that helped propel him to this moment. Higher (divine) conscious intention caused this man to be positioned in this very moment, ready to experience this profound interaction. It was an intended higher conscious interaction—and even though it was not consciously known to this man, he was still moved by that intention. I don't for one moment think that this man came to meditation because of his mother. He came because something inside of him knew he had to be there in that room, for whatever reason. His act of showing up was only the method by which he positioned himself for the moment to occur, but he still had to consciously accept this moment so the higher awareness would open (recognizing his son was really present). This man's acceptance that his sweet child's essence was present and not forever lost to him through physical death shattered his walls of grief, softened his spirit, and allowed the full vibration of love to be released within him.

This experience most assuredly created a new destiny for this man, as it altered the path that would shortly have unfolded (his breakdown) if this spiritual intervention had not occurred. This man had moved the gauge of acceptable (normal) reality that night within his own conscious awareness, and in so doing, he released the way he had been living his life for the past ten years and awakened a new reality through higher conscious interaction.

Our energetic, individual consciousness is always connected to what we love because love is the vibration that is all consciousness. Jonathan knew his father needed assistance, and I knew Nana needed assistance because nothing ever breaks the bond of love—not even death.

Always we long for goodness, joy, love, and beauty to last—and it does, but not in mortal flesh. It lasts through our ability to manifest the reality of our conscious beingness through every moment we are experiencing, through every connection of love. Love is not a gift bestowed upon us in random, fleeting moments. Love is the essence of our beingness, eternally ours to experience.

Just because it is not normal or cannot be fully explained, we must not ignore the signs of our true nature displayed all around us. Paranormal experiences are really just instances where we are able to perceive the quantum world (paranormal reality) that simultaneously exists with our own classical world (normal reality). We don't slide in and out of reality; we only awaken aspects of our awareness capable of perceiving other states of consciousness simultaneously occurring.

As we continue recognizing and unfolding the full measure of our own conscious awareness (our higher self), we begin seeing and experiencing signs that "reality" and even our destiny are not as set in stone as we perceive them to be.

Chapter 11

Fate vs. Free Will
Fate = Predestined Possibility; Free Will = Choice

> *Through our free will we are always*
> *choosing from the spectrum of fate.*

> *A fated crossroads is where predestined*
> *paths cross at a predestined event; and*
> *free will allows us to switch from the*
> *path we are traveling to a different*
> *predestined path, altering the*
> *destiny that manifests.*

Who of us hasn't struggled with the concept of fate vs. free will? This question goes to the heart of whether we are bound by forces beyond our control or able to inject conscious choice, our own free will, into the equation of how our life unfolds.

I've thought about it many times in my life, especially after realizing a crossroads between these two forces (fate and free will) was experienced.

Everything is intended—fated—in the sense that there are *predestined paths* that are available to us as we are living our lives. All paths that may open, all realities that may manifest, and all destinies that may be fulfilled are *fated possibilities*. Thus, through our free will we are always choosing from the spectrum of fate.

The choices we make are influenced by everything we, as soul divinity, have experienced (the events) as well as the way we flowed through the events (our emotions, our attitude, and our awareness).

Our soul divinity holds intention for what can be experienced in our lifetime as part of the divine destiny intended through all conscious experiences. This intention creates all fated possibilities, including all of the predestined paths that can possibly manifest. These paths allow us to experience life on the highest vibrational frequency (love and spiritual awareness) all the way through the lower vibrational frequencies (ego identity and desire).

Since we are able to experience simultaneous, multi-level awareness, intended purpose and destiny are experienced on many bands of consciousness, usually unperceivable to us at the time. All predestined paths carry intention (purpose) and flow through intended destinations (destiny) that allow us to exercise free will in opening the fated possibilities that manifest.

Thus, free will and fate work in concert to manifest the realities and destinies we live through the predestined paths we choose. Our soul knows all possible choices and anything that can manifest into reality, thus our waking conscious, our subconscious, and our higher conscious are all involved in free will as far as impacting the choices we make.

Our soul's intention as well as our free will open up possibilities, but always we are vibrationally tethered to the predestined path we are following. And although the choices along the predestined path always remain in harmony with the purpose and energetic intention of the path, our vibrational frequency can shift through our experiences, our choices, our attitude, and our awareness. For this reason, and because nothing we are to experience is absolutely set in stone, any and all predestined paths have *fated crossroads.*

Fated crossroads are junctures on the predestined path we are traveling where a *predestined event* is occurring and an alternate predestined path is "crossing" our path. At these fated crossroads, we have a choice available to us to either remain on the predestined path we are following or shift to a different path.

These fated crossroads are intersections on our predestined path where we can choose to experience our life in a different way and/ or on a different vibrational frequency. There are many reasons these fated crossroads open. It may be that we have grown in awareness and no longer need to attract certain experiences that are on the path we are traveling, or they may open so we can experience something more intensely in order that we more fully comprehend a pattern, concept, or awareness. They may open because we intend a different life for ourselves than the one we are living.

All fated crossroads are significant points on our predestined path where our choice, whether made consciously or unconsciously, can alter the course of our life—sometimes dramatically. These fated crossroads are on every predestined path, in every life, and they are always in harmony with the divine destiny we are unfolding through our free will and conscious awareness.

Very often we over-identify with our life or our present reality to the point we misperceive the value our experiences have in relationship to soul consciousness. This type of perspective would cause us to view our life experiences as the end and all to everything and not as tools to trigger awareness and opportunities to help us awaken more consciously. Experiences always trigger insights registering somewhere within us that will consciously surface when and as appropriate to our unfoldment.

We will experience many, many fated crossroads in our life; and all predestined paths chosen are purposeful and valuable in what they allow us to experience.

For instance, we are in art school in Chicago and we fall in love with someone while visiting Italy. This is a predestined event, a fated crossroads where predestined paths are crossing, allowing us to exercise free will in the choice we make and the destiny that unfolds. The predestined path we are currently following carries an intention that we will graduate from art school, remain unmarried, and become a famous artist. The other predestined path opened at this fated crossroads allows us to choose to quit art school, remain in Italy, marry the person with whom we have fallen in love, and teach art to college students. Each predestined path will afford us very different experiences and different destinies.

To many people, the life of fame and wealth would appear to be the better destiny, while others would view the life of sharing art, beauty, and love as much more desirable. But each path is profound in what it awakens in us and valuable to the soul through the purpose it serves. Although we do not often perceive the higher purpose of our experiences or the life we are living, everything we choose matters, and purpose is always being served through the awareness we gain.

A fated crossroads is much like a railroad switch between two train tracks. This switch allows a train to smoothly transition to another track and change the route it is traveling because the destinations along a different line are not accessible to the train unless the switch is thrown and the train transitions to the other track. It is the same with fated crossroads.

Fated crossroads can be subtle or obvious. The more subtle fated crossroads are those that open due to a shift in our awareness or our intention to experience a different way of life. Other fated crossroads are more obvious because they involve major events, like changing jobs or getting married.

There are even some major fated crossroads where we will either experience or avoid something that could cause our death. Sometimes we may consciously realize we narrowly escaped death—a close call. Other times, we will just sense that something significant transpired in our life. Since these types of fated crossroads can impact our souls continuing on through this incarnation as well as our human conscious awareness and physical embodiment, there are often higher (divine) consciousness warnings to help us realize what can occur—and even divine intervention to save our lives.

Free will, choice, can seal one destiny as well as open another one by allowing us to move beyond a fated crossroads. The following two events reflect how choices made at these types of major fated crossroads can manifest very different destinies.

Bob was an elderly man who was loved and well respected by all of us who knew him. One evening, when a large group of us were gathered, I received the following energetic thought from higher consciousness that I was instructed to share with Bob: "Tomorrow, someone will ask you to help them move something very heavy. Do not do it or your heart will fail."

Everyone present heard this message, as Bob had asked that it be shared openly in front of the group, and many people were gathering around Bob expressing their concern.

Although the message was clearly a warning, I asked Bob if he understood the deeper meaning being conveyed. Bob replied that he very much understood that Universe was warning him that he could die, and he promised me there would be absolutely no heavy lifting.

Bob sensed my deep concern and assured me that as someone who had gone through major heart surgery in the past and had a weak heart he fully understood the danger of lifting something heavy. He hugged me, thanked Universe, and told me not to worry, that everything would be okay.

Late the next evening, I received a phone call telling me that Bob had died earlier that day. A neighbor had come over and asked Bob to help him lift and move a refrigerator—a big, heavy refrigerator. Bob helped this neighbor and died shortly afterward from heart failure (a heart attack).

This was a difficult experience for me, not only because I would very much miss Bob but also because I couldn't reconcile why Bob had ignored the warning. Eventually, higher conscious interaction helped me to realize that all the warnings in the world won't prevent what someone chooses to experience, as each of our lives is ultimately ours to govern. Bob consciously chose to ignore warnings from three different points of consciousness: his own, mine, and Universe. Why? It wasn't because he didn't understand the danger, as he clearly did. For reasons only known to him, Bob chose to lift that refrigerator and in doing so, sealed his fate, even though Universe had made him consciously aware of the danger, affording him the opportunity to choose another predestined path and a different manifested destiny.

This was a profound experience, but it was not the only time I've personally experienced interaction with higher (divine) consciousness warning someone of a fated crossroads where death could occur.

Once, I awakened from a dream about my mother traveling in Boston, Philadelphia, and New York on business. In the dream, her car skidded off a high bridge at nighttime, due to rain and slippery roads, and plunged into the water below and she was killed. Although she was alone in the car, I was energetically there, sensing everything. It was the first time I realized how dark and cold water is at night after you flow down past the surface. There are no visible lights, and it is cold and horribly frightening.

The dream was so real that it kept me awake the remainder of the night. My mother had never traveled with her job, but in the morning she confirmed that she was scheduled to attend training seminars in those identical three cities the following month. She had not yet told anyone, not even my father.

Over the years, I had shared dreams with my mother that had proven accurate, so she had an established foundation of belief in my dreams, and to my great relief, she chose to cancel the business trip.

My mother's choice to cancel her trip may also have been influenced because she has held a lifelong terror of bridges—so much so that it was extremely frustrating, as children, riding in a car with her any time a bridge of any type or size loomed ahead. It didn't matter the height or length of the bridge. As soon as she saw the bridge on the horizon, she would straighten up, grip the wheel, slow down to near stopping, and yell at all of us to be quiet while she concentrated. Concentrated on what? It was a little bridge, for cripes' sake. Nonetheless, she freaked out.

Several years later I connected a dot about this precognitive dream and my mother's fear of bridges when learning a famous actress had drowned. It was reported in the news that the actress had a lifelong fear of drowning—so much so that she avoided water. Yet, the night she died, she was on a boat on the water and died of drowning.

Immediately, I realized the terror my mother held about bridges was due to an unconscious knowing that she could someday die by her car skidding off a bridge (as in my dream). This event was predestined, a fated crossroads, and my mother, as a soul, knew it. She didn't consciously remember how her death could unfold, yet every time her physical consciousness was confronted in this lifetime with a bridge, she experienced angst and fear. On some level below the surface of her conscious mind, she recognized the danger bridges posed, even though there was no event in her current lifetime that had caused that fear. There is no doubt in my mind that my mother's fear of bridges stemmed from her unconscious knowing that a bridge was somehow involved in her possible death.

So, instead of dying at that major fated crossroads, my mother made a conscious choice to change her destiny by not attending those seminars. Her destiny was altered, and she went on to eventually retire and enjoy daily interaction as a grandmother to my sister's child, who loves her very much. I was very grateful that Universe afforded my mother an opportunity to choose a different destiny by making her consciously aware of a different predestined path available to her.

We are always being assisted along the pathways of our life, but ultimately, just as with Bob or my mother, it is still our choice to decide the course our life flows and the destinies that unfold.

Although we use them to convey the same meaning, fate and destiny are not quite the same thing. Fate is really a palette of potential experiences that can occur. Once we make a choice from this palette of potentiality, that choice leads to a manifested destiny. Therefore, destiny is what results from the fated choices we make.

The confusion comes in because we typically think of our destiny as the only pre-fated course our life was destined to take. This is not necessarily so. The misperception occurs because we are unable to perceive all the alternative destinies that would have manifested had we made other choices.

For instance, in Marilyn Monroe's case, one might conclude, "She was always destined to be one of the greatest movie stars of all time, an iconic sex symbol." Not necessarily. She could have also been destined to be a happy young wife and mother. We recognize destiny after it has been fulfilled; yet, we do not see all the other fated possibilities that could have easily resulted in a different manifested destiny.

Most often we make our choices based upon our identity, our ego, and our desires, without thinking about it. All of us do it, and there's nothing at all wrong in this approach, as these choices still manifest valuable experiences and insights, stirring conscious awareness.

But once I began focusing on why certain events were manifesting in my life, I was able to consciously perceive a correlation between my choices and the reality I was living. The more consciously aware I became, the more I realized my life wasn't just a series of random events without purpose. There were connections; there were patterns.

One aspect of our predestined paths that we do not often consciously perceive is that every path carries purposeful intention, and each intention carries a series of events (a pattern) we will experience in order to awaken awareness. Actually, each predestined path carries many purposeful intentions, which means there are many different patterns we can experience on any predestined path.

It becomes very exciting once we begin recognizing the pattern within our experiences because then we have an opportunity to change that pattern; we don't have to keep repeatedly living it.

Our normal method of recognizing a pattern is to repeat it often enough (sometimes lots and lots of times) that we become consciously aware that we are reliving the same experience. Patterned experiences may present themselves differently in appearance, but they end up mirroring an identical vibrational experience we have previously encountered. A perfect example of this is repeatedly attracting the same kind of boyfriend or girlfriend. They all may look different (the packaging), but each one carries a similar vibrational theme that we are experiencing over and over. It can be anything from disregard to abuse, as it is a pattern unique to us. And amazingly, even when someone else recognizes our pattern when it pops up in our life again, we do not see it. This is because it is our awareness to gain—not someone else's, and until we are ready, the awareness light does not turn on, no matter how often other people keep flipping the switch for us.

Most importantly, we are not experiencing these patterns because we deserve to suffer. We are experiencing them to enlighten us to the fact that something within us is attracting these situations. Once awareness awakens, we can neutralize the vibrational pattern we are attracting by acknowledging, healing, releasing, or resolving the cause of this pattern.

Imagine there is a rotating beacon of energetic light on top of your head. It is there because of your conscious or unconscious intention to attract certain situations into your life—situations that help you awaken awareness and shift your conscious perspective. Once your consciousness shifts, so does that energetic beacon, and you no longer attract the same situations; your life (and you) shifts to a different frequency.

The most phenomenal option available to us is that we don't have to wait until we are living the repercussions of our choices to comprehend what we are attracting and why. Conscious attention, reflection, and perception can play a significant role in shifting our lives and manifesting different outcomes. Utilizing energies of attention and reflection makes us consciously aware of a pattern we are repeatedly experiencing. Then utilizing our innate sense of perception allows us to recognize an approaching pattern before we are involved in experiencing it fully, allowing us to make different choices. In this way, we begin consciously living in tandem with the moments we choose.

Often, though, the pattern is easier to recognize than the reason we are attracting it. For instance, we keep attracting superiors in our jobs that don't recognize our abilities and undermine our efforts to be successful. If a pattern keeps repeating, it isn't about the manifested realities (being demoted or passed over for promotions). It is about the intention (purpose) of the pattern, which may not be about experiencing success or disappointment at all. This pattern may really be affording us an opportunity to realize that we have never followed our heart and taken a job we enjoy, but rather we choose jobs based upon what we think will please another or make us feel validated in our life.

Choosing to be more consciously aware can help us to recognize energetic patterns before we have to experience their effects in our life.

Imagine that when you first meet someone new who interests you, you could recognize him or her as part of a repeating pattern—for example, the pattern of attracting an emotionally aloof boyfriend or girlfriend. The minute you consciously recognize this pattern, it would be like being in a store when the "bargain" special is announced. There would be lights flashing and buzzers sounding, warning you that this person is definitely not going to be what you emotionally bargained for, no matter how much you wish it to be otherwise. Would you ignore the warnings and choose to engage in a relationship with this person? Hopefully you would choose otherwise so you could focus your conscious energy on reflecting why you are repeatedly attracting this same energy (pattern) into your life, especially if you find yourself still energetically (physically, emotionally) attracted to this type of person (aloof). Eventually, through attention (recognizing a repeating pattern before you become too involved); reflection (engaging in techniques to reveal why it is occurring); and intention (shifting your conscious focus on more harmonious experiences), you will energetically release the pattern, shift your vibration, and attract more positive relationships.

Discerning our available choices becomes as invaluable to us as consciously intending the realities we will manifest.

Think of the spectrum of fated possibilities as an energy band of everything available for us to experience. By choosing to be more consciously aware, we begin to recognize patterns in our experiences through the choices we have made and the results that occurred. Once we begin perceiving patterns in our life, the energy of discernment is activated in our conscious awareness. Discernment allows us to perceive through our experiences instead of viewing our experiences as events that happen to us that we cannot control.

When we hold a conscious intention to perceive what may really be occurring in an experience and why, we are utilizing discernment, and we are not only consciously sorting through the meanings in the experience but also the choices available to us in what or how we experience.

Think of discernment as being in the movie theater of your mind where a past, present, or future experience is being projected up on the big screen. The conscious intention of reflecting this experience back through your conscious awareness is an act of engaging in discernment in order to perceive the pattern, the choices, and possible results carried within this experience. In this way, a window is opening in your conscious awareness where you are able to utilize discernment in conjunction with the experience to perceive the cause or purpose of this particular experience through the lens of higher awareness. This would be like hitting a "conscious pause button" when an experience is first unfolding in your life and you are able to discern (perceive) why it is appearing and the many potential ways the experience can unfold before you experience it fully. In this way, you can then more consciously choose if and how you will continue to interact with the experience.

Discernment activates a state of higher self-awareness that allows us to grow stronger and more connected in our ability to perceive, to discern, the choices available to us in our lives. Thus, discernment becomes an invaluable tool when exercising our free will because it allows us to make better, more conscious choices that will not only affect and alter the realities (experiences) we live but also the predestined paths we follow, and, ultimately the destinies that manifest.

The more we consciously engage in the process of discernment, the easier it will be for us to dial into our higher consciousness (higher self) and begin exercising free will to better manifest the life we choose to live.

Destiny is only a fated possibility until it manifests and everything is really about our free will working in concert with fate, destiny, and intention through the choices we make. Together all those aspects as well as how we experience our lives—our thoughts, emotions, and attitude—embody the co-creative nature we experience and express in unfolding the realities and destinies we live.

Imagine you are in a traumatic car accident. You experience not only the event but also many emotions: panic, fear, helplessness, etc. You physically heal, but you don't really move on with your life because you are drawn back to reliving the experience every time you find yourself driving on the same street or under similar circumstances. One day, someone tells you that you chose this experience. You immediately think, "*What nonsense! What an outrage! Who in his right mind would choose to experience a horrible car accident?*" You don't believe for one minute that your free will, your choice, caused this accident. The driver who ran a red light at the intersection and hit your car caused this accident.

In reality, the events we experience unfold through a series of choices we have made all along the predestined paths that we are traveling. We may not have consciously chosen it at the exact moment that it occurred, but somewhere along the course of our life, the choices we made have led to us being on the current predestined path we are experiencing. And this event, the car accident, was always a fated possibility that could occur on this particular predestined path. On some level of our consciousness, we were aware of the possibility of this accident when we made our choices—as soul divinity knows everything that can possibly occur in the lifetime—and we still chose this particular predestined path because of the purpose it will serve in our awakening.

Sometimes, though it is difficult for us to imagine, one purpose of a predestined path may be to experience (or witness) hardship or suffering. We do not experience suffering because it is deserved, but because in our suffering we are oftentimes enlightened as to what binds us that needs to be released—or inspired as to what needs to be recognized or embraced. Maybe experiencing this car accident will help us recognize that we are in an unhappy relationship that needs to be ended, or we will be inspired to become a physical therapist and help others recover from debilitating injuries.

The ultimate purpose divinely intended for us is not the experiences themselves; it is to consciously awaken. Our experiences are the tools of our conscious awakening; they can trigger awareness or act as catalysts for change.

But even if we don't think we have a choice in what we experience, we do have a choice in how we experience. *How* we live our life is as much about free will as *what* we live in our life. We should be joyfully traveling along our path, but often we feel dragged from one experience to another or trapped in our life by the reality of our circumstances. Attitude, like many things, is always our choice, even if we do not consciously realize we can choose.

We can't point a finger at anyone else for choosing our attitude, because we alone choose it. That's exciting in the possibilities it presents because our attitude can change the effects any and all experiences have on our lives, releasing us to live more joyfully.

Often we think that holding on to our attitude about a situation serves a purpose, but it doesn't. The event is over, and nothing we do will change that it happened. An event is only intended to occur once, to live once, but it can live on forever in the way we view it. We can choose to experience it over and over in our thoughts, our emotions, and our attitude; or we can choose to only live it once by viewing it as an experience and choosing to utilize our thoughts as a way to understand the purpose of the experience.

The only thing we can choose about an experience that has already manifested is how we will view it. This is a very important aspect of exercising our free will that we often ignore.

Attitude is everything, and it is within my power to control, so when I find I am choosing fear or pain or anger, I can choose to consciously feel love, peace, and joy no matter what is transpiring. Though it is not always easy, it is always my choice. And even if I am not able to change what is happening, I can change how I am reacting to it.

Our higher consciousness knows all of what is to transpire on the predestined paths we are unfolding. And once we are more consciously aware and energetically aligned with our higher consciousness, we can consciously get on board our ultimate destination train of awakening and remembrance and not only act as co-conductor, shouting out stops (intended destinations) along our predestined paths, but also as co-engineer, controlling our routes (manifested realities).

It is always within our ability to affect the realities we live, and by developing and utilizing our tools of intention, attention, perception, reflection, and discernment, we can learn to recognize energy as it is manifesting or even before it manifests, thereby more consciously choosing not only what we experience but also how we experience in order to unfold our highest possible destiny in any moment.

Even if we are not always consciously aware of the choices we make, choice is always ours. The sooner we recognize this truth, the sooner we can begin consciously impacting the realities we live because *we can't ever control our destiny if we don't believe it is ours to control.*

Chapter 12

Co-Creating—Shaper of Reality and Manifested Destiny

*If reality were set in stone, it would
matter nonetheless for we can
shape even stone through
our conscious intent.*

Though we don't usually, if ever, realize it, we are co-creators of our reality, of our destiny. We do not move randomly, willy-nilly through our lives. But when we are more centered in ego identity, we may not consciously recognize the powers at work in our life or the opportunities available to us through choice.

Every reality that manifests is done through co-creation between divine consciousness and us, but *us* isn't just our waking conscious self. It's also our subconscious mind and our higher consciousness (higher self).

We can even learn to consciously affect the future reality that manifests through our intention. Reality is not set in stone. It moves as our consciousness intends. Even though we are the conscious co-conductor of our life, we more often view ourselves as the caboose. It is not true. It is just a misperception, based upon our limited awareness of our own divine beingness.

Usually, we drift along day-by-day, not really aware of how much our conscious intention interacts with the reality that manifests. Co-creating, manifesting our reality, is a very natural process—one where we sometimes don't even realize we are doing any intending at all. Intending seems to happen on the subconscious level, such as with breathing or influencing our behavior and the choices we make. Intending also happens on the waking conscious level, such as every time we reach for a bar of soap or decide to call a friend. Hundreds of intended interactions every day bring about a result—a resultant reality—all flowing toward intended destinies.

Typically, though usually unbeknownst to us, there is another consciousness also involved. We sometimes glimpse it if we happen to experience something profound. But because we don't understand what was experienced, we often view this type of experience as divine intervention. It is divine intervention, but it can also be something else at the same time: higher (divine) consciousness interacting with our waking awareness.

Most of the time we don't recognize higher conscious interaction, as it can appear to be many things: intuitive thoughts, feelings, precognition, etc.

For a long time, I just threw all of my intuitive thoughts and feelings in the precognition pile, to be investigated more thoroughly at a later date. But eventually, I began recognizing that sometimes higher conscious interaction altered the reality I was experiencing. And then, quite remarkably, I also realized that an initial conscious intention on my part had also been involved in manifesting a specific reality. Once those thoughts, those dots, connected, an amazing realization occurred within my conscious awareness:

Reality is *shaped* by conscious intention.

It is possible to manifest a consciously intended reality in the immediate moments we live by learning to work in concert with higher conscious interaction, our own intuition, while in waking consciousness.

The following rather ordinary event was the conscious catalyst that turned on the light and revealed this phenomenal insight.

Dog"ged" Conscious Intention

One day my husband and I were walking our three dogs in a local park. On the very first loop around, I saw a large dog run up the street next to the park and disappear around the corner. It was troubling, as I perceived the dog was lost and in danger from traffic. I consciously intended to watch for the dog, catch it, and reunite it with the owner.

As we finished our walk and were loading our dogs into the car, I glanced to my left and saw the lost dog running through a yard next to the main thoroughfare. We drove over to the area, and just as we pulled into a parking place, I saw the dog resting by the side of the road a few feet ahead. This was a very large dog with a collar that had neither tags nor a place to hook a leash. I was happy the dog allowed me to approach her, pet her, and wrap my hand through her collar to prevent her from running. The dog was docile and seemed comfortable with me, so I opted to hold her while my husband went back to the house to drop off our pets and pick up a regular leash we could loop through her collar and dog treats to entice her.

After my husband pulled away, I realized that the prospect of finding the dog's owner would most likely be arduous and stressful to the dog, and it was not the reality I wanted this sweet dog to experience. So, as I stood by the side of the road, I consciously planted the intention that this dog's owner would see me, recognize his or her dog, and they would be reunited. This intention was driven by my compassion to see this dog safely reunited with its owner as soon as possible, an intention I lovingly and trustingly held it in my mind and heart. I just knew it was going to happen.

Within a minute or two, a very strong feeling came over me that I wasn't on the right side of the road. The thought then came into my mind that I must get this dog across the road and stand on that side of the road and I must do it now. Though I didn't know why I needed to cross the road, I never doubted my higher consciousness was speaking to me though my intuitive thoughts and feelings, because it just felt right. But actually crossing this road was very tricky, because I had no leash with which to control the dog and she was not at all interested in being walked or pulled across the road. An uncooperative, large dog is rather difficult to manage without either a leash or an established relationship.

Eventually, I was able to safely maneuver the dog across the road, mainly due to sheer will and the luxury of enough time to coax and prod her, as there was no traffic. And although I followed my intuition to cross this road, it made absolutely no logical sense for me to do so. It would now be very inconvenient when my husband returned, as there was no place on this side of the road for him to park and load the dog. This meant I would either have to re-cross this road with the dog or walk this dog several hundred feet to a side street with parking. Either of these options would be difficult—not just because of the traffic, but also because the dog collar was loose and I risked the dog pulling her head completely free and escaping.

But as I was standing by the side of the road, I pushed all of these thoughts out of my mind, focusing instead on my feeling of love and conscious intention that the owner and dog would soon be safely reunited. I did not predetermine how the dog and owner would be reunited. I was leaving that up to Universe, trusting it would just all unfold as appropriate.

I'd only been standing on this side of the road for a few minutes when I turned my head to the left and noticed an approaching maroon van with a little boy hanging partway out the window beginning to slow down. As the van rolled to a full stop in front of me, right in the middle of the road, the side door slid open and the little boy yelled, "Hey, lady, what are you doing with my dog?"

My response was to just smile, as I was very relieved, and the little boy's indignation was cute. As his unwavering stare was demanding an answer, I explained to both he and his mother (who was driving the van) that I'd seen the dog running, assumed it was lost, had managed to catch her, and I was just standing here waiting for them to come by. The little boy narrowed his eyes and looked like he wasn't buying any part of my story. He was one tough sale.

Meanwhile, the dog had barked a couple of times and began wagging her tail so strongly she was knocking me sideways as I began guiding her to the open doorway of the van. As the dog jumped into the van and was greeted with a big hug from the little boy, the mother expressed concern about how the dog had managed to escape the yard, as the dog had been securely locked behind the gate when they left for the store. This little boy's mother was very happy her son, leaning out the passenger side window, had recognized his dog standing next to me, and she thanked me for helping.

A short while later, my husband returned and was happy to learn of the dog and owner reunion. When I imitated the outrage of the little boy at seeing me with his dog, we both laughed in amusement. Then my husband pointed out that had I not crossed the road, they would have passed right by without noticing their dog, as that side of the road is not only dark, due to low-hanging tree branches, but also lined with parked cars that would have obstructed the dog from view by anyone driving by.

There is no doubt that my conscious intention and following my intuition shaped the reality that manifested. Why else would my intuition have guided me to stand at that particular section of road rather than closer to the side street where I originally noticed the dog? And why else did I feel the strong impression that I must get that dog to the other side of the road, which was difficult, illogical, and inconvenient? Setting and holding my conscious intention with love, and initiating action based on a sense of knowing (crossing that road), co-created the reality that manifested. Higher consciousness (perceived through intuitive thoughts and feelings) working in concert with my conscious intention and waking awareness was the co-creative process that transformed a fated possibility into a manifested reality.

Many people may choose to view this event as coincidence, which I completely understand. But I know otherwise. Accepting that a conscious intention has manifested into reality is not important for other people to believe, but it is very important for the person consciously intending it to believe. I could have just as easily dismissed this experience as coincidence and never recognized how much my conscious intention and my intuition was involved. But this time, I very much consciously realized exactly what had occurred, and my conscious awareness activated an energetic circuit that will only make this co-creative connection stronger and stronger as I learn to work more consciously with the possibilities.

To me, the word coincidence is the main deflector of higher conscious connectedness. Many of us toss experiences into this coincidence category because we have no idea how it could be otherwise, and this is the very category that stunts our higher conscious growth.

This story is a perfect example of an ordinary, everyday occurrence turning into something quite extraordinary. This experience was a fated crossroads, a predestined event. I was there, the dog was there, and the owner would be passing right by us. Two predestined paths were intersecting with two vastly different realities that could manifest. On my current predestined path, a quick reunion here would not have occurred, as the dog and I would have gone unnoticed by the passing owner. And I could have easily spent a day or longer tracking down the dog's owner and reuniting them.

In order to take advantage of the alternate predestined path—the alternate reality available—I had to make a conscious choice to follow my intuition and relocate the dog and myself to the other side of the road so the dog could be noticed by the passing owner and reunited.

My intuition, through a higher conscious impression, created the opportunity for an alternate fated possibility to occur and to experience a different outcome—a different reality if I chose to act upon it by crossing that road, thereby positioning myself for it to occur.

How many of these simple fated crossroads do we just flow through every day without consciously recognizing?

Reality is not fixed. It is shaped—even moment-by-moment—by our intention and our choices. And although many of our intentions may not manifest because they are not part of the current intention our soul divinity is holding or an intended purpose of the predestined path we have chosen to experience, there are still many other intentions and choices available to us.

It was phenomenal to experience such a defining, subtle moment. I had personally witnessed and experienced the magnificence of higher consciousness and waking awareness co-creating a reality "shaped" by conscious intention.

Chapter 13

Nothing About Us Is Coincidental

Although we do not yet consciously realize it, everything we have ever experienced—all the way back to the Creation of collective human consciousness—was divinely designed to trigger awakening of our divine nature within our conscious awareness. The purpose of being in human consciousness is to remember what we have forgotten—the true nature of our beingness, our "spiritual identity."

A good analogy may be to imagine you are a master builder, capable of creating wondrous structures—beautiful and functional—and the winner of many awards and recognition. On a business trip in Europe, you are involved in an accident where all identification is lost and you awaken in a state of complete amnesia. You don't remember your name, where you live, or anything about your life. You can't remember who you are—your identity.

One day, a few months after you physically heal, you take a job as a carpenter in order to provide money to live. When you pick up a hammer to fix something, a memory comes flooding into your consciousness, unveiling a piece of your identity. As a result of each experience and challenge, your awareness continues to unfold, bringing more and more aspects of your true identity. Then one day, full remembrance of all that you embody floods your consciousness, and the truth is made known to you. The master builder is fully awakened, fully unfolded in conscious awareness and expression. *You remember.* And you are at peace because you know, you remember, exactly who you are as a person. And even though what you experienced while in a state of amnesia was oftentimes profound and beautiful, there was always a longing within you to remember your true identity. Nothing gained through any experience could satisfy that longing.

It is the same for each of us while experiencing human consciousness. We long to remember our true nature, and all acts undertaken are toward that ultimate end. Nothing experienced while in a state of spiritual amnesia, no matter how profound or wonderful, will satisfy our longing to remember.

We must consciously realize we are experiencing a state of amnesia only. We do not need to learn how to become anything. Just like the master builder, we already are; we need only remember to unfold the knowing of our true spiritual identity. All of us, even now, are in various stages of awakening and remembering.

Our life provides the setting and our experiences afford us the opportunity to develop a conscious relationship with our own higher self. Therefore, it is important to be attentive to the sounds, feelings, thoughts, impulses, or impressions of higher conscious interaction. In this way, we begin to perceive our awakening consciousness.

But just what is consciousness?

That is a question that is impossible to answer, though not impossible to ponder. The origin of consciousness is unknown and is a far more analytical wormhole than the "which came first, the chicken or the egg?" syndrome. We can physically touch the brain, which we associate with the mind, which we associate with consciousness. But it is just an association, as consciousness doesn't really have all that much to do with the brain, although that is where it appears to reside in our body—or so we think. Consciousness really resides everywhere within us and around us. It resides in every molecule of our physical body, in every emotional feeling, in every thought wave, in everything around us, so to believe consciousness is harnessed inside a specific organism is inaccurate. Consciousness doesn't really reside anywhere. It is nonlocal. Consciousness is tethered to us, as we are tethered to it.

Discovering your own higher consciousness is like finding out you have a traveler stowed away inside your beingness—one that doesn't need either your permission or a ticket to ride. All consciousness requires in order to move is intention. Most of the time the dynamic between consciousness and intention is something that is vast and mysterious—unknown by us and certainly unperceived. But there are times, through awakening our awareness, that we can personally witness this phenomenal masterpiece of our divine beingness—conscious intention made manifest.

The ability to alter or define reality becomes more obvious once you begin experiencing the subtle energetic interaction between conscious intention and higher conscious thoughts and feelings while in waking awareness. Is it possible to manifest through conscious intention? Yes, of course it is. We do it all day, every day, though we are usually unaware of the relationship of conscious intention to manifestation. Can we utilize this innate ability to shift the flow of our lives or manifest our dreams? Yes. Absolutely. But first we must recognize it is occurring. Sometimes it naturally happens in a way that awakens the potential within us long enough for us to consciously grasp the possibilities. Then, through focus and attention, we will become witness to the power of conscious intention to transform our lives, our spirits, and our realities.

For many years, the intention part of consciousness was not at the forefront of my mind. My focus was on reflection and perception to open and deepen my relationship with divinity and my higher self through intuition and expanding my waking conscious awareness. And although I had utilized intention in changing my life or manifesting a certain outcome in a situation, I'd never really connected the natural flow and easy manner in which conscious intention can shape reality, nor the barely perceivable manner in which it had manifested throughout my life.

Recognizing that reality can be altered by conscious intention and fate is altered by conscious choice (free will) was a huge breadcrumb.

I realized nothing about us is coincidental.

We are divinity's intention form, and that divine intention form is our very own unique soul consciousness.

Because we are focused on identity, physicality, ego, and desire, we are slow to grasp why we were shaped through divine design in the first place.

It was not to become anything but rather to reflect the truth of ourselves back to us—awakening and remembering what has always been and what will forever be.

Divine consciousness ... us.

Part 2

Creation

We have come to think of Creation as when our seen universe physically came into being (the big bang theory, etc.) or when we, as human beings, were created in physical form by divinity. Either way, to us, Creation is often considered the point at which we and our seen universe began through happenstance or intention.

But what if there never really was a beginning to Creation in either of those senses or even a beginning to divinity, for that matter? What if Creation really wasn't an initial burst of energy that exploded our seen universe into existence or divinity's touch, with finger pointing, giving life to human beings or even when physical matter came into being?

Instead, what if Creation is how divinity intends to awaken itself and the original act of Creation is the point at which divinity intended this divine design to unfold?

It is true that Creation was intended by divinity, but Creation is not when we as consciousness came into being, as we have always been; nor is Creation when human beings first appeared in physical form, as that was always divinely designed to unfold at a specific point in collective human consciousness.

Creation, as related to us, is the point at which we, as collective human consciousness, first unfolded in divine consciousness and began journeying as Avatars of Consciousness™ in order to remember our divine nature. The Creation of collective human consciousness is the divine design intended to bridge and awaken us to what we have forgotten—our own divine All-at-Once Consciousness.

This is the truth of our Creation as collective human consciousness (our "beginning"); and our ultimate "birth" into conscious expression as a form divinely designed to captivate our consciousness while simultaneously awakening it and setting it free ... our soul divinity in individual human consciousness expression.

Chapter 14

Destiny? Oh, I'd Almost Forgotten

*All physical matter manifests from divine
energy—the conscious vibration of love.
Thus, love is all that ever "matters"
(materializes).*

Throughout all my experiences since moving to Florida, I had been seeking truth. By seeking truth, light (conscious awareness) had come in hundreds of profound and insightful ways. Eventually, with that light striking so many chords in me, awareness opened to actively seek love—not just accept that love comes but seek what comes from being love through conscious intention.

Originally I did not perceive the higher awareness carried in the benevolent words, *Seek truth and light will come; seek light and love will come; seek love and all will come,* for that awareness existed in a space I had not yet conceptualized. Eventually, I was able to perceive a deeper truth ... *love is all and all is love.* I realized that even though our perception makes it appear differently, all physical matter manifests from divine energy—the conscious vibration of love. Thus, love is all that ever "matters" (materializes).

The ability to perceive and express love in every moment is impeded by beliefs, experiences, emotions, and attitudes, which act as clouds coloring love's natural vibration. Until the clouds clear, the purity of the vibration of love will not be consciously realized.

Only the vibration of love remains constant and perfect. Matter is not constant; it is ever changing through conscious intention. It forms, falls away, and is formed again. Although matter does not remain constant, all matter carries at its core the conscious vibration of divine love in any and all manifested appearances. Therefore, if we could seek to find love in any experience—in any situation, no matter how contrary to love we perceive the experience to be—we would

99

be energetically in harmony with the pure vibration of love in any experience without either the reflection of outward appearance or the lens of our own perception. In doing this, it may not outwardly appear that anything has changed, but a significant transformation will be triggered. Once we can look into the heart of any feeling or experience and see only love, we will eventually be only love. This will make all the difference in our awakening and how we live our life, as the constant vibration of love will be held within our conscious awareness; love will be our conscious center.

I've begun to think of seeking love like learning to ride the wave of love. Sometimes I catch the wave; sometimes I can't seem to get my footing because I'm too attached to the outcome of a situation; and sometimes I lose my balance and fall—I cave in to my fear. But someday I fully expect that I'll no longer have to seek love at all; I will just be love. Then I will have fulfilled the divine destiny intended for me—intended for all of us.

A few years ago, I found myself holding a focused, conscious intention to more actively unfold my spiritual awareness and energetically pursue my spiritual path. As typically happens when our intention becomes consciously focused, I found myself drawn to certain places or people. On one particular day during this time, I found myself moving through a bookstore enjoying the energy when I unexpectedly found myself conversing with a lovely blonde woman newly awakened to her spirituality. She was alive with the frequency of wonderment, and it was truly beautiful to behold.

As we were talking, my awareness traveled to a part of her body where I perceived a traumatic physical issue that had recently been cleared. While I was verbally sharing this message with her, she exclaimed, "Oh, that is so true. This wonderful acupuncturist has done amazing work on clearing it, and she has also helped me very much with chakra balancing."

My entire energy field began vibrating. I just knew, finally, this was the acupuncturist I was destined to meet. The reason I say finally is that since receiving Universe's message, I had not intentionally tried to find this acupuncturist. Instead, when the occasion arose, I sought acupuncture as a modality of healing, which had not happened all that often, I used only four acupuncturists over the years, and none of them provided chakra balancing, nor seemed the least bit open to the concept.

Although I never stopped believing, it had certainly been a long time between receiving Universe's message and its possible fulfillment. It had been so long, in fact, that the thought had faded to the back burner of my mind unless I was experiencing some physical problem that required an acupuncturist.

Today, while standing next to this woman, I was vibrating like an energetic tuning fork struck by the impact of pure knowing that this was the acupuncturist who had been foretold me while reading on that beach so long ago.

As the blonde woman was writing down the acupuncturist's contact information, she threw in an, "Oh, by the way." The acupuncturist was no longer taking new patients. *What!* After awaiting this moment, seemingly forever, I was now being energetically met with an "accepting no new patients" sign. Over the years, I'd heard these words before, and never once was I able to see a practitioner no longer taking new patients. But in the next instant, my inner knowing told me not to worry; I would be her client.

On the following day, I telephoned the acupuncturist's office and learned she was still accepting new patients. Although I'd have to wait a couple of weeks for my initial appointment, the waiting was no problem, as I was absolutely certain this was the acupuncturist who would open my destiny.

A few weeks later, during my initial appointment, I learned that chakra balancing can be done after all of my impeded organs have been cleared of any blocked energy. I was so excited to finally be at this moment in my life that I could hardly contain my enthusiasm. Although I couldn't jump right in and go straight for chakra balancing, I was feeling reassured that it would happen soon. So, I was in. The other reason I was in? It was because this holistic practitioner, whose name is Angela King, carried an energetic vibration of confidence, compassion, and perceptive insight. Immediately I perceived the strong, bright light of her beingness—a light that is not only pure and clear but also erudite and intuitive. There was a sense that I could trust her, as she is warm and caring—not in a mushy, overly sentimental way but in an open and honest way. I sensed a spiritual strength in her that sprung from a foundation of truth, love, and the vibration of one who is willing to move to the rhythm of Universe. Never had I experienced this kind of energetic reaction to any of the other acupuncturists. I was convinced this was the time, this was the place, and this was the acupuncturist who would open the destiny I was always intended to live through chakra balancing.

For a moment, I sensed my higher consciousness chuckling in the background—and I, a little while later, would realize that there was definitely a little joke being played, though not by Universe, but a joke we all sometimes play on ourselves.

Chapter 15

Knocking at Destiny's Door

My acupuncture treatments had started. After the intake process and physical exam, Angela outlined that she would be using acupuncture to revitalize the flow of energy to my organs, improving function and well-being. In addition to acupuncture, she would also be using an additional technique to pinpoint and clear subconscious emotional blocks held in my body's organs, which interfere and restrict harmonious energetic flow throughout my body. Once the organs are all clear, chakra balancing is an option.

I tried to contain my excitement while Angela was explaining everything and reminded myself of a printed cartoon from many years before. The gist of the cartoon depicts an owner reprimanding his dog for bad behavior, with the owner assuming his dog clearly understands his every word. Basically, the owner said something like, "Bad dog, Fido! Don't chew shoes, Fido." In reality the dog heard the words like this: "Blah blah, Fido! Blah blah blah, Fido."

Just like the dog, all I was hearing when Angela was talking was, "Blah blah, chakra balancing! Blah blah blah, chakra balancing."

It's not that I wasn't interested in healing and releasing subconscious blocks, but in all sincerity, all I really cared about was getting on with whatever would manifest my destiny through chakra balancing. End of story. The rest of what I would experience was just to allow me access to chakra balancing. I didn't see any harm in getting a little healthier, but it was not my main focus.

Angela recommended that we work on clearing and rebalancing my liver, thyroid, kidney, stomach, heart, and adrenals. All I could think as Angela was explaining the treatment course was that chakra balancing was just around the corner.

In my first treatment session, Angela used acupuncture to treat the energy and physiology of the liver organ while simultaneously utilizing another technique to ascertain if there were any subconscious emotional blocks also impeding the liver's functionality and energetic flow. Though the technique being utilized was not a procedure with which I was familiar, I was familiar with muscle testing (kinesiology), which was a key component of the procedure. Many years prior my chiropractor had utilized kinesiology/muscle testing to help successfully diagnose and treat an aliment.

This particular kinesiology technique (NET) was intriguing in that it allows access to the subconscious mind to pinpoint energetic emotional blocks associated with a particular organ or point on the body while moving the practitioner and client through a process of determining the associated emotion, origin of the emotion, and original emotional theme that caused the subconscious block. Once key aspects are revealed, a clearing process is then utilized to release the subconscious block. It sounds simple enough; a nonintrusive method to access my subconscious while working in concert with my conscious mind and my body's kinetic energy through muscle testing to release emotional blocks.

I'd soon learn that this procedure was far more profound than just releasing emotional blocks in order to increase energy flow and organ functionality. Releasing subconscious blocks affects all areas of our lives, especially our emotional responses to our experiences, which in turn affects the very choices we make on a daily basis.

The first session utilizing this technique was interesting in that it went back to an issue when I was twenty-two years old involving my father and my relationship with a boy my father strongly disliked. Although I consciously and emotionally connected with what was revealed in the session, I didn't really perceive anything all that extraordinary about the process. My perspective changed dramatically the following week.

In my next session, Angela and I were working on clearing a subconscious emotional block in my thyroid. We had determined the blocked *present-day emotion* associated with the thyroid was *overly sympathetic*. Angela had determined that overly sympathetic was the congruent emotion by posing a list of emotions associated with the thyroid to my subconscious while muscle testing them for congruency.

After Angela established the blocked emotion, she then began posing concepts and muscle testing for the role being expressed when the emotional block was experienced. The role was a way to pinpoint the expression that was involved in the emotional block, such as child, college student, lawyer, wife, mother, etc. To keep it simple, I began thinking of "role" as the hat we are wearing at the time the emotional block occurs.

The congruent *role* associated with the blocked emotion in my thyroid of being overly sympathetic was that of me expressing as a *mystic*. Once this role was established, Angela then moved on to pinpointing the present-day emotional theme. The present-day emotional theme is basically the way a particular set of circumstances or a situation emotionally impacts me at the present time in my life. It is my emotional response to a situation. It is not just the emotion of being overly sympathetic but the way in which I am experiencing that emotion that creates the emotional theme.

An extraordinary part of this technique of interacting with the subconscious is that the information will typically just bubble up from my subconscious and come into my mind. Once that happens, I speak it out loud and Angela muscle tests it for congruency. Most of the time the information is traditional, but sometimes what comes from our subconscious can be very unusual and unexpected. I was about to experience the unexpected in this session, which was only my second session with Angela.

The *present-day emotional theme* that unfolded in this session and was muscle tested with my subconscious and indicated to be congruent was that, "I was overly sympathetic to people and attached to the outcome of my spiritual interaction with them as a mystic."

This made perfect sense to me, as I had stopped doing spiritual work due to my inability to detach from people and their suffering. My overly sympathetic nature wanted the difficulties people were experiencing in their lives to instantly be okay. This emotional theme was definitely one to which I could relate and that rang true.

The next part of the session addressed the origin of this emotional theme. The origin is the point when this emotional theme first occurred—when this emotion first became blocked within my subconscious. The origin of an emotional theme can be present-day only or it can originate at a prior time. When a present-day emotional theme originates at a prior time, it means that I've experienced this same emotional theme, this identical emotional reaction, prior to the present day. It isn't just isolated to the here and now. The reason it is important to pinpoint the origin of the emotional theme is because it energetically connects the present-day emotional theme all the way back to the original time it occurred so that the entirety of the subconscious emotional block is cleared, not just one event.

My subconscious indicated, through muscle testing, that the *origin* for this emotional theme was prior to present day. This meant that Angela now had to work backward querying while muscle testing from the present day backward to conception in order to determine the congruent age in my current lifetime when the emotional theme of being "overly sympathetic to people and attached to the outcome" first occurred in my subconscious.

Think of an indication of congruent as when the subconscious accepts information as being harmonious in relation to the subject matter being muscle tested. For instance, when we were muscle testing for the role in relation to the present-day emotional theme, mystic was indicated as congruent whereas wife was indicated as incongruent. An indication of incongruent is when the subconscious rejects the concept as harmonious to the subject matter being tested. To keep it straight in my mind, though it isn't the precise meaning of congruent and incongruent, I began thinking of "congruent" as when the subconscious accepts a concept as accurate and "incongruent" as when the subconscious rejects a concept because it is inaccurate.

Posing concepts as statements to the subconscious and then muscle testing these statements for congruency or incongruency is a way in which to engage the subconscious mind in dialogue to eliminate information and pinpoint specifics relevant to the subconscious emotional block.

In this day's session, Angela was working backward to pinpoint the original timeframe associated with the present-day emotional theme, and the process of querying the subconscious, while muscle testing is extremely rapid. I was amazed when I consciously realized this process had rapidly moved me through my current lifetime all the way back *before* conception, and the original emotional theme of "being overly sympathetic and attached to the outcome" didn't originate in my current lifetime. It originated *five lifetimes ago.*

Once my subconscious indicated that five lifetimes ago was the congruent origin for the present-day emotional theme, Angela paused the session. Angela then expressed surprise that I'd gone back to a past life so soon in my treatment plan, as it was rare. She shared that she'd only previously experienced a handful of sessions where the origin of the subconscious emotional block wasn't in a current lifetime but rather in a past life. I, too, expressed surprise, but I wasn't uncomfortable with the concept of past lives, because I'd already experienced conscious remembrance of a few of my past lives during my current life. I told Angela it was just unexpected to move so fluidly past conception and right into past lives without any perceived barrier; I was just momentarily taken off guard.

Angela explained that when she reached conception and my subconscious had not indicated any age in my current lifetime as congruent, she had posed the statement "prior to conception" (preconception), which was indicated by my subconscious to be congruent. The indication that preconception was congruent to the origin of the emotional theme meant that the origin was prior to conception or in a past lifetime. Angela explained that she then began posing timeframes and muscle testing for the congruent past lifetime. When she posed the timeframe "one to ten lifetimes ago" to my subconscious, muscle testing indicated that this timeframe was congruent. Then, in order to pinpoint the specific lifetime involved in the original emotional theme, Angela began to query and muscle test the individual lifetimes between one and ten until my subconscious indicated that five lifetimes ago was congruent.

Although past lives are not a traditional aspect of this particular technique, Angela believes in allowing a person's subconscious to take him or her as far back as necessary to pinpoint the origin of the emotional block, even if that means into past lives, because as a professional practitioner, she is there to facilitate the process while always remaining neutral and objective.

I thought it was important to let Angela know that I was open to whatever my subconscious deemed appropriate—even past lives. Also, I shared with Angela that I didn't ever view the purpose of experiencing past lives as entertainment. Always when I had previously experienced a past life, the information was never conveyed from my higher consciousness for entertainment or ego identification but rather because the past lifetime experienced was relevant to something occurring in my current lifetime. These past life experiences were always profound and instrumental in healing or clarifying an issue in my present lifetime.

After our brief discussion, Angela continued the session, and we were now posing concepts and muscle testing my subconscious for the *role* related to the original emotional theme of being overly sympathetic and attached to an outcome five lifetimes ago. Angela instructed me to just relax and focus on the role, five lifetimes ago, and just allow the thoughts to come into my mind. I was then to speak these thoughts out loud so Angela could pose them to my subconscious and muscle test them for congruency.

Almost immediately, the thought *midwife* came into my mind, and I spoke it out loud. When it tested as congruent (accurate) with my subconscious, I was a little surprised because I'd never been interested in anything related to "doctoring."

Amazingly, the following thoughts then flashed through my mind, which I spoke out loud to Angela; and all of which tested as being congruent with my subconscious: "Five lifetimes ago, as a midwife, I was overly sympathetic to women when they suffered hardship or loss during pregnancy, and I was emotionally attached to the outcome of babies being born (if they were healthy or died) because of how that outcome would affect the mothers and their lives. These feelings were affecting me personally as well as impacting the function (midwife) I was trying to perform in that lifetime."

Wow, it's not the same role (mystic vs. midwife), but the essence of the emotional themes was identical. I was "overly sympathetic to people and attached to the outcome," whether it be the outcome of my interaction with them as a midwife—healthy babies in a past life—or the outcome of my interaction with them as a mystic—happy lives in my current lifetime.

Once I consciously recognized the energetic correlation of the present-day emotional theme (in my current life) to the original emotional theme (in a past life), a big light came on in my mind. I clearly recognized the impact of this particular emotional block in my current lifetime—not only in my discomfort around newborn babies but more importantly, when doing my spiritual work.

Any time I was interacting with people spiritually and I perceived that they were going to experience hardship, I immediately felt what they felt. Although I hadn't realized it before, I was definitely overly sympathetic and emotionally attached to the outcome of the difficulty on people personally and on their lives. I constantly found myself worrying and stressed out by what they were experiencing— as though I was energetically experiencing it myself. The more I experienced this type of emotional reaction, the more reluctant I was to engage with people. It eventually inhibited all spiritual interaction with others because of my inability to emotionally detach from what they were experiencing. Although I knew my reactions were not appropriate, I couldn't seem to control them and found myself immersed in these feelings to the point that my emotions were deeply affecting not only my ability to function as a spiritual being but also my peace of mind.

I found this session intriguing, as I could so easily see the similarity in the emotional theme in my current lifetime and the emotional theme five lifetimes ago. Angela explained that even though the roles will vary, the original emotional theme and the present-day emotional theme will always carry the identical feelings, though what is creating those feelings—the circumstances—will be different. The circumstances involved in the emotional themes can be different because it is not the circumstances themselves that create the block. Rather, the emotional block is created by how we are emotionally responding to the circumstances. Angela shared the concept that when we go back to the origin of an emotional theme we aren't looking for an exact replication of events or details, because that doesn't happen. Rather, we are looking for the basic emotional theme experienced. In this case, it was overly sympathetic and attached to an outcome.

It was then that I realized that the emotional theme is not about the details that color the emotions but only about the nature of the emotions being experienced. This helped me to better recognize the emotional themes and more easily understand their correlation to each other and why these events were energetically linked in my subconscious. The details can be dramatically different, but the basic emotional themes are always the same, as that thread of emotional similarity is what causes the subconscious mind to link the original and present-day emotional themes.

I felt very surprised by what I experienced in this session, though I could clearly see the connectedness. Angela explained that once the origin of the emotional theme is pinpointed, she would query my subconscious as to whether any additional details were needed or if there were any additional blocked emotions related to this emotional theme. In this way, it's like an energetic net sweeping over the situation, including anything the subconscious deems relative, from the present day back to the origin, so everything is included when the emotional block is cleared from my subconscious.

Angela then posed statements and muscle tested my subconscious. My subconscious indicated that there were no additional emotions or details needed to clear this emotional block.

We were now ready to move through the process of clearing this subconscious emotional block. This process was the same in every session. Angela positioned my finger on the organ pulse point, located in my wrist area, involved in the emotional block (in this case the thyroid). She then placed the palm of my hand on my forehead, which she explained is my body's emotional center. Angela next instructed me to close my eyes and think about the original emotional theme involved in the subconscious block. The process of consciously holding the original emotional theme in my mind while I was simultaneously contacting the organ pulse point and my body's emotional center released the subconscious emotional block. Once I felt at peace about the emotional theme, Angela instructed me to open my eyes and she would then retest my subconscious to verify that the emotional block had been cleared.

The clearing process is very simple and takes no longer than a few seconds to a couple of minutes; and amazingly, once released, the emotional block will be wiped from my subconscious and with it the negative effects it had on my choices, emotions, attitude, and life.

Angela retested the original emotional block to confirm that it had been released and the session drew to a close, but that was definitely not the end of the experience. Although I found the session interesting and I could very much relate to what I had experienced, that was not the reason I became completely confident in the validity of this process for clearing subconscious blocks. The reason I became a believer was what happened after the session. Energetically I was feeling more optimistic, energized, and happier than I had in quite a while, almost as though emotional blocks carried an energetic weight that had been lifted from me with their release. It was obvious that something profound and powerful was happening in these sessions. Blocks were definitely being cleared. The proof was not just my muscles verifying (through kinesiology) what my subconscious was clearing but also how I immediately felt, thought, and reacted differently.

A few days after this session, I was interacting with someone who was going through a difficult issue in her life. Amazingly, I was empathetic and able to interact with this person, sharing spiritual insights without feeling overly sympathetic or attached to the outcome of the situation. I was surprised to find that these negative emotional reactions were no longer affecting me. This dramatically changed my life, as I was now able to engage and interact with people regarding spiritual matters in a more positive manner for both them and myself. I will always be empathetic to people, because that is just my nature. But now I am no longer feeling emotionally bound to their experiences in an unhealthy way—triggered by a subconscious emotional block originating long ago adversely affecting such a major part of my life.

Interestingly enough, releasing this emotional block also brought a sweet little side effect in that I am no longer reluctant to be around newborn babies. And though it certainly doesn't carry the same life-altering impact as being able to spiritually interact with people, it is yet one more verification of how releasing subconscious emotional blocks can change your emotional reactions, freeing you to more harmoniously express your true nature in the circumstances of your life.

There was no doubt about it—dramatic changes were occurring in my life. One of the most unexpected, surprising changes was that I just found myself feeling happy. I had forgotten how the sensation of happiness feels when it is just naturally occurring from within and not triggered by outside influences, such as an amusing situation. Something phenomenal was happening. Not only did I feel much better, but my emotional reactions to situations were also changing. It is difficult to describe, but there was a renewed sense of my self. I had feelings of peace and happiness that I had not felt in a long time, and I knew it was because of what was occurring in these sessions.

This experience prompted me to want to learn more about this unusual technique. Before my next session, I expressed interest in learning more about why this technique worked—the theory behind it, etc. Angela shared information about the technique, studies, and the science behind kinesiology and the subconscious, as well as various ways she had personally utilized this technique as a tool to facilitate healings. I came away from that discussion completely confident in Angela and the validity of this technique to clear subconscious emotional blocks. Later I realized that my belief in what I was experiencing allowed enlightened awareness to unfold clearly within my consciousness, without fear or doubt ever entering into the experience.

An example of how remarkably our lives can change by releasing subconscious emotional blocks was a situation with my husband that had been ongoing for over a year. While working with him in our business, I had become increasing agitated whenever he asked for my help in solving a problem. This was very bizarre behavior, and although I very much disliked the way I was acting and felt terrible about it, I couldn't seem to either consciously control my reactions or change my behavior.

Quite surprisingly, without every having voiced this issue to Angela, it came up in one of my early sessions as a present-day emotional block. In the session, the original emotional theme causing this subconscious emotional block was revealed and cleared, and this behavioral issue was just gone. These emotional reactions and behavioral responses were never again experienced by me or displayed toward my husband. That in and of itself absolutely confirmed the validity of this type of technique, as previously I had consciously tried very hard to change my behavior, with absolutely no effect.

Angela explained that a current life situation with a similar emotional theme to one blocked in the past will trigger emotional responses we don't seem to be able to control.

All I knew was that our relationship had been significantly affected because something imperceptible was igniting these responses in me, though I couldn't understand what or why—or even how to change it.

Clearing this subconscious block allowed me the freedom to express and interact in a way I truly intended without the negative influence of a previous event. It was a life-changing experience, not only because a negative situation affecting my life was cleared but also because I realized the adverse impact subconscious blocks can have on our relationships and our lives.

These types of energetic benefits were so remarkable that I had completely overlooked the healing effect of these subconscious clearings on my physical body. Not only was I feeling better mentally and emotionally because of cleared subconscious blocks, but I was also feeling better physically. No other personal proof was ever needed. The immediate changes in how I was feeling, my emotional reactions, and my improved relationships was resounding verification that this particular technique worked. It inspired me to continue with this process and utilize this technique to clear out anything in my subconscious that was interfering in my ability to experience a better life.

It was an exciting concept and one I embraced. There's something extremely viable and personally very powerful about being able to use your own body's consciousness through muscle testing and interacting with your subconscious to determine the cause and then to clear subconscious emotional blocks—all the while in a waking conscious state.

For most of my life, I had been consciously engaged with higher conscious awareness, but now I realized there was another aspect of my consciousness in play—an aspect that existed below the surface of my conscious awareness, significantly influencing my life. Although I'd had encounters with my subconscious before my sessions with Angela, I had no idea of the true impact our subconscious has on our lives.

The procedure Angela was utilizing initially appeared to be just a technique to restore healthy energetic flow to my body, but I was learning that any system that allows interaction with the subconscious is a lot more significant than immediately realized or valued.

Imagine that for the first time in your life, you find out that your choices and emotional responses, including self-sabotaging behavior, are being significantly influenced from an aspect of you that you cannot see, you cannot hear, and with whom you cannot speak. But this aspect controls the programs (the patterned emotional reactions and therefore, your choices) that are running in the background of your life. And if your subconscious mind is currently running a program that is incongruent or in conflict with your intentions, it can significantly impact not only what you live (experiences and choices) but also how you live (emotions and attitude). Once a programmed response is held in the subconscious, it isn't easily removed. The subconscious program must be accessed through some form of conscious awareness before it can be changed. It's like having the huge mainframe of your awareness locked behind a vault door. Once you open the door, you gain access to the mainframe and can change the program. But until then, you are stuck in an emotional pattern of response, caused by a previously experienced unconscious influence that is overshadowing your life.

Discovering you have a method to access your subconscious is like learning you have new communication service to a previously remote area of your own self. You can now energetically throw open that vault door and engage in dialogue with your subconscious to find out why the current program is running. Then you can efficiently and effectively clear (release) the counterproductive program and cleanly install the new program you consciously intend through affirmations, prayer, higher conscious insights, etc.

Though I was just at the beginning of conscious interaction with my subconscious, it was a significant moment in my life—one where I realized this type of communication with my subconscious was both insightful and capable of altering the entire way in which I was living my life now and in the future.

The acupuncture treatments and therapeutic release of subconscious emotional blocks continued until one day a few weeks later, Angela told me that we were done with clearing all of the targeted organs, and if I was still interested, we could now pursue chakra balancing.

There had been so many remarkable sessions where I was able to experience immediate changes in my life that I had completely forgotten that I was originally here just for the chakra balancing.

The higher conscious thought from years before immediately flooded my mind: "Someday an acupuncturist will open up your destiny."

Someday was finally here!

Chapter 16

That's It?

Finally, my long-awaited moment was here. This was the day. Angela was going to do chakra balancing, and I was going to have my destiny revealed. What was my destiny? My energy was abuzz with hope and excitement. Though I didn't know what to expect, after all these years of waiting, it was going to be wonderful!

Angela had me relax on the table so she could place the acupuncture needles in my chakras. As she was doing this, I was consciously trying to calm myself down so I was more peaceful during the experience, as my heart was pounding and my mind was racing. As Angela placed the last needle, she asked me if I was comfortable and then told me that she would turn down the lights and return in approximately thirty minutes. Yep, thirty minutes of profundity were about to happen. I was expecting this to be unbelievable. The show was about to begin. I'd now see my destiny unfold right before my eyes. I was almost goofy I was so excited, as you can well imagine.

As I was relaxing in this peaceful room, I was running through all the ways that Universe may communicate. My mind was very active, and I'd noticed that my body was definitely vibrating from the energy moving through my chakras. I was also seeing colors, which was not unusual.

I was still mentally enthusiastically exploring all the phenomenal possibilities when I was surprised by Angela's return, as the chakra balancing session had come to a close.

Wow ... That's it? What destiny opening?

To say I felt devastated would be the understatement of the century. After all these years of highly anticipating this moment, it was absolutely nothing like what I expected. In my mind, I fully expected to experience an extraordinary destiny-revealing event—not just a heightened sense of energy flowing through my chakras.

But from somewhere deep within me, I knew the original message from Universe was still accurate. (I'm loyal, that's for sure.) I assumed that Angela, though profound in many other ways, must not be *the* acupuncturist. There was no other choice available to me, as I must trust my higher inner guidance; but at this very moment I was in the middle of full-fledged disappointment.

At the same time, I realized profound things were happening in these sessions—things that were helping me, changing me, and releasing me from blocked emotions; things that were improving my physical health, personal life, and spiritual connectedness. So, I decided that I was going to just forget about the destiny thing, as that would manifest when it was appropriate and I was going to definitely continue with these sessions, as I'd already experienced remarkable changes in my life. This technique was unlike anything I'd ever experienced. Many techniques promised results that may well have occurred, but they were far too subtle for me to consciously recognize as working. On the other hand, this energetic technique was phenomenal.

As Angela was removing the last needle and my disappointment had settled to an acceptable level, she suggested that in our next session we move on to a variation of the technique that tests how congruent (harmonious) our affirmations (intentions) are with any programs or emotional blocks we are holding in our subconscious.

An affirmation is basically a statement in the affirmative (positive) that conveys a belief or an intention that you want to experience in your life, for example, "I am okay living abundantly and being spiritual."

The technique Angela suggested sounded intriguing, as I'd been using affirmations for years and had personally experienced their powerful effect in my life. It would be interesting to see if I had any subconscious emotional blocks interfering with the intentions behind my affirmations. Could releasing subconscious blocks cause my intentions to more rapidly manifest or unfold in even more profound ways? It was exciting to think that releasing subconscious blocks may boost the affects of the intentions I was holding.

Imagine, you begin seeing an acupuncturist for one thing and you receive healings in areas you didn't even know were afflicted and find yourself once again happy, peaceful, and excited about your life. It was a great feeling and one I wish everyone could experience, because I think all of us are open, beautiful spirits that get overloaded, overwhelmed, and impacted by being in such a difficult place as an earthly incarnation.

What I was experiencing in these sessions was so personally transformational, it was as if an energetic line was delineating the before and after snapshot of how I was living my life. In the before shot, I felt like I'd gone ten hard-fought rounds and had lost momentum. I was lethargic, a little dazed from some pretty hard-hitting emotional experiences, and disconnected from my joy. In the after shot, I felt like I'd been infused with energy, hope, and optimism. Now I believed I was not only going to win this game of life but I was going to love my life no matter what happened. Lethargy was gone, replaced by a revitalized spirit of well-being, along with my natural ability to flow with the punches while keeping my balance and my sense of humor. I was once more enthusiastic, joyful, and spiritually centered.

All I could say was that I was definitely feeling renewed, as though a breath of fresh air had come into my life. Most importantly, I realized it wasn't too late to feel energetically reconnected with my center, my true self. It's never too late to re-embrace your life because the moment you feel energetically reconnected to your true self, you want to joyfully experience your life rather than merely go through the motions of being alive. It's the difference between energetically experiencing your own life force as the catalyst in your life versus feeling as though you and your life are being tossed around by the winds of circumstance and change.

So much had happened over the years that I didn't even realize how slowly my life force had diminished until I felt it resurge inside of me. That's how energetic disconnection from our true self happens—slowly. It's not suddenly where one day you're happy and vibrant and the next day you're sad, disengaged, or listless. Who wouldn't recognize that drastic of a change? Dulling of your true self is insidious, sneaking up on you one experience at a time, until one day you just act and feel differently. Sometimes you vaguely remember a different you, a happy you, but you can't really discern when it all shifted or why. How many of us feel this way? I'd wager many.

Are you energized and confident and filled with joy? That is the way we're supposed to live, but that sense of ourselves can be hijacked when we're older through accumulated piles of experiences smelling to high heaven of loss, disappointment, and sadness. Eventually we give up believing it will ever change, and that's when we succumb to the notion that we will never, ever feel any better. Hope fades, taking our joy with it.

Our sense of our true self can also be hijacked when we're young through devastating interactions with people or situations that steal our light, our joy, and our hope—hiding it away from us, someplace deep inside. When we're young, we don't realize how fragile our true self is to the heartbreak we experience or the abuse we suffer or the inappropriate choices we make due to peer pressure. Our youth makes us feel invincible, but it is not our youth that creates our feelings of strength, purpose, and enthusiasm. It is our connection to our light, to our core essence. The dulling of our connection to our light and sense of our true self happens in many ways, but the effect is always the same—we begin drifting from our true self, from the core within us, and we no longer experience "joie de vivre" (which translates as *joy of living*). Our life force is diminished by cloaks of protection we wrap around our hearts, our minds, our bodies, and our spirits. At some point, we begin living life as though it is an obstacle course rather than an extraordinary trip. We need to be riding through life with our heads out the window, feeling the wind in our hair and the sun on our face, looking forward to the adventure. Instead, we are hunkered down in the back seat, eyes closed, just praying the ride takes us someplace good soon.

I had no idea how hunkered down I had become until I experienced my natural exuberance once more. It was fantastic!

These sessions made me very aware that subconscious emotional blocks must be influencing the predestined paths I was traveling, the choices I was making at fated crossroads, and the destinies that manifest.

But besides blocking me from what I wanted to experience, could these subconscious emotional blocks also be serving an unperceived purpose in my life?

Although I did not yet perceive the more profound role of our subconscious, I am very much focused on alleviating subconscious emotional blocks originating in this lifetime as well as in the past so I could more readily manifest my true physical and spiritual potential.

Surprisingly, emotional blocks aren't just created and carried within our subconscious mind because of past life or current life events. Sometimes a subconscious emotional block is created from anticipation of something we will or won't experience in our current lifetime.

The first one of these types of sessions begins with a subconscious emotional block affecting my stomach. The blocked *present-day emotion* is *stifled,* and the *present-day emotional theme* is that, "I am feeling stifled from Spirit and not moving in the flow."

Stifled from Spirit was a very unusual concept to experience, as I was only expecting blocked emotions to involve issues related to my physical life. Yet in this session, it was apparent that subconscious blocks could relate to spiritual essence as well as physical form.

When we muscle tested for the *origin* (first appearance) of this present-day emotion of feeling stifled from Spirit, it went back to *conception.* Then, incredibly, my subconscious indicated that the congruent *original emotional theme* was that, "I didn't want to incarnate, as I felt incarnation would stifle me from the flow of oneness."

What a remarkable emotional theme to encounter in one of my earliest sessions. Although I hadn't known exactly what to expect, experiencing something so spiritually focused, and even profound, was completely unexpected. Angela also expressed surprise at encountering this type of subconscious emotional block.

Does this emotional theme mean that I was already in oneness before incarnating and my physical incarnation would stifle me from feeling that connection to oneness, from experiencing the flow of oneness? I'm not exactly sure what this emotional theme means, but it is fascinating to be experiencing a conscious perspective held by my soul at the energetic beginning (conception) of this lifetime.

It was only the beginning of my sessions with Angela and I was already getting glimpses of my soul, which I found personally intriguing.

This emotional theme really resonated with me, as it confirmed to me that we don't consciously enter our current lifetime as babies who are unaware. We, as souls, are very cognizant of what lies ahead and behind us as we incarnate.

The concept that we know what lies ahead of us was very evident in another session I experienced a short time later. In this particular session, the subconscious block was from my heart holding a *present-day emotion* of being *frightfully overjoyed* in my current *role*, expressing as a *mystic* in this lifetime. The specifics of the *present-day emotional theme* were that, "I was joyful at interacting with Universe as a mystic while at the same time frightened of the responsibility and of doing something wrong."

Frightfully overjoyed was a perfect way to express how conflicted I felt when doing spiritual work. On one hand, I felt the bliss of being spiritually connected while at the same time fearful I would misinterpret something being energetically conveyed through higher consciousness. Constantly, I questioned my relationship to divine consciousness, the information, or the outcome because of my fear of getting something wrong. This caused me to not only feel personally conflicted but also distracted and even exhausted through constantly fighting my fear.

But now, in this session, I had hope that this block would be cleared, allaying my fears so I could more fully experience bliss when interacting with Universe. (And that's exactly what happened. The "fright" part of frightfully overjoyed was gone, leaving me able to fully experience joy.)

Once the present-day emotion and emotional theme are identified, we then move on to pinpointing the origin (original occurrence) of the present-day emotional theme of feeling overjoyed at doing something while frightened of the responsibility and of doing it wrong.

Angela and I had determined, through muscle testing, that the *origin* for this *emotional theme* was *conception,* but we hit a snag trying to identify the specifics surrounding the original emotional theme.

Specifics can involve the role you are expressing (artist, accountant, soldier, etc.) as well as anyone involved with you in the role you are expressing, such as family, friends, and others. When Angela queried my subconscious as to whether the category of "family, friends, others" was relevant, my subconscious indicated that the category of "family" was congruent to the original emotional theme.

Okay. As Angela explains it, family can either mean "family you made" (family that originates from you, such as husband, children, grandchildren) or "family you came from" (such as mother, father, grandparents).

Pretty simple. Through muscle testing, my subconscious indicated that *family you came from* was congruent with my subconscious; yet, when we tested mother, father, grandfather, grandmother, or any other term associated with family you came from, nothing was testing as the congruent concept.

Angela retested "family you came from," which was still testing congruent (accurate). This was very perplexing, as we had tested for and exhausted all traditional family member roles. Angela paused the session and instructed me to close my eyes, forget everything, relax, and just let the thoughts come into my mind. Quite surprisingly, the term *spiritual family* immediately flowed into my mind from a higher conscious thought and out of my mouth. Angela immediately tested this concept, and it was congruent. This was the term (spiritual family) my subconscious was resolute about us identifying.

This is a perfect example of the profound higher conscious interaction that was occurring in my sessions. The concept of spiritual family as part of the "family you came from" was an extraordinary concept and one that Angela had never previously encountered as part of this technique. And although I'd always sensed there was a group of spiritual beings around me, I'd never consciously thought of them as my spiritual family.

It was amazing to realize that my own subconscious mind not only recognizes a group of beings not physically present on earth as the *spiritual family you came from,* but also that this spiritual family is somehow energetically involved in a subconscious emotional block. This insight was more than a little mouth dropping for both of us. Not only were my sessions now involving very unusual spiritual overtones, but I was also beginning to consciously perceive that much more higher conscious interaction was occurring than I initially realized.

At this point in the session, we had determined that the emotion of being frightfully overjoyed originated at conception and somehow involved my spiritual family. We were now muscle testing concepts to determine the original emotional theme. Once again, almost immediately, a higher conscious thought flowed through my mind, and when muscle tested, my subconscious indicated it was congruent. The congruent *emotional theme, originating at conception* was that, "I am *joyful* at what I am to do in this lifetime; yet, *fearful* of the responsibility and of letting down my spiritual family."

Angela then queried and muscle tested my subconscious. No additional details were needed, and there were no additional emotions connected to this emotional block.

We immediately moved on to the part of the session where we release the emotional block, repeating the technique previously used.

After the session ended, all I could think was, *Wow, that was really unusual.* It was intriguing to now be consciously aware of my spiritual family and to know that my spiritual family was somehow connected to what I was to experience in this lifetime. Did this emotional theme mean that my spiritual family would somehow share in something I would do in this lifetime? When I get back to the spiritual realm, does my spiritual family hold up little cards, rating how I've done? Not hardly. But it does make sense to me that my spiritual family must somehow energetically share in my life experience. Why else would something I'm doing in my lifetime be able to cause my spiritual family's let down? Maybe I'm the "designated driver" for the journey of this lifetime and my spiritual family is sharing in the "ride," but they are not directly responsible for either the "route" I take or the way I handle the "vehicle."

I can't help but wonder about what I'm in jeopardy of either doing less than expected, not doing at all, or doing wrong in this lifetime. Yipes! Have I already missed the window of opportunity? Have I already done something that will impede the event from manifesting? Thoughts poured into my mind and went everywhere.

This session involved a lot more than merely snippets of information about a subconscious emotional block. It was like having a sneak peek at what I, as a soul, was holding in my consciousness as I was embarking upon my current lifetime. Looking into the life ahead of me at that moment of conception, I was simultaneously anticipating joy at what I was to do; yet, I was fearful of what might happen and how it would affect my spiritual family.

As I was having these thoughts, I realized that this session had unexpectedly presented me with an opportunity to possibly affect my destiny by holding a conscious intention that whatever it is that I committed to do in this lifetime will not only be done but be done well.

In thinking back on these types of sessions, I realized that the origins of these present-day emotional themes were at conception. To me, conception is the energetic beginning of a lifetime, so how could there already be a subconscious emotional block before anything in the current lifetime has even been experienced? The block isn't from something that already happened, prior to conception, or we would go back into a past life for the origin. No, the subconscious emotional block is *at* conception. To me, this can only mean that it's caused from something we are anticipating will or won't happen in the lifetime ahead.

After experiencing these two sessions, I realized that an emotional theme originating at conception is a telltale sign that we have entered our current lifetime predisposed to a frame of mind. Any emotional block that occurs at the moment of conception is significant in what it reveals about how we are perceiving the lifetime ahead of us. These type of subconscious blocks can give us profound insight about who we are as souls as well as how we are perceiving our self in relation to the lifetime we are about to experience and the emotional challenges we will encounter along the way.

Here I was expecting to open up my destiny through chakra balancing, which had basically been a wash; yet, amazingly, I had stumbled onto a profound technique that was speaking volumes to me personally and spiritually.

Though I did not realize it then, no stumbling was ever involved. Rather, I had merely arrived at the moment pre-destined by Benevolence for the *knowing* that graced me as a child to begin unfolding within my waking conscious awareness.

It was a knowing destined to not just awaken in me, but in all souls.

Chapter 17

Letting It Ride

One night, a short time after beginning the new therapy with Angela that involved testing affirmations for congruency with my subconscious, I was drifting to sleep when a gentle knowing came over me regarding the higher conscious thought, "*Someday an acupuncturist will open up your destiny.*"

For the first time, I realized that the words "chakra balancing" were never a part of Universe's message to me. I had always just assumed that chakra balancing was associated with the message, as I was reading about a person experiencing phenomenal spiritual awakenings through an acupuncturist doing chakra balancing.

This conscious awareness took me by complete surprise, as I had never previously realized that my own mind had made the leap to chakra balancing as being the modality for my destiny opening. Universe only "spoke" of an acupuncturist—there was no mention of the method used ... I had just *assumed* it was chakra balancing.

Just before falling asleep, a thought filled my mind, *Angela is an acupuncturist. Let's just see if that destiny thing is still going to open up through her—if she is the one foretold me by my higher conscious awareness so long ago.*

Immediately, I felt myself smile as I realized that oftentimes we lead ourselves one place (acupuncturist) because we are convinced of why we are going (chakra balancing), only to find we are actually there for an entirely different reason—a yet unperceived purpose.

Finally, I understood why I sensed my higher consciousness chuckling. This was the little joke I had played on myself. I assumed I was at an acupuncturist to experience chakra balancing when that was merely an energetic hook to bring me to this particular place to experience whatever Universe and my soul have in mind—regardless of my intent and focus.

As my last waking conscious thought merged into my sleeping breath, my heart was at peace thinking that maybe in this lifetime I would still get to experience that long-ago promise from Universe. Maybe even now I was firmly on my destiny path; maybe we all are, always.

Chapter 18

Our Subconscious: Vault, Gatekeeper, and Key

In reflecting on the sessions I'd been experiencing with Angela, I began to detect emerging central themes in some of my past lives, even if the specific roles were different. A few key central themes were energetically entwined with emotional blocks related to written or verbal expression of my spiritual nature.

For instance, in past lives where I was a spiritual teacher, author, or mystic, there were emotional blocks in these lifetimes about being recognized by people for my spiritual teachings, writings, or abilities. Some of these emotional blocks were created due to a fear of being persecuted; others were due to people identifying with me personally instead of the spiritual message I was conveying; and still others involved a fear that the spiritual messages I conveyed would not be accepted because of my background—humble beginnings, no formal training, etc.

Considering how much of my focus in this lifetime has been on spirituality, it shouldn't have surprised me to find that I had similar emotional issues in my current lifetime as those in past lives related to expressing my spiritual nature, especially now when I understand that some emotional reactions in my current lifetime might be influenced or even triggered by subconscious blocks created from experiences in the past.

It was easy to identify with these past life issues, as I had already experienced these same fears in my current life when doing spiritual work out in the world. If I remained in a safe environment or in a small group of people with whom I felt comfortable, everything was fine. But when I found myself among people seeking me out for spiritual interaction due to growing recognition of my spiritual abilities, these subconscious blocks were triggered. Once that happened, it was only a matter of time before I found some excuse to step back from my spiritual work and retreat to the safety of a hidden life. There was strong subconscious resistance to being recognized or associated with my spiritual work.

There was also an intriguing group of lifetimes related to spiritual missions I was not able to fulfill where an aspect of the emotional theme involved my spiritual family holding a belief that I was the one to perform the task based upon my identity.

This specific term, identity, also kept popping up in a few sessions involving a soul issue related to spiritual self-identity. This concept revolved around my reluctance to embrace my individual essence, as my entire focus was on divinity rather than myself. Adoration and love of divinity were so strongly held within my soul consciousness that I did not desire to experience my self-identity at all, choosing rather to fully embrace divinity to the denial of self.

Once this issue of identity clarified itself in my waking conscious awareness, I realized that the issue of identity was interwoven in other emotional themes already experienced in quite a few of my earlier sessions.

It was really fascinating to realize our current lifetime can reflect central themes we have carried throughout many incarnations—or even a deeply-held soul issue. But in order to perceive these themes, we have to have the dots to connect. I realized those dots could be found by accessing our subconscious emotional blocks.

Everything experienced in these sessions involving my subconscious helped me to realize that not only does our subconscious hold the information (the vault), but it also releases it (the gatekeeper) in the manner that is appropriate for what needs to be cleared (the key). Amazing, isn't it? Our quiet, reticent subconscious is vault, gatekeeper, and key.

At some point in this process, I had begun wondering why the term "lifetimes ago" was accepted as congruent by my subconscious when I wasn't always physically incarnated in human form. Sometimes the past lifetime involved me expressing as a spiritual form, an essence, or a vibration, but always my subconscious allowed the term lifetimes ago to be acceptable when moving back through past lives (preconception). There is no doubt in my mind that the term lifetimes ago applies in a way that the subconscious accepts, as I personally experienced many sessions where terminology was rejected by my subconscious. My subconscious was not just letting this term, lifetimes ago, slip by.

Eventually I realized I had been looking at this terminology too narrowly, through the perspective of my human consciousness. A lifetime was consciously perceived by me to only mean when I was physically incarnated on earth, experiencing a life in human form. But then I realized that human embodiment wasn't the common thread in all the lifetimes I experienced, as I wasn't always in human (physical) form. Sometimes I was in spirit (essence) form or energy (vibration) form.

The common thread in any lifetime was consciousness. We are always conscious while in any state of being. Every time we incarnate or extend our conscious beingness as a new expression, whether as human form, spirit form, or energy, it is perceived by our subconscious to be a *new expression of conscious beingness* (lifetime).

We, as human beings, think of a lifetime as relating only to physical incarnation because that is the form we now hold in our current life expression. But our subconscious mind is able to view the entirety of what we have consciously experienced as every form of expression, no matter what form we held. So while human form is an embodiment that characterizes physical incarnation on the earth plane, it does not define all conscious expressions nor lifetimes.

Consciousness is the only common denominator in any expression of beingness, and our subconscious accepts the term lifetimes ago no matter the expression/role (human being, spirit form, or vibrational energy) and no matter the location (earth or another location).

As my sessions continued, a surprising higher conscious thought came into my mind: *Our subconscious is not just ours alone, but rather our subconscious is simultaneously the universal collective unconscious.*

Up until this time in my life, I've never thought of my subconscious—that part of me that seems to be controlling my unconscious self—as being the collective unconscious. I'd always thought of the collective unconscious as more of a group of all unconscious (unmanifested) thoughts and feelings that existed somewhere in Universe. Although I hadn't really ever thought of collective unconsciousness simultaneously existing within me as my subconscious, it really made sense for several reasons.

It explains why anyone who is sensitive is able to discern past, present, and future information and events about people they are energetically connected with in person, by telephone, or by merely focusing on their energy. Sensitive people are tapping into the universal collective unconscious—the all-knowing awareness carried within their own subconscious beingness.

They are not connecting with some magic place outside of themselves through a gift only they possess. They are reaching inside themselves to a space of consciousness that holds all the information ever known in Universe. The gift is not that they possess this ability; it is that they are utilizing an ability that everyone possesses. Sensitives have just awakened to a natural ability within themselves that others may not yet have perceived.

Once, when I was first beginning to awaken to my spirituality, Universe conveyed the energetic thought, *Your footsteps will echo in the hall of records.* At the time, I had no idea what the term "hall of records" meant but thought of it as the space where all knowing—all past, present, and future information—is held. Although I didn't believe it was a physical place, such as a library, I'd always conceptualized it to exist outside of myself, accessed through higher consciousness—as though I was reaching up into the ethers of Universe, through my higher mind, to touch it.

Now I realize that divine "all-knowingness" is carried within each and every one of us, accessible through our own subconscious.

Think of it as though we are always mainlining allness and all aspects of consciousness (collective unconscious, collective conscious, higher conscious, subconscious). Everything—all knowing—is carried within each of us. We need only learn to allow ourselves to consciously perceive the typically imperceptible within us. In this way, our own waking awareness is the bridge within us between **all that is** (exists) and **all that is known** consciously.

Our subconscious is the key to unlocking our inner knowing, our blocks, our destiny, and all knowing. It stores the information of our soul, of our mind, and of our experiences, as well as that of all souls—all consciousness.

Another reason I came to believe that our individual subconscious is, in fact, the collective unconscious all of us are simultaneously experiencing is from something revealed in one of my earliest sessions. In this particular session, the block in my subconscious was not caused by my emotions but by emotions and an emotional theme belonging to another person.

This session changed how I perceived consciousness. It was no longer perceived as being isolated within me, but rather my subconscious (our subconscious) is interwoven as the consciousness of everyone and everything.

In this thought-provoking session, my *present-day emotional theme* was that, "I was *overjoyed* at being a channel for God yet, *fearful* of the responsibility and of doing something wrong and displeasing God (frightfully overjoyed)."

The *origin* of my present-day emotional theme went back before I was born, *two months in utero* (in the womb), to *my mother's* blocked emotional theme of: "being overjoyed at becoming a mother, but fearful she would displease God and he would take her child."

My mother's fear (not mine) of displeasing God was imprinted (blocked) in my subconscious all the way back to when I was first beginning this lifetime, influencing my entire life.

My subconscious block was not originally created by my own fear but by another person's fear. For this to occur, our individual subconscious must simultaneously be the collective unconsciousness of all beings—all energy. Otherwise, how could someone else's emotional theme not only be known within me but also blocked within me? For this to occur, it makes perfect sense that we are all interconnected as one consciousness.

All energies, all expressions, and all existence are interconnected. But connected by what? It really can't be anything other than consciousness. Conscious, unconscious, subconscious, higher conscious—it doesn't matter, as it is all still awareness, consciously perceived or not.

Although I'm sensing it is true that we are all connected through the collective unconscious, I'm wondering why I'm not experiencing unlimited emotional blocks belonging to many other people (the entire collective) within my own subconscious. Why isn't every emotional block ever created within anyone not popping up in my subconscious?

Higher conscious thoughts began flowing through my mind, and I realized that another soul's emotional blocks can become our own subconscious blocks when our natural empathy with each other becomes sympathy. We are all empathetically bonded with each other, but if we experience the emotional intensity of another's experience so deeply that the empathetic line is crossed, then whatever the other soul experiences is mutually shared by us and can become emotionally blocked within us.

The nature of empathy is "to understand" another person's feelings, whereas, the nature of sympathy is "to share" another person's feelings. Immediately, I realized why the subconscious emotional block (in one of my first sessions) related to being "*overly sympathetic to people and attached to an outcome*" had created such a tremendous impact on my life. I had crossed the line between empathy and sympathy when I was spiritually interacting with others. I was not just empathetically caring and understanding of what they were experiencing; I was sympathetically experiencing their suffering as if it were my own. Empathy and sympathy are both energetic expressions of caring, but sympathy can sometimes be so intensely felt that the suffering of another becomes energetically imprinted within us. Now I more clearly understand what a tremendous blessing it was for me to have been able to release that particular subconscious emotional block.

This is an important message for all of us. We should always be empathetic—understanding and caring—but when we sense we are crossing the line, it's time to explore what is creating that overly sympathetic reaction. For me, it was a need to personally help alleviate suffering, and my sympathy became a badge reflecting my degree of personal commitment.

There's nothing wrong with wanting to help someone and even being personally committed, but it is how you facilitate that help that reflects if you have crossed the empathetic line. You can significantly impact another person's life, but you shouldn't do it by living their path as yours—which is inappropriate for both you and them.

A beautiful example of this is something done by three caring souls: Carolyn, her daughter, Jessica, and Carolyn's sister, Sharon. They saw the suffering of a homeless man and decided they might be able to help him to change his own life. The easy thing for them to do would have been to just give him handouts, but they realized money wasn't what this man needed. He needed his life back. They chose, through the grace of their hearts, to help him find a way that would alleviate his suffering, not just put a bandage on it. They weren't looking to feel good about themselves or receive praise. They were looking to help a man reclaim his life—a man who had touched their hearts.

This man, who had lived on the street for years with his beloved dogs, is now living in his own home with secure employment. Why? All because a soul walked by and gathered like-spirited souls to find a way to help this man alleviate his own suffering.

This is a perfect example of alleviating another soul's suffering without crossing the line. They held a conscious intention that if he wanted to change, they would help him. Their hands were extended to him in empathetic support, but always he had take the action necessary to facilitate the change. Never was it a case of them pushing him off to the sidelines of his own life while they fixed it for him.

We can make a tremendous difference in other people's lives. But it's important to remember that we must always honor the path of the soul. It is their path ... not ours. And we should never make it ours. We have our own soul path, and we should always honor that as well.

For the first time in my life, I now understand why so many things have impacted me. This session and these thoughts from higher consciousness perfectly clarified the difference between empathy and sympathy in my mind, my heart, and my spirit. That knowing will make all the difference in how I live the rest of my life. And maybe it will make a difference in how you live yours too.

It was all so very intriguing—this relationship between our own subconscious and the collective unconscious—that I couldn't help but wonder about all the possibilities available to us when we learn to really tap into the unknown within each of us.

At this point, it seemed to me that everything fell into the category of either conscious or unconscious. But in the back of my mind, there was a nagging little thought that I am missing something and that it wasn't at all as straightforward as either conscious or unconscious.

Though I didn't really understand what I could be missing, I filed these thoughts away. My mind was the library housing all these thoughts, and my consciousness was the vigilant librarian, sorting and cataloging all of the mental cards and notes—sometimes frantically—not knowing what would eventually unfold but somehow sensing I was positioned on the event horizon of a new conscious awareness.

Chapter 19

Pulling a Thread in the
Tapestry of Divine Consciousness

*Truth is often what we perceive through our
own reflection, rather than what we perceive,
experience, and express as our true state
of beingness. Until we stand as our
true beingness and not outside
of it, we misperceive our own
beingness to be whatever
"truth" we perceive.*

Imagine that your essence, the very fabric of your being, is a
thread. This thread runs through all experiences, all lifetimes, and
all expressions of consciousness held within each soul's center. It is
the divine thread that has unfolded the space of consciousness in
which we now exist—in which we have always existed. And that
space of consciousness can reveal our very beginnings because it is the
consciousness all of us are holding.

The expression of divine consciousness is as varied as the number of
stars in the seen universe, but at its core, the reason for that expression
can only be one truth. That truth is what I had searched for my entire
lifetime, and I think that is what each of us is seeking, though that
intention can be well hidden from our conscious awareness most of the
time.

Many years ago, I wrote the following higher conscious thought:
Truth is a multi-dimensional lie; what you believe depends on your angle.
It seemed the message in these words is that we have come to believe
truth to be something based upon our perceptions or our experiences.
But what if *truth just is* and until we are standing as truth and not
outside of it, we will only be able to perceive aspects of truth based
upon our angle (our consciousness, our experiences, our perceptions)

rather than truth itself? If we are standing at any angle to truth, then truth is distorted through our perception, and once distorted, we are viewing a mistruth or in effect, a multi-dimensional lie.

What if the message of these higher conscious words is that we have never perceived or experienced truth in its purest form? What if we have based everything we know, going all the way back to our beginning, upon a misperception that we accepted as true because of our inability to perceive the entirety of our own pure truth, our true beingness?

The thought that truth was skewed by my perceptions held me captive for many years, creating a search for pure truth. Often over the years, when I thought I'd arrived at truth, I would sense, "No, that's not it either. I'll know when I'm there, as it will ring so true that there will be no doubt and I won't be able to glimpse any other perspective that seems more real." So on I searched.

Isn't the truth of "who am I?" at the heart of what all of us are seeking? It is a search that involves us experiencing, processing, and then experiencing some more as we journey through lifetime after lifetime as Avatars of Consciousness. To me that is the magnificence of consciousness; our ability to follow impulse, logic, intuition, and theories—accumulating what we perceive to be just random bits of information—until a thread of conscious thought links all those pieces into an entire knowing that has always been sitting right there in front of us, just waiting for us to consciously realize it.

This lifetime is the rarest of lifetimes. We are more fully conscious in this lifetime than we have ever been. It is an amazing time to be living. Yet, we get so caught up in making a living or trying not to succumb to negative forces all around us that we don't realize how blessed we are to be here, right now, at this time and in this space. We have forgotten that we chose to be here. Why? For many of us, it is because we want to consciously awaken and claim our birthright—our divine conscious nature.

Hold on to the concept that we, as souls, may not yet have recognized the pure truth of ourselves. Hold on to the concept that this lifetime is the lifetime we will have that conscious awareness so we can begin to release from illusion (multi-dimensional lies) and embrace our truth.

For me, the search began in earnest the day I found myself perceiving everything I was experiencing as a thread within the tapestry of divine consciousness. There had been far too great a number of profound experiences in my life for me to pass them off as merely coincidence without any greater purpose. And as I began pondering the purpose behind my life, it seemed as though a thread connected everything. Then, as I began consciously and energetically pulling on that thread to see where it would take me, I was hoping it would lead to me to the ultimate purpose of my life.

At one point, I thought the thread had led me to acupuncture for chakra balancing in order to open my destiny, the purpose of my life. But that didn't seem to be the intention. Instead, the thread led me to a profound energetic technique to clear subconscious emotional blocks, assumingly to heal my physical body so I could enjoy my life and my true self more fully.

But that, too, wasn't the destination intended by that divine thread, and as I moved backward, searching for the origins (first occurrence) of my subconscious emotional blocks, I wasn't at all surprised to find that they went back three lifetimes ago, and twelve lifetimes ago, and even thirty-three lifetimes ago. But imagine my surprise when I kept going back: fifty lifetimes ago; ninety-nine lifetimes ago; 499 lifetimes ago; and even 599 lifetimes ago? (When was that, I wondered?)

It made sense to me that there would be unresolved issues or emotional blocks in my past lives. Why not? What's so different about then (back in past lives) or now? But experiencing past life blocks to clear aspects of my physical embodiment, my emotions, my individual personality, and even my soul wasn't the only intention that divine thread was revealing or where it would consciously lead me.

Quite incredibly, my longing to find answers kept me following that thread until it eventually led me all the way back to the beginning of collective human consciousness. But even when standing in that extraordinary moment, I wasn't able to fully comprehend what was being revealed.

At each point where a conscious awareness was awakened in me, I sensed there was a profound correlation between the various aspects revealed, but I wasn't able to tie it all together, because key pieces of information remained dormant, held within my unconscious awareness. And until fuller knowing awakened within me, I was unable to perceive the interconnectedness of all those moments of awareness.

We tend, through our human perception, to assume that if we have had an awareness that we are perceiving the allness involved in the awareness. But this is a misperception created by our need to always assign definition to everything we perceive, not realizing that our definition is limited by our scope of view. Our view is created by how we relate a new conscious awareness to everything we already know. We do not perceive in relation to *everything that is* (exists). Rather, we only perceive in relation to *everything that is known within us*. The vast difference is that we are only able to perceive after we have experienced. We can sense before we experience, but we cannot connect dots and perceive the depth of something until it has been experienced and awakened within us. It must be made known within us before we are able to perceive the depth of the awareness. Thus, oftentimes we move through life assuming we know all we need to— until we sense a deeper meaning or an unexplored connectedness.

At many points along the way of unfolding this conscious knowing within me, I was limited by the borders of my own waking consciousness, and the interconnectedness of information to my soul and to divine consciousness was not immediately perceived. Although I thought the tidbits of awareness were profoundly interesting, I only initially viewed these pieces as snapshots of me. I didn't realize that those snapshots weren't just related to me, as a person and as a soul, but that they were actually clues in unraveling the great mystery of all of us as collective human consciousness.

Even when standing at the very threshold of collective human consciousness, clarity of all that I was experiencing didn't immediately come. Why? It was because the thread in the divine tapestry I was holding could only transport me to the moment where the enlightened knowing was to be found. But the knowing itself had to unfold through my own waking consciousness; it would not happen by me just standing in the moment.

True knowing can only awaken within us by pulling the moment through us, energetically, rather than holding the awareness outside of us as a snapshot of the experience. It is the difference between hearing or reading a truth and feeling and knowing a truth. Reading a perception or hearing a concept does not activate conscious knowing; it only activates conscious awareness. Knowing must be experienced energetically in order for it to touch the subtle energies of our own being and trigger remembrance within us of that knowing. Having our eyes skate over a passage in a book does not activate knowing; it only activates conscious awareness. And conscious awareness alone does not awaken us—it only leads us to the moment where knowing can awaken us.

For example, consider when you are having a conversation with a friend where you are sharing something relevant to him or her, and he or she immediately dismisses what you are saying by responding, "I know, I know." Your friend's response may be a sign that he or she doesn't know but rather that he or she is just consciously aware of what is occurring. Why is he or she aware? Maybe because this subject has been previously broached with him or her by you or someone else in an effort to help him or her, but your friend has not personally pulled the energetic knowing contained in the experience through him or herself. He or she is just experiencing the snapshot of the moment, not the energy of the moment itself and is unable to perceive the depth of energetic knowing carried in the moment. And most importantly, maybe he or she isn't consciously ready to know, as there are other things that must be experienced by your friend first—things of which you or other people are not aware.

When this happens, don't be frustrated. Instead, shine the light on your own self and try to perceive something that you, too, may be assuming you know but do not. We all have 20/20 vision when it comes to other people's issues while being blinded to our own. Therefore, grace must always be extended by all of us to each other when it comes to what we perceive about others in relation to what they perceive about themselves, because it might not yet be the proper time for them to know. This way, grace will always, then, likewise, be extended to us when it is not yet time for us to know.

Knowing comes from an energetic connectedness to an awareness, not just a knowledge that the awareness exists.

The profound knowing held within the confines of my very own consciousness—tethered there, as a thread within the tapestry of divine consciousness—was only known when I was energetically pulling it consciously through me.

For instance: What is an enlightened awareness contained within the tapestry of divine consciousness?

It is this: We are not only an individual thread, but we are all the individual threads as well as the entirety of the tapestry, all at the very same moment (All-at-Once Consciousness).

Some of you have just perceived this example as a conscious awareness, and some of you have energetically experienced this example as a conscious knowing. Connecting to how you experience can be as insightful as what you experience. Why? It reveals what we may be resisting or avoiding because we intuitively sense what we know long before we ever energetically experience the unfolding of that knowing within our consciousness.

Why aren't we allowing our knowing to come forth into our consciousness? It may be because we are not ready. Other experiences must occur; other awakenings must be consciously experienced.

Many of us sense the knowing that we are the divine thread in the tapestry of divine consciousness, but we just don't yet consciously remember what we already know. But when our conscious remembrance of what we have always known occurs, we will have pulled the energetic knowing of our divine nature consciously through us ... and we will be awakened to our remembrance.

Chapter 20

Glimpsing the Cornerstone of Awareness

It is impossible to remain in a conscious state of perfection if you hold anything outside yourself as being more perfect. By doing so, perfection becomes a goal to attain rather than a state of being, which always places you outside seeking rather than just being.

Many changes had occurred in all aspects of my life over the past three months. No longer was I held hostage by a personality altered by fear and doubt, as I was going about my life doing positive things that I had been unable to do for a number of years—maybe even my entire life.

The release of a major subconscious block about writing had opened up a wonderful new world. Plus it was an incredible testament to the credibility of this type of process, as any of my previous attempts at writing had always been met with frustration or self-sabotage.

Can you imagine what your life would be if suddenly you were able to pursue your heartfelt intentions by alleviating unperceived emotional blocks? Just by interacting with your own subconscious, you could manifest your intentions and experience phenomenal changes in your life. It is almost too amazing to believe, but it is true.

Of course, there are always those who may choose to pooh-pooh the validity of this type of subconscious technique. I completely understand their skepticism, as it does seem rather unbelievable that something so simple could effectuate such remarkable changes. But it is true. Each of us knows, deep within ourselves, when something has shifted, and I knew that I was now experiencing my life as never before. I had regained my sense of joy as well as a deep connection to my true self. Results made me a believer, grateful for the experience, while the profundity of these sessions captured my attention.

Many of my sessions had yielded unexpected spiritual insights, and I began to very much look forward to these revelations. But nothing was to captivate me as much as the sessions that began happening around the spring of 2009, not only because of the information being revealed but also because there was now a rhythm, an order, to when and where each session was to take me. It was so consciously transformational and spiritually uplifting that I didn't worry about anything except showing up and letting my soul and higher (divine) consciousness guide.

Prior to this time, Angela and I had been using affirmations that we had constructed centered around my intentions concerning various areas of my life, such as spiritual, financial, marriage, career, etc.

One day during this period, I was sitting in the waiting room, meditating before my session began. I briefly meditated before all my sessions as an energetic transition from the activity of daily life to peacefully centering myself for interaction with more subtle vibrations. While I was meditating, a beautiful light was filling my third eye, and my mind was receiving higher conscious thoughts about love. Then, as I was coming out of this meditation, a very specific affirmation was imbued in my mind through energetic thought from higher consciousness.

Instead of using an affirmation on our prepared list, I opted to utilize this specific affirmation that I perceived through higher conscious awareness. Unbeknownst to me, this would be the jumping-off point of an extraordinary shift in my sessions. From this point forward, my sessions were not just atypical, in that almost every session went back to a past life, but they also involved a mystical component where both my subconscious and higher self worked in concert with my waking conscious mind to unfold concepts deeply moving to me emotionally, spiritually, and consciously.

I would begin the session with a specific affirmation from higher consciousness. Then, once I was in the session, my higher consciousness worked in harmony with my waking conscious mind to convey extraordinary concepts, terminology, and insights that were posed and muscle tested with my subconscious for congruency—all of which contributed to unraveling the complex emotional themes held in these lifetimes. Not only did the affirmations reveal subconscious emotional blocks related to extraordinary concepts about all of us as souls, but there was also a timing as far as when and how the information unfolded. My subconscious would take me back—through a particular affirmation given by higher consciousness—to a specific cluster of lifetimes, revealing interwoven concepts throughout the cluster (typically a series involving three lifetimes) before moving on. The order in which I experienced the lifetimes in the cluster was random, but there was always cohesion between the lifetimes in these clusters.

This process, experiencing one cluster of lifetimes before moving to a new cluster, very much helped me to consciously perceive correlations between the *cluster lifetimes*—even though I was well into the second cluster of lifetimes before I consciously recognized this pattern. (Eventually, I learned that these cluster lifetimes always involved major shifts in consciousness.)

There was no way to miss the divine intention behind what was happening. It was like being on a carpet of information that was designed to unfold as it did and when it did. I just utilized a specific higher conscious affirmation, and the rest naturally occurred.

One of my first experiences with one of these type of cluster lifetimes began one morning by using a specific affirmation received through higher consciousness. My subconscious indicated that this affirmation was indeed incongruent, which meant there was a subconscious emotional block. Muscle testing has determined that the *present-day emotion* involved in the subconscious block is *inefficient*. The congruent *present-day emotional theme* was that, "I am feeling inefficient when working because I feel torn between obligation to others versus what I feel I am supposed to be doing. The emotion of inefficiency was caused by feeling like my energy was split between two worlds: what I feel obligated to do (working with my husband in business) versus what I felt I should be doing (spiritual work with Universe). And I'm feeling as though I can't do both equally well (efficiently) at the same time."

Muscle testing confirmed that there was a prior original time when this emotional theme first occurred. As we began our search backward for the *origin* of this *present-day emotional theme*, I was once more in preconception and muscle testing took me to a lifetime that was *999 lifetimes ago*. After having already experienced quite a few unusual sessions that went back over 599 lifetimes ago, I was comfortable with the process and not shocked by a timeframe this far back.

Just before Angela started testing for the role being expressed in this lifetime, 999 lifetimes ago, I wasn't really expecting to be anything other than a human being on Earth. But that's not what happened. For the first time in all my sessions, I wasn't human, and I wasn't on earth.

Imagine that your subconscious rejects the words "human being" and "earth" as being congruent (harmonious) with a subconscious emotional block created 999 lifetimes ago. It causes you to come to a screeching halt in these type of sessions—that's for sure—because you don't initially know what else you could have been if not human on earth.

Fortunately, the term *in spirit* came into Angela's mind, and when she posed it to my subconscious, it was congruent with the *role* I was expressing. But Angela and I didn't get off that easy, as my subconscious indicated that more details regarding this role of "in spirit" were needed. This is where we hit a bump, as the few typical concepts that popped into my mind—such as spirit guide— were not testing as congruent. This created an unusual, unexpected mental impasse, and we were forced to begin posing and testing many atypical concepts (let your imagination run wild here for a moment). During this process, I had to consciously remind myself that the term "lifetime" is perceived by our subconscious to be a new expression of conscious beingness. I couldn't let myself get mentally hung up on the fact that the role I was expressing as was not a human being on earth.

Eventually, Angela (my hero!) put forth the word "master," which muscle tested as accurate, but my subconscious still would not let us move on without clarifying the location (which we knew was not earth).

We began thinking about where else I could have been in a lifetime 999 lifetimes ago. After muscle testing a few of my thoughts that were incongruent, Angela uttered the phrase "another dimension," which she then posed to my subconscious and which muscle tested as congruent to the location.

So, at this point in the session, we determined that in this particular lifetime *999 lifetimes ago*, I was a *master in spirit in another dimension*. After we tested for the role (master in spirit) and the location (another dimension), I was hoping more information would unfold, as I wondered how that dimension correlated to earth, but to my disappointment, no further details were needed or forthcoming about either the role or the location.

In these sessions, I try never to get caught up in identifying with a role or an expression, as they are stepping-stones to revealing the emotional theme. I've learned that although the details can be interesting, the purpose of the session isn't about unearthing the entire story of the lifetime. It's about revealing components of the emotional theme necessary for the subconscious to release the block, and when tested, the subconscious will always indicate whether additional details are needed.

As we continued through the session, posing statements and muscle testing my subconscious, the following additional information related to the *original emotional theme* was revealed by my higher consciousness and all muscle tested as congruent: "999 lifetimes ago, I am a master in spirit in another dimension. My spiritual family is involved. And a natural disaster is about to occur."

At this point in the session, I was perplexed as to how the present-day emotional theme could possibly relate to an impending disaster involving my spiritual family. I had no idea why my subconscious took me back to this lifetime, as I couldn't see any correlation, any subconscious link, at all. But the correlation was spot on once the particulars of the original emotional theme were revealed.

The following specifics were conveyed through higher conscious thought and all tested as congruent regarding the *original emotional theme:* "In this lifetime, 999 lifetimes ago, my spiritual family believed that I would be able to prevent a natural disaster that is about to occur based upon their perception of me—my identity. Although my spiritual family wanted me to attempt this feat (prevent this disaster), I was there, in this specific lifetime, to fulfill a different function (the details of which were not clarified). Even though my spiritual family believed I could simultaneously perform both tasks, I did not believe I could do both efficiently. So, I was feeling torn between a sense of obligation to my spiritual family to try and perform the task they desired versus what I felt I was supposed to be doing in this lifetime."

An "obligation to others versus what I felt I was supposed to be doing." This original emotional theme tied perfectly to the present-day emotional theme!

This was a profound confirmation of the credibility of this type of subconscious technique. Initially, I had no idea how the present-day emotional theme could correlate to this past life, 999 lifetimes ago; yet, as the session unfolded, the reason my subconscious had made a connection, a link, between the present-day emotional theme and the original emotional theme was very obvious.

Not surprisingly, muscle testing revealed that I wasn't successful in performing both roles, as I felt ill equipped to be doing both simultaneously. I was feeling inefficient in relation to how I perceived my own abilities versus the magnitude of the task.

The session ended with me clearing this emotional block in only a matter of seconds. I was momentarily amazed that something so easily cleared could be held so deeply and for so many lifetimes within my subconscious.

The details in this session helped me to consciously realize that this technique for releasing subconscious emotional blocks is a valid way to dialogue with my subconscious; my soul. This session was corroboration of the validity of this technique. The proof was that even when I could not perceive how the original emotional theme related to the present-day emotional theme—and I honestly didn't believe it did—it was proven to be profoundly accurate once the session unfolded and the details were known.

My personal life significantly changed after this session. I no longer resisted doing both business and spiritual work, nor did I worry about what I was supposed to be doing or if I was doing it efficiently. The tremendous pressure I had been feeling in my life was gone and was replaced by a knowing it would all just work out. (And it did.)

After this session, I was intrigued by the fact that we exist in other dimensions in forms or roles that may or may not be similar to that of an earthly experience and there are a group of beings that we consider to be our spiritual family that are sometimes involved, sharing in the experience.

Obviously, our lifetimes are linked in a way that allows our subconscious to experience it all no matter when, where, or what occurs—whether on earth or in another dimension; whether as spirit or human form.

I was wondering what else we experienced and where else we had been throughout the unfolding of our lifetimes, as it was fascinating to learn that we aren't always experiencing as human beings on earth.

New Session in Same *Cluster*, Originating 1,001 Lifetimes Ago

A session usually began with Angela muscle testing for the emotion and present-day emotional theme that was part of the subconscious block negatively affecting body, mind, or spirit. Once the emotional theme was established, Angela then tested to determine if the emotional theme was present-day only or if there was a prior time this same emotional theme had occurred in my subconscious. Angela always tests to find the origin, the original point, when the emotional block first energetically occurred in my subconscious. Angela explained to me that pinpointing the original emotional theme is important to clearing the entirety of the subconscious block from the present day all the way back to its point of origin. I conceptualized clearing a subconscious block much like pulling out a weed, in that you want to make sure you get the root (origin) in order to release the entire emotional block.

All sessions begin in present-day. If muscle testing my subconscious indicates there is a time prior to present-day when the emotional theme first occurred, we must then move from present day backward to pinpoint the origin, with Angela testing ages in my current life for congruency until she reaches conception. If Angela reaches conception without my subconscious indicating any point (year of age) within my current lifetime as being congruent, then Angela must continue moving backward past conception and into "preconception" or past lives.

Once in preconception, Angela continues querying the subconscious while muscle testing for an indication of which point (lifetime) is congruent. For example, Angela may say, "One to ten lifetimes ago." If the subconscious indicates through muscle response that this timeframe is congruent, Angela then breaks down the set of numbers, querying and muscle testing the subconscious, until the specific lifetime is identified as congruent.

Angela then retests the lifetime indicated to establish it is congruent to the subconscious in relation to the original emotional theme before moving on to uncovering relevant details of that emotional theme.

Mentally, as we are moving backward in preconception, it can sometimes be a little tricky keeping the timeframe of past lives in order. For instance, twenty lifetimes ago was experienced prior to three lifetimes ago. (Something I experienced three lifetimes ago was more recently experienced than something experienced twenty lifetimes ago.) The higher the number, the further back the lifetime. So, a lifetime twenty lifetimes ago is further back than a lifetime three lifetimes ago.

The session on this day began with me utilizing a specific affirmation from higher consciousness, and muscle testing of my subconscious indicated there was an emotional block associated with this affirmation in the lung area of my body. Angela now had to determine the specific emotion involved in this subconscious block affecting my lung. To do this, Angela utilized a list of emotions associated with the lung area and she began posing these emotions to my subconscious while muscle testing each one for congruency in order to lock in on the specific blocked emotion.

In the session on this day, my subconscious indicated that the *present-day emotion* associated with my lung was *grief*. Once the emotion was pinpointed, the related emotional theme either bubbles to the surface of my mind from my subconscious or just flows into my mind as a higher conscious thought—and it's usually easy for me to discern the difference. But on this day, it felt as though all of my consciousness was involved in this experience—as though there was no difference in consciousness between my subconscious and higher consciousness. It was almost as if they were one and the same.

The thought that was flowing through every part of my consciousness related to the *present-day emotional theme* was: "I am experiencing grief from the pain of separation, as nothing feels as good as oneness with God."

I wasn't at all surprised that this thought was the congruent present-day emotional theme, as I was experiencing a very strong emotional response as this concept was flowing through my mind.

When we began muscle testing for the *origin* of this *present-day emotional theme*, I was expecting it to be conception, as that was where I first encountered an emotional theme related to oneness. But the origin wasn't at conception but much further back. The origin of the emotional theme ended up going back *1,001 lifetimes ago*.

I didn't know exactly what to expect, but muscle testing indicated that I was not a human being. What, then, was I in this lifetime, 1001 lifetimes ago? Almost immediately the higher conscious thought "energy/spirit form" flowed into my mind. Typically, when I express a concept in our sessions, Angela then verbally restates the concept while simultaneously muscle testing it with my subconscious for congruency to the emotional theme. So, when this *role* of *energy/spirit form* was accepted by my subconscious as congruent, all I thought was, "Okay, energy/spirit form is a little unusual, but it's probably some type of spiritual energy rather than an incarnated human being."

Next, Angela began muscle testing to pinpoint the *original emotional theme* back in this lifetime *1,001 lifetimes ago*. And the emotional theme that rapidly flowed through my mind from higher (divine) consciousness was that, "as this energy/spirit form, 1,001 lifetimes ago, I am grieving over being separated from God. I'm feeling tremendous grief at my loss of connection with God and oneness."

For the first time in any of my sessions, I experienced an uncontrollably deep emotional reaction when this emotional theme consciously came to light. Instantly, I was emotionally transported back to this moment and was experiencing the emotional theme as though I was spiritually connected to it and emotionally living it right now. Tears began flowing down my face, my heart was aching to the point it felt broken, and my lungs were feeling constricted by grief. I was crying almost uncontrollably, which shocked me. But I realized it could only have been caused from a deep wound within my subconscious that had just been consciously exposed. The emotional reaction was so spontaneous that I was struggling to keep myself in check. Imagine you feel as though you are going back to the very moment where you felt yourself separating from all that you love. It felt as though I was being ripped open in grief and loss from the experience of being separated from God and oneness.

I wasn't just experiencing sadness; I was experiencing devastating loss. Even though I eventually began to feel more composed, I was not having an easy time controlling my emotions, which hadn't ever happened before.

As Angela continued the session, she told me that muscle testing has just revealed another emotion associated with this original emotional theme.

The *second emotion* associated with this original emotional theme was *deserted/forsaken*. Immediately, higher conscious thoughts revealed that, "I was feeling forsaken by God. I couldn't fathom why I was experiencing separation because my adoration of God was so absolute. I had no sense of anything else, not even of self."

As the concept of being forsaken by God was coming into my mind, my entire beingness began to shake, as though this emotional theme had triggered an energetic remembrance. For the first time in my life, I was experiencing the feeling of being forsaken, and it was a devastating emotion.

I was absolutely mortified at being forsaken by God. One moment I was experiencing a beautiful, blissful oneness and the next, I perceived myself to be deserted, forsaken by all I loved, utterly alone—grieving my loss.

Even in writing these words, my eyes begin to tear as I feel the heartache of others when they are deserted by someone they truly love—when they suddenly and unexpectedly find themselves forsaken and not at all comprehending how or why it happened. All that comes into your mind at this time is, "Why, oh God, why?"

Understanding why becomes paramount in your mind when you experience this depth of emotional devastation because you think, "If I can understand why it happened, then maybe I can fix it and get back to where I was before." Finding out why is the glimmer of hope we place in our hearts that we will eventually be able to recapture what was lost. The loss is so deep and so complete that it is impossible to imagine getting over it. All you can imagine is getting back what was lost.

It was then that I realized this subconscious emotional block might explain why there had always been such a profound need in me, even as a little girl, to make a deep, conscious connection with the benevolent perfection I have forever adored. Even as a child, I experienced a longing to be with divinity that was sometimes difficult to understand and often painfully felt. The sensation is hard to describe, but it felt as though I was trapped in the middle of a mind that couldn't remember and a heart that couldn't forget.

In this session, I was experiencing this emotional theme as though the devastating loss of being separated from God had just struck a raw nerve in my soul. It was so overwhelmingly real that I no longer felt warm, loved, protected, and blissful. Now I felt scared, alone, and so absolutely forsaken that I couldn't find any place inside of me that didn't ache for what was lost.

Of course, I was crying once again in the session, but this time, my mind, my consciousness, was also silently experiencing the crushing spiritual pain of separation that was coursing through me. It was as if there was no difference between the pain I felt in my heart and the pain I felt in my mind—as though consciousness and love were both experiencing this loss to the same degree.

This was the deepest spiritual pain I've ever experienced; and I found myself speaking thoughts out loud, unable to keep them inside. It was then that I sensed all of us in the room—in one way or another—were empathetically connected to this moment. And although I know that crying can be an emotional release, this feeling was not caused by an emotional release but by an emotional connection to this very moment of separation.

By now, I felt so emotionally and spiritually drained from experiencing my worst nightmare, separation from God, that all I was hoping was that it would end soon.

Just as I managed to rein in my emotions, Angela once more muscle tests for any other associated emotions, and my subconscious indicated that there was yet another emotion. Immediately I was hoping that all my body's emotional responses were behind me.

Thankfully, the *third emotion* of feeling *self-conscious* didn't trigger any deep emotional response from me. Higher consciousness revealed very little about this emotional theme, only that, "I feel aware of individual self separated from oneness consciousness."

For just the briefest of moments, as this thought hit my mind, I experienced a feeling of absolute aloneness. Only a moment before I felt as though I was enjoying blissful unity; and now, a heartbeat later, I was totally alone. Instantly, I shifted from a sense of oneness to an isolated sense of only self.

By this point in my session, I had begun feeling a little robotic in my interactions with Angela, so I didn't immediately grasp that muscle testing had just revealed a *fourth emotion.* What now? The fourth emotion was *timid,* and immediately the following emotional theme came into my mind from higher conscious thought: "As a result of now perceiving my separation, I am feeling timid and shying away from God. I love and adore God, but I am now feeling in*timid*ated by God's beautiful essence and perfection; I am no longer feeling our blissful oneness connection."

As muscle testing confirmed this emotional theme was congruent, my only thought was, *I hope that's it.* And it was.

This ended up being not only my longest session but also my most emotional one (big understatement). When the original emotional theme was revealed, I consciously realized it was profound, but I was shocked by the sheer magnitude of my emotional responses to something that went back 1,001 lifetimes ago. This speaks volumes about how traumatic this event must have been for me, as a soul. And really, why wouldn't it be traumatic? What can be more devastating to a soul than experiencing separation from benevolent oneness— separation from all they love; grieving not only their loss of connection, but also having to cope with the devastating feeling of being forsaken? Four distinct emotions (grief, forsaken, self-conscious, timid) were interwoven in an experience that was so energetically devastating to me as a soul that I was still feeling the aftershock of that experience even in the present day.

Because of my innate knowing that we are all connected, there is no doubt in my mind that this experience—separation from benevolent oneness—is something that all of us as souls experienced and we are even now living the effects of our feelings of separation.

Finally, we moved into the clearing part of the session and I was very consciously focused on releasing all of these intense emotions that originated so long ago. For the briefest moment, a thought flashed through my mind that I had been afforded a rare opportunity to forever release this emotional block from my consciousness. I was not this forsaken spirit—grief-filled by separation from divinity—in my current lifetime. Rather, I'm that little girl of nine who fully and profoundly experienced divinity without any sense of separation, who has grown into a woman who is absolute in her knowing that divinity is love, we are love, and our true beingness is never separated from either divinity or each other. We are never alone—the entirety of divine energy is our benevolent companion.

Nothing was ever so personally compelling or touched me so deeply as connecting through my own body, mind, and soul with this moment, as this was the first time I'd ever consciously experienced separation from Benevolence in any of my sessions.

Deep within my heart, I planted my conscious intention that the release of this subconscious block experienced over 1,001 lifetimes ago would help me feel more connected to oneness, as I longed for it still.

This day's session was the very first session I ever experienced that was related to any of the cluster lifetimes, although I didn't know it at the time. This was the session that I went into after that beautiful meditation in Angela's waiting room—when I first went off the program sheet and began utilizing only affirmations directly received from higher (divine) consciousness.

Experiencing this session launched me as never before into a conscious intention to really understand what, exactly, had brought about my feelings of separation, and that thought, "*What caused my separation?*" was to be a conscious catalyst for all that eventually unfolded.

Even before this session, throughout my life I've felt a need to understand why we are in human embodiment, separated from Benevolence. Although I've always felt a strong affinity to spirituality, I've never followed a scripted spiritual path, as nothing has ever resonated more true nor captured my spirit more than the deep inner knowing of Benevolence carried within me since childhood.

Meditation, prayer, and holding the vibration of love within my consciousness are undeniably beautiful bridges to divinity and to my soul—to oneness. But is that bridge really what heals the cause of separation, allowing oneness to occur? I wonder.

After lifetimes spent reincarnating, where we follow spiritual disciplines given to us by enlightened beings of great spiritual depth, why isn't there greater understanding about our deep-rooted feelings of separation? Our feelings of separation are at the core of why we all feel so much fear, suffering, and longing; yet, there doesn't really seem to be a clear-cut reason for the cause of our separation or the purpose for our being on earth, experiencing all these lifetimes.

Deep in my heart, I believe a lot of us—maybe even the majority of us—have been here many, many times, and some part of us is enlightened to the fact that our spiritual paths may not completely get us where we intend. There is a subtle knowing carried within me that the path to enlightenment may not just be about reflection or following a spiritual discipline.

What if all the consciousness and vibration raising only gets us a microscopic hair away from true oneness, because it is just a more enlightened bandage on a deeper issue related to separation?

What if all of the acts undertaken by us, as souls, have been based on misperceptions in our consciousness that will not allow us to experience true oneness until we perceive the truth within our own self-conscious awareness? Then, when we apply the tools for raising consciousness and our energetic vibration, we will be more able to consciously experience our oneness in living expression.

What is the real reason we feel separate?

Mentally I've worked through many concepts, especially the ones like "we are separate because we are imperfect" or "we are separate because we are evolving." But if, in fact, divinity is perfect and fully actualized and fully realized and has always been so at all moments, then how can either of these reasons be correct? They can't; yet reasons like evolving and imperfection are the foundation for how we go about seeking our oneness.

Another concept is that the way to oneness is to rid ourselves of what we perceive to be holding us back through human embodiment.

But if human incarnation is holding us back and we were all these things (perfection/oneness) before entering human consciousness, then why did we enter human consciousness in the first place?

These are the thoughts that have nagged at my still mind for years. I'm hoping that releasing this deeply-felt subconscious block will help me feel more connected to oneness until I can find answers to these questions.

And although I would never have believed it at the time, this was only the beginning of truly astonishing sessions that were not only related to my individual consciousness but also the consciousness of all of us as a collective.

New Session in Same *Cluster,* Originating 1,001 Lifetimes Ago

In this day's session, I was using an affirmation from higher consciousness related to accepting who I am as a spiritual being, an affirmation that tested as incongruent with my subconscious, indicating there was a subconscious emotional block interfering with the intention of this affirmation. The *present-day emotion* was *false self-assuredness,* and the *present-day emotional theme* was that, "although I perceive myself as a spiritual being, I also doubt my spiritual beingness as I have fears, insecurities, and questions."

Once again, the *origin* of this emotional theme went back *1,001 lifetimes ago* when I was expressing (*role*) as an *energy/spirit form.* The *original emotion* was that same feeling of *false self-assuredness,* which basically means I'm assuring myself that something is true while at the same time feeling some doubt about it.

Just then, as the *original emotional theme* began to flow through my mind as higher conscious thoughts, I began to sob. My mind and my heart were hurting so much that I was momentarily wondering if there is something physically wrong with me. But then I realized it was just the intensity of my feelings—brought on by my conscious connectedness to this moment—to conscious awareness of the original emotional theme.

This session only just started, and it was already emotionally intense. It reminded me of the same level of spiritual pain I experienced when I previously went back to this very same lifetime, 1,001 lifetimes ago. This lifetime must have been very devastating to me as a soul, as I

155

was still feeling emotional waves of what was lost flowing through me even now.

I was trying to speak the original emotional theme that was moving through me as thoughts and feelings, but it is nearly impossible because I was crying too hard to speak clearly. Angela encouraged me with body language to just take my time.

Finally, I was able to convey the *original emotional theme, 1,001 lifetimes ago,* which Angela immediately tested and found to be congruent: "1,001 lifetimes ago, as this energy/spirit form, I completely adored God and did everything right (or felt that I had); yet, I was still experiencing separation from God. Not being able to experience God in the immediate moment was extremely traumatic, and I couldn't comprehend why I was no longer in oneness. I couldn't fathom either what I'd done or what had happened to cause my sense of separation, and I was trying to assure myself it would all be okay. Yet, I was also feeling doubt about it really working out (false self-assuredness)."

As soon as I was able to verbally express this original emotional theme, my crying began to subside, and I felt very relieved that the emotional intensity of this session seemed to be finished.

We then cleared this emotional block, and as I was holding a mental picture of this original emotional theme, a torrent of thoughts began flooding my mind. Then a sense of absolute stillness filled the room, and I realized Benevolence was conveying energy to my mind as thoughts—extraordinary thoughts about the true cause of my separation; thoughts that flabbergasted me while simultaneously reverberating as true.

Incredibly, the true cause of separation was not due to something I'd done wrong or as a form of punishment or because I was unworthy, but because of how I viewed my own essence. I had missed the entire point of oneness by admiring divinity to the exclusion and denial of self.

My own identity, my own perfection, as a spiritual beingness had been negated when I shifted my focus to living through divinity rather than as my own essence. The purpose of oneness was not for me to suppress my essence in lieu of divinity or forsake myself through loving divinity but to fully be who I am and to love myself as I love divinity.

Divinity intended for me to experience the full magnitude of my own essence so I could truly feel absolute joy as our oneness. But instead, I viewed my spirit as nothing and divinity's as everything—all of which negated the beautiful point of oneness.

The divine intention of oneness is to be our own sacred divinity—not to just experience divinity's beingness but also be our divine nature.

I was shocked by these thoughts. I'd lived my entire life loving divinity with all my heart, holding this love in my consciousness, assuming this was the pathway home. Now I was learning that oneness is not just about loving divinity; it is also about simultaneously loving yourself as you love divinity. This is a concept that I had not only disregarded as a human being in my current life but also as a soul in past lifetimes, and I absolutely believe that most of us disregard this concept. It's so much easier to love that which we perceive as more perfect or divine rather than our self, and it's even harder to perceive ourselves as divine.

Then, divine conscious thoughts unfolded the most shocking concept of all: "My perception that God was more perfect than me had elevated God to a place of worship above me. By elevating God, I negated myself, and in so doing, I was not able to perceive the truth that my light and God's light were the same. God and I were one light, one vibration without separation. By perceiving God as a higher vibration, a more perfect vibration, feelings of separation naturally resulted."

Just as this thought was finishing, the following higher conscious thought immediately flowed into my mind:

> "It is impossible to remain in a conscious state of perfection if you hold anything outside of yourself as being more perfect. By doing so, perfection becomes a goal to attain rather than a state of being, which always places you outside seeking rather than just being."

In my life 1,001 lifetimes ago, my consciousness was unable to recognize that my own essence, my own light, was identical to that of the divine. And my act of perceiving something (divinity) as loftier, more perfect, or purer than me had consciously placed me in a state of feeling separated from perfection.

A British friend of mine has used a word that perfectly sums up my feelings in this session: gobsmacked. Once she explained that the word "gobsmacked" means you are utterly astounded to the point of being stopped in your tracks, speechless. All my life, I've perceived divinity as above me, a Benevolence to be adored. But right now, in this session, everything I had believed about divinity and my relationship to divinity was shifted to a place I couldn't fathom. Gobsmacked doesn't even come close to describing my feelings. One part of me was sensing this concept was truth, and that part of me was standing dumbstruck in the middle of my consciousness. Meanwhile, another part of me, resembling a horse someone is trying to bridle, was vehemently tossing its head from side to side, refusing to comply.

Over and over I wondered, "How can the concept that divinity and I are identical be accurate?" As someone who has always placed God above everything, nothing within my own conscious framework could ever have prepared me for this moment. And I have to be honest, divine consciousness has revealed an insight about divinity and I being identical that I was intuitively sensing is true, but the part of me that's lived an entire life with a huge misperception—divinity is above me; and perfection is outside of me, something to be gained—is fighting this concept tooth and nail.

But even while fighting and resisting, something about this insight hit a chord that resonated deep within me as true. As much as I wanted to toss it aside, I couldn't, because that's not the way I'd ever reacted when faced with a new perception that may shatter a prior belief. But I imagine many of us feel the same way, in that there has to be a willingness to transition to different states of consciousness in order to gain enlightened awareness. This willingness must also carry the flexibility to change when it is apparent a belief is incorrect. If we can't recognize a higher truth when it presents itself in our life—even if it means we'll have to change or let go of something we cherish—how can we ever stand in higher vibrations or in enlightenment? We can't.

It's not about being right, which is more a validation type of energy; it's all about what is true. Right and true aren't always the same thing at the same time. Although getting it right is important, staying true, living in truth, and doing right by that truth is the most important thing.

In this session, I realized that what I had always perceived as truth wasn't really the highest truth, and I now had a conscious choice to make. I could either dogmatically cling to my established position or I could choose to let go of my current perception and allow a higher truth to come forward.

That's what's difficult about being human. We're insecure about letting go of something we cherish or hold as true unless we have something else to fill the void. In this case, I didn't have anything to fill the entirety of the void; but nonetheless, I knew this concept was truth. Even so, I was reluctant to release my need to adore and worship divinity as perfection above me. But a lucid moment broke my quandary of consciousness when I realized that I didn't have to release my love of divinity. All I had to do was love myself as I love divinity. In this way, there is no conscious separation.

When we compare ourselves to an ideal (divinity or even others), we perceive ourselves as "less than," creating self-loathing and separation. Once we begin perceiving our divine nature, we can love ourselves and each other as divinity, eradicating the perception that divine perfection is outside of us. Then we will no longer perceive ourselves as separate beings from divinity or each other.

We don't have to abandon our love for the divine in a presence we spiritually embrace (God, Christ, Buddha, Source, etc.). We just have to embrace that we are all identical in essence, none more perfect than another; there is no separation; and we must consciously add ourselves and all others to the equation of love. We can go right on loving the divine, but we must also consciously hold the knowing that divinity, and we, and all are, in truth, one vibration without separation.

This is not easy, as we have all had the misperception of separation imbued in our consciousness—but it is possible. Now when I think, *I love divinity*, I add *as I love myself and all others*. This way I can hold love for divinity in my heart while consciously recognizing there is no separation in essence between divinity, myself, or anything.

I eventually accepted, though reluctantly at first, the concept that divinity and I are identical in nature; but if divinity and I are one already, then why am I living on earth, trying to attain the state of oneness? Is it because earthly incarnation causes the sense of separation and we have to consciously recognize that we are one even when experiencing human embodiment? Or is it really something else entirely that causes the feelings of separation and the reason for all these physical incarnations? Why am I really here?

After clearing this emotional block, these were the thoughts I carried from this session into my very next session—a session that was to bring a revelation that would prove to be the cornerstone of an extraordinary new unfoldment of awareness.

New Session in Same *Cluster,*
Originating One Thousand Lifetimes Ago

This session began with me sharing with Angela that it was sometimes difficult for me to express in the role of a wife as well as that of a spiritual being. There were times when it felt virtually impossible for me to be both identities at the same time. This was a very bizarre thing to even be talking about, but nonetheless, that was the topic this particular day due to something personal I was experiencing.

Even though it would have been typical for us to choose an affirmation that targeted this type of issue, Angela decided to instead check my heart area for physical issues or emotional blocks, as I was feeling very strong physical discomfort in my heart while sharing these thoughts with her.

Muscle testing revealed that there was no physical issue but there was a subconscious emotional block in my heart, with a *present-day emotion* of me being *dogmatically positioned.* The *present-day emotional theme* was that, "I was dogmatically positioned that I could not be both a wife and spiritual being at the same time because they can sometimes be opposing concepts." (To me "dogmatically positioned" means that I'm holding a strong opinion as if it is fact, but it may not be fact at all.)

My subconscious indicated through muscle testing that the *origin* of this *present-day emotional theme* went back *one thousand lifetimes ago,* when I was expressing as *spirit form* with a blocked *emotion* of me feeling *dogmatically positioned.* As we continued muscle testing to clarify the *original emotional theme,* I was amazed by what came into my mind as a higher conscious thought and out of my mouth: "I am dogmatically positioned that I can't be *all* and *one* at the same time."

It wasn't the emotional theme that caused me to marvel at the synchronicity of the moment. Rather it was that even though we didn't use an affirmation about being two things simultaneously, we were directed by my subconscious and higher consciousness to that very issue. Synchronicity took us where we were intended to go no matter what course we set.

Again it was apparent that higher guidance was definitely overseeing these sessions. Otherwise, what made me start talking with Angela about the inability to play both roles (wife and spiritual being) on this particular day, which happened to be the very next session after the one related to 1,001 lifetimes ago? It was neither coincidence nor chance—that's for sure. (This is when I realized I was experiencing a cluster of lifetimes, somehow related.)

The session was very brief, and a thought popped into my mind that "all and one" is about viewpoint or perspective rather than duality—which made no sense at all to me.

Although I didn't realize it at the time, my ever-present higher consciousness and subconscious had just given me a huge breadcrumb—actually, a baguette-sized breadcrumb: *all and one simultaneously.*

My subconscious then indicated, through muscle testing, that there were no additional details needed—an indication that we could now move on to the process of clearing this subconscious emotional block.

After having completed what I believed to be the most insightful series of sessions I will ever experience (999–1,001 lifetimes ago), I would have liked to disregard some of the concepts revealed, as they were contrary to what I deeply believed my entire life. But I couldn't.

When I say that we must sometimes set aside ideals to which we are deeply attached, it comes by way of my own experience, and an inability for me to do so at this time would have brought about completely different results. I would have never seen a more enlightened truth, as I would have been too caught up in my own identification and attachments to allow a different truth to unfold.

Later on I discovered that these insights not only altered my conscious perception but also shifted a deep misperception within my soul and took me an entirely different direction in consciousness, one I was already fated to experience—one that would yield answers to my most soul-searching questions.

Where was I heading? Back to a point in consciousness where everything was revealed in a way that blew open my mind; interconnected my spirit; and solidified my knowing that ***the state of perfection is just a thought away***.

Chapter 21

Leaving Behind the Misperception of Separation

Serendipity does not result from happenstance.
Rather, serendipity is what places us in those
moments where fortuitous events occur.
Divine design has many faces;
serendipity is just one.

When you are involved in an unusual event, it is sometimes difficult to comprehend all aspects of the experience while in it. Some things are obvious; others are more veiled. Over the years, I've recognized that I'm perceiving on different levels while experiencing the unusual. I've come to think of this state of awareness as *lucid perception,* as it's similar to what you experience when lucid dreaming. When you are lucid dreaming, you are fully lucid, observing the dream while also experiencing the dream. Though you don't usually realize it at the time, when you are lucid dreaming, you are holding two states of consciousness simultaneously: dream consciousness and higher consciousness. If you were just in dream consciousness, you would not know you were dreaming until you had awakened. By consciously realizing you are dreaming while in a dream, you are simultaneously experiencing higher consciousness and dream consciousness.

Oftentimes I'm in a state of lucid perception while going about my life. It feels as though there is another consciousness simultaneously experiencing what I am experiencing. There is. It is our own profound, yet subtle, higher consciousness or higher self. Our higher self (*lucid observer*) is able to perceive the more veiled aspects or nuances of an experience that may be slipping by our waking awareness unobserved.

The most wonderful part of experiencing lucid perception is that subtleties that are normally whizzing past my waking conscious mind are not lost. Experiences are being perceived through this other, more lucid state of consciousness, and that higher conscious awareness is known to me as clearly as if it is my own waking conscious thoughts and feelings.

This is what was happening in my sessions with Angela. Most of the time I was aware of higher conscious interaction, where my human consciousness was simultaneously aware of higher conscious insights normally imperceptible to me. This type of interaction has been ongoing throughout my life, and I'm very familiar with the subtle, heightened state of consciousness that is naturally interacting with my waking conscious mind. It isn't like there are two minds present; it's more accurate to say that my normal waking mind and higher mind are simultaneously one and the same.

Interaction with our higher consciousness is always occurring, but until we are more awakened, we don't consciously recognize it. As one begins to consciously recognize higher conscious interaction, one is more able to sense the subtle difference between normal waking conscious and higher conscious thoughts and intuitive feelings. Think of lucid perception as when we are simultaneously experiencing our own all-knowingness (higher consciousness) while in normal waking consciousness.

When I'm experiencing lucid perception, I don't try and make things fit or predetermine the meaning or outcome. I simply allow all my senses to absorb various energies—sensory input—while experiencing and thinking at the same time. Many times profound insights come into my mind, or the angelic being that has been my life-long companion is present and injects concepts to ponder or words of advice. Other times, I am thinking while experiencing in a way that opens up many channels of higher conscious awareness wherein I am able to perceive the connectedness of the experience to other events or thoughts. A lifetime of interacting in this way between Universe and myself has netted wonderful experiences and profound insights, along with tons of loose ends that don't seem to go anywhere at all.

Initially, when I began balancing the energy of my body through acupuncture while also testing for and releasing subconscious emotional blocks, I was not in an open, lucid conscious mode. This was because my consciousness was entirely focused on chakra balancing and the destiny it would unfold. I was in a very focused, attached state of conscious "lockdown" awaiting the "wow" moment that I just knew I was going to experience in chakra balancing.

Consciously identifying what I expected to experience (the opening of my destiny) created a predetermined attachment to a specific outcome that affected higher conscious awareness. Although higher conscious insight still occurred—as nothing we do or don't do can prevent that from happening—I was not as consciously aware (lucid perception) that it was occurring.

To better experience higher conscious interaction, you have to let your mind go and flow without identifying what or how you will experience or attaching to a predetermined outcome. It is difficult to experience lucid perception if you are already consciously pre-determining what you will experience—what you will know.

Once I realized that chakra balancing might not be my soul's ultimate intention, I consciously opened myself to going with the flow. I realized that my desire for one outcome was merely the cause for me being in a certain space at a certain time to experience something else. This happens all the time. I think I'm doing something for one reason only to find there was a different intended purpose than what I had originally perceived. When I realize the desired outcome that initially drew me to the experience is not going to manifest, it can be confusing or even disappointing. But I've found if I detach from my desire and continue on through the experience, something unexpected and wonderful often happens. A beautiful insight or some sort of "aha" moment occurs.

I'd always thought of these as serendipitous moments—assuming that something fortuitous had unexpectedly unfolded while I was seeking something else. But I have come to realize that serendipity is not accidental at all, though we tend to associate the manifestation of something wonderfully unanticipated as brought about by happenstance (being in the wrong place at the right time sort of thing).

An example of this is something that happened to me once when I was looking for a new job. I had seen an ad in the paper and telephoned to inquire about the position. After a brief discussion, I'd been asked to come in the following morning for an interview. The job was in a neighboring city, and as I was writing down the address,

I had a picture in my mind of the exact location of the building. The next morning, I arrived for my interview and found that I had "accidentally" gone to the wrong location. Somehow, I had gotten the address mixed up in my mind and arrived at a building nowhere near the correct location. It was so bewildering to me as to how I could have made such a mistake that the look on my face must have caused the receptionist to ask me what was wrong.

As I was explaining my error to the girl at the front desk, a managing partner of the CPA firm walked by to get a drink of water at the fountain and overheard my conversation. He introduced himself and told me that it was strange that I had shown up at their office for a job, as they were planning to run an ad for an assistant to the office manager, who was about to take maternity leave. The partner then asked me if I was interested in applying for the job. I was surprised but said yes. I ended up getting hired that day and went on to work for them for over eight years, shortly replacing the office manager, who decided she preferred to stay at home and enjoy her new baby.

So, although I wrote down the correct address, I ended up going to the wrong location. Initially, I had absolutely no idea how I could have made such a mistake. Then I realized that serendipity brought me to the wrong place at the right time for me to secure a wonderful job that I loved—a job that had not yet even been advertised. I was thrilled by my luck. Everyone, especially my father, seemed to enjoy the story, as they thought it both strange (how it happened) and wonderful (how it ended up). That description perfectly sums up the nature of serendipity ... strange and wonderful.

At some point, I began to realize that serendipity is always occurring—even when we don't consciously recognize it.

We think of serendipity as the fortuitous result of a chain of accidental events rather than perceiving serendipity as the hand that orchestrates and guides the way the events unfold. Serendipity is what places us in those moments where fortuitous events occur. Divine design has many faces; serendipity is just one.

Recognizing serendipity at work in our lives is when we peer behind the veil of conscious awareness and perceive the hand of divine design weaving the circumstances of our lives. Even now, at this time in our lives, we are not experiencing chance events. There is divine design to all that we experience—no matter how we perceive the intention of our journey.

Once we begin to believe we are always where we should be at every moment, then we have to allow and even learn to embrace unexpected experiences, even in the face of our own disappointment.

It's neither about being oblivious during an experience nor about trying to fit square pieces of understanding into round holes of experience. When we are experiencing something we don't quite understand, we often try to find explanation for it in the present when the purpose may actually be linked to the past or even the future. By being willing to let our higher awareness guide us when we find ourselves trying to force logic into the situation, we are trusting that answers not found in the present will eventually come.

Though it is sometimes difficult, we must try not to jam an answer that doesn't fit into the equation of the experience as our way of snipping off loose ends that don't tie up so we can just conveniently file the experience away—out of sight and out of mind. Consciousness is an open file and remaining open while we are experiencing—without predetermining either where it will end up or how it relates—allows us to gather dots of awareness to be connected to other dots at some point in the future.

Although only a few months had passed since I began these sessions, I'd already realized there are several puzzles in process. There was the puzzle of just my physical body and current life and why certain issues had manifested. Interwoven in that puzzle were other pieces related to issues involving my soul and why I had chosen to incarnate many times in similar roles with variations of specific themes.

Then one day, light began to shine on the idea that the way in which the issues unfold in our lives through our choices and our perceptions may be unique to each soul, but at the heart of all of us, there are similar soul issues.

As I came into my next cluster of sessions, I was not expecting anything except more threads—some that I hoped would eventually be woven into a connected fabric of insight.

And though I did not yet understand how the threads connected, there was a feeling of acceleration in the information being revealed and a sense of connectedness to everything being experienced.

New Session in Next *Cluster*

Going into this day's session, which was the next session following the cluster lifetimes of 999–1,001 lifetimes ago, I was not really thinking anything in particular except that I was fascinated by what had transpired, as it seemed I'd moved into something quite incredible. In these sessions, my subconscious had taken me back over one thousand lifetimes ago and I was experiencing subconscious emotional blocks that related to very spiritual concepts about divinity, oneness, perfection, separation, being all and one simultaneously, and most profoundly, how divinity and we are identically the same essence.

Because I am still experiencing unusual energetic discomfort in my heart area, Angela began this day's session by testing my chakra points for any type of physical or emotional imbalance. Muscle testing revealed there was a subconscious emotional block in my *root chakra* related to a *role* I would play in the future as a *spiritual teacher*. Angela and I were now moving very rapidly through determining the emotion and emotional theme. The *emotion* was *loftiness* (other people's), and the *emotional theme* was: "other people viewing me as lofty and focusing on me as a person rather than on the essence of the message." (Even though Angela and I were flying through this session, I realized that I'd never before encountered a future role, and although the terminology wasn't lost on me, I wasn't sure of what it actually meant.)

The concept that anyone would view me as loftier than them is not only contrary to my beliefs, but it also tends to shift focus from the spiritual message to me personally.

Once, when I was just beginning to share higher conscious insights with others, a familiar angelic presence conveyed the following energetic thought: "Remember, my dear, do not allow yourself to be put on a pedestal and do not put yourself on one either, as no one is more special than another, only more aware of the blessings all embody."

That beautiful insight helped me to never lose sight of the spiritual truth that no one (even those appearing more gifted) is ever more special than anyone else. Some are just more "awake" than others.

And no one should be penalized for sleeping in!

Back in the session, we still needed to determine the origin of this subconscious emotional block and the original emotional theme involved. As Angela and I began muscle testing to pinpoint the *origin* for this *emotional theme* related to other people perceiving me as *lofty*, we were surprised that it went back *1,999 lifetimes ago.*

Wow! My mind couldn't even grasp the reality of what would be involved in a lifetime over 1,999 lifetimes ago, which is a jump of one thousand lifetimes from my last cluster (999–1,001 lifetimes ago). (See what I mean about feeling an acceleration going on?)

The timeframe momentarily surprised us, but we continued flowing through the session—or tried to—but we found it extremely difficult to establish what my subconscious was trying to reveal about the role involved in the emotion of loftiness, back at this origin, 1,999 lifetimes ago. We muscle tested the concepts that I am human, spirit, and master, with no hit as far as congruency with my subconscious.

The only way to describe what we were experiencing in this particular session was that my subconscious was adamant that the proper terminology must be used, for it was not allowing us to move on without pinpointing the exact role I was expressing. Several minutes lapsed where we pondered and then posed and muscle tested many concepts related to my role in this incarnation, 1,999 lifetimes ago. (The word "incarnation" is used only in the sense of entering a conscious lifetime, not necessarily meaning entering physical embodiment.)

Finally, Angela instructed me to just completely relax without thinking about anything and let's just see what comes through. A few moments later, these words began to come forth: "state of consciousness, spirit form, new soul."

When we posed and muscle tested *state of consciousness, spirit form, new soul*, my subconscious indicated that this entire phrase was congruent with my *role*, my embodiment, at this time, 1,999 lifetimes ago. We tried testing each of the sets of words separately, but only the entire phrase—all three sets of words—was indicated by my subconscious to be the congruent role.

It was not only very obvious but also interesting that we were directed by my subconscious to pinpoint precise definitions that, at times, were paramount to the overall information being imparted. We never tried to pull out more information than the subconscious wanted to impart, nor did we ever ask yes or no questions.

There is a technique to testing subconscious congruency, and Angela always professionally follows that procedure while simultaneously being gifted in her ability to identify areas to explore, phrase statements to pose to my subconscious for testing, and interpret the language of the subconscious. Angela can best be described as a *subconscious linguist;* she is an amazing person and practitioner.

The words "new soul" made all of our heads pop up, and our minds were on full alert as we began exploring this lifetime, 1,999 lifetimes ago, when I was expressing as state of consciousness, spirit form, new soul. We assumed we understood the terms "state of consciousness" and "spirit form," but the term "new soul" carried an energetic vibration that was captivating our consciousness. Although I was not voicing my desire, there was no doubt I wanted to jump right in there and interrogate my subconscious with a spotlight and rapid-fire questions to get to the bottom of this concept. But we didn't, as it wasn't appropriate to engage the subconscious in conventional dialogue. Instead, Angela once again muscle tested to verify that all three of these terms (state of consciousness, spirit form, new soul) were the congruent role, which they were, and we began moving through the process of identifying the original emotional theme.

At this *origin, 1,999 lifetimes ago,* the blocked *emotion* is *loftiness* and the *emotional theme* that flows into my mind and tests as being congruent is: "I am focusing on the magnitude of Creator's beingness rather than on the essence of oneness. I am caught up in viewing Creator as loftier, while feeling that I am "less than" Creator. This view is causing me to feel as though I am leaving behind the state of Creator's perfection, as I was being birthed into this state of consciousness, spirit form, new soul (the *"birth of the new soul"*).

Wow! Higher consciousness is incredible and capable of conveying insights that would otherwise seem impossible for us to perceive. Then, to my utter disappointment, my subconscious indicated that no further details were needed. (I would have definitely liked more details.) "Birth of the new soul? Leaving behind the state of Creator's perfection?" But with no choice afforded us by my subconscious, Angela and I moved on to the process of clearing this emotional block and then testing to confirm it had been cleared.

Even though separation wasn't the direct emotional theme, it wasn't a stretch to see it was the causative factor.

The higher conscious insight, *birth of the new soul*, conveyed in this session was too astonishing to fully comprehend. Never had I expected to find myself consciously aware of this point (the birth of the new soul). But it makes perfect sense that I would find myself taken back here, as it would be shocking if "leaving behind the state of Creator's perfection" didn't cause a subconscious block. (Although I did not yet realize it, this event—the birth of us as new souls—was a major shift in consciousness, impacting all of us.)

But the view that we are leaving behind Creator's perfection— virtually being exiled into a different state of consciousness—is a misperception. This conscious misperception was caused because we do not perceive our true nature. And it is this type of conscious misperception that we have experienced from the beginning of collective human consciousness all the way into the present day— misperceptions that not only create subconscious emotional blocks because of our conscious perception of an experience but also create layers and layers of illusion in our consciousness and in our lives.

Even though all of us, as souls, may experience an identical event in consciousness—such as the birth of the new soul—we do not always experience identical emotional reactions. Our reactions are created by how we perceive an experience in relation to our conscious awareness, and that is unique to each of us. One soul may view an experience as devastating and hold on to it for an eternity, while another soul may be less attached to the experience and energetically release from it immediately. It's important to always remember that how we view an experience and how others view it may not be the same. Once we consciously recognize that all of us may be viewing and experiencing an identical event through our own unique conscious perspective and emotional filters, it will be easier for us to extend grace to others as well as ourselves. This mindfulness will help us to better understand our own path and how we move through the experiences of our lives, while at the same time honoring the uniqueness of every soul's journey—a journey of awakening we all empathetically share.

During the session, there was no conscious realization of why my subconscious had linked the emotional theme related to my future role as a spiritual teacher with the original emotional theme, back 1,999 lifetimes ago. But as the session was coming to an end, I realized that the very thing that I didn't want people feeling about me in my future role as a spiritual teacher (loftiness) was exactly what I had been feeling about Creator in this past lifetime. And in both emotional themes, the message of oneness was entirely overlooked.

This realization not only brought the message of this session consciously home to me, it also reflected the profound veracity of this energetic technique as I clearly recognized why my subconscious had linked these two emotional themes. In both emotional themes, the focus was not on the spiritual truth conveyed through the nature of our oneness. The focus was on that which reflected this truth (Creator, etc.), rather than on the truth itself. The truth is that we and that which we perceive as loftier are identically the same essence of oneness, so no one can ever be "less than" or "greater than" anyone else.

After the session ended, we discussed this unusual terminology (state of consciousness, spirit form, new soul) and wondered what exactly was occurring in this particular lifetime, 1,999 lifetimes ago. Although we didn't fully comprehend the phenomenal glimpse we had just been given into the truth about all of us as souls, we must have all sensed something, because none of us wanted to engage in conjecture. It's as though we didn't want our predisposition to any concept to taint the purity of what might be revealed in future sessions.

I was very happy that my husband and I had been sitting in on each other's sessions, taking notes, and eventually recording them, as I believe the conscious exposure of these sessions was greatly contributing to the transformations both of us were experiencing in our lives and in our consciousness. It was like we were being double exposed to a radiating field of love and consciousness.

If Universe was trying to get my attention, it worked, as I felt I'd just been gobsmacked awake from my sleepwalking state of consciousness. Although I wasn't sure of what exactly had awakened me, I knew something phenomenal had just occurred, and it wasn't just me. Angela and my husband also seemed to be experiencing the same thing, as there was a crackling of excitement in all our energy fields and a light in our eyes that was not there previously.

All of us were sharing the same extraordinary moment of conscious clarity, as though we had just experienced a sneak preview of the coming attraction of something spiritually sacred and consciously profound.

New Session in Same *Cluster*, Originating 1,999 Lifetimes Ago
The following week, just before my session, I was seated in the waiting room, meditating as I usually do. Although I received no higher conscious thoughts pertaining to a specific affirmation for the upcoming session, I did experience a dramatic increase in energy in my heart area. Over the past several days there had been a gradual increase in energy around my heart, but now, just as my session was about to begin, the intensity spiked to a point I was no longer able to ignore.

Due to the level of physical discomfort I was experiencing, Angela decided to test my heart chakra point for any physical issues or subconscious emotional blocks. Muscle testing confirmed there was no physical issue, but there was a subconscious emotional block, and we were surprised by how long it took to pinpoint the role.

Once again, my subconscious seemed to have a specific term related to the *present-day* role it wanted clarified. The role was difficult to pinpoint because it was rather atypical in nature. The *role* that was ultimately revealed and tested to be congruent was that of me as a *child of God*. This is not a concept that one would normally think of as a role (such as doctor, singer, scientist, etc.), but there was no doubt that this was the precise terminology my subconscious intended us to identify. (The reason the subconscious was resolute about this precise phrase was apparent once the original emotional theme was revealed.)

Although I'd heard the phrase "child of God" before, I've not ever consciously thought of myself in this manner at all, so landing on this particular term was very surprising. It was just one more example of the interaction with higher consciousness that was occurring.

When the blocked *emotion* in the *present-day* was revealed, it was that of *false self-assuredness*. The congruent *present-day emotional theme* was that, "I, as a child of God, am assuring myself that by the end of this life I'll be able to connect back (be reunited) with God and oneness, while at the same time doubting I'll really be fully conscious enough for that to happen."

Once the present-day emotional theme was pinpointed, Angela posed the statement to my subconscious about whether this emotional theme was present-day only or originated in a prior time. A prior time was indicated by my subconscious to be congruent, and once again, the *origin* was *1,999 lifetimes ago*. It's apparent there were some very intense emotions being experienced in this lifetime, 1,999 lifetimes ago, so I was not really surprised something related to being a child of God and reunited with God and oneness would go back, once more, to this lifetime.

In this lifetime, 1,999 lifetimes ago, the *emotion* was the same as the present-day emotion of *false self-assuredness,* and the *role* I was expressing was *state of consciousness, spirit form, new soul.* (Just as a note, information is never assumed to be the same in any lifetime previously experienced. When Angela posed the concept and muscled tested for the role in this particular session, once again nothing but the multi-part phrase "state of consciousness, spirit form, new soul" was accepted by my subconscious as congruent.)

As we began the process of pinpointing the *original emotional theme* relating to false self-assuredness, the higher conscious thoughts that immediately flowed into my mind and all tested as congruent were: "On one hand, I am assuring myself that I am being birthed for a positive purpose—as we are seeds of Creator's light—but at the same time, I'm feeling as though I'm being expelled from Creator's perfection. Would I ever return? If I did return, would it be the same? Am I ever going to be this fully conscious again?"

This was a profound emotional theme to experience, and once it was revealed, it was clear why my subconscious was so resolute about us identifying the term "child of God." If back in this lifetime, 1,999 lifetimes ago, I was considering us to be "seeds of Creator's light," then child of God is a perfect way to epitomize our beingness. No doubt about it, our subconscious is mysterious; yet, when it intends to reveal itself, communication is always precise, relevant, and even profound.

But almost immediately after this original emotional theme was revealed, I experienced a deep feeling of, "Why bother?" I instantly recognized a familiar feeling I'd experienced many times in my life.

Haven't we all experienced these *"why bother?"* thoughts when trying to figure out how to unravel the mysteries of us and Universe and thoughts about how to be one with divinity? Sometimes I feel like giving up before I even start because it all seems just too complicated, cloaked in mystery, and unverifiable.

Usually these types of reflections begin with a random thought about divinity or the purpose of life. Then as I move through the process of comparing intuitive concepts with logical reasoning, I eventually find myself overwhelmed with pessimistic thoughts like, "What's the point? By the time I get back, everything will have changed—or I'll be so changed, I won't even be able to get back." Always my thoughts start out very optimistic, and then doubt creeps in and I begin feeling too overwhelmed to continue.

Now I realize that this very theme, originating 1,999 lifetimes ago, was subconsciously contributing to deflating my optimism. It was akin to subconscious water thrown on the fire of my conscious optimism. I realized that I'd been fighting on two fronts: *first*, keeping my optimism alive, and *second*, not giving in to my feeling that I'll never be conscious enough to return to oneness.

Once this emotional theme was identified as congruent, Angela then muscle tested to ascertain if there were any additional blocked emotions associated with this original emotional theme 1,999 lifetimes ago. My subconscious indicated that there was *one other emotion*. It was the feeling of *inefficiency*. The related emotional theme was: "I felt inefficient because I don't have all the pieces in order to put everything together and find cohesiveness, and without those pieces how was I ever going to get back efficiently?"

This second emotional theme also really resonated with me, as in my current lifetime I feel the need to understand how everything fits together and interrelates. Even when learning something new, I'm never just concerned with the scope of my task. I always want to understand how all the pieces work together in the entire process.

Even in childhood, I was obsessed with solving mysteries (Universe, God, life) by trying to detect the details or find the missing components. And this need seemed to be satisfied, in my youth, by reading. By the time I was thirteen years old, I'd already read the Bible three times, most of the non-fiction books in my grade school library, as well as many other books. I read constantly, and though I didn't read just mysteries, they were among my favorites. It was challenging to figure out who did it before the end. These books trained my young mind to cull through information, pay attention to the details, and utilize logic and intuition. I learned to tie pieces of details together, weighing what was important, while setting other details aside, realizing that some pieces distract you by sending you on a wild goose chase.

Always when reading, I was looking for the clues that linked everything, allowing me to pierce the veil and solve the mystery. This was easy to do in books designed to give you the pieces, like mysteries, but it wasn't so easy to do in other things, such as life.

Although I was trying to remain optimistic, my fact-finding mission in human embodiment didn't appear to be going so well. I'd run into an apparently insolvable enigma. The pieces that would help me to pierce the veil of mystery were also hidden behind that same veil. Normally, only the answer is veiled, but in this case, both the answer and the pieces were veiled.

There's no doubt that this subconscious emotional block had a tremendous impact on my current lifetime. It was easy to imagine the extraordinary benefits that I or anyone could gain by alleviating this type of unconscious influence in our lives, as no one on this planet can be entirely immune from the impact of emotional blocks. I know I wasn't. The proof was this very session.

For a moment I consciously intended that releasing this subconscious emotional block would alleviate my "false" self-assuredness, leaving me feeling absolutely "assured," confident, and trusting that I'd find my way back to divinity and oneness by the end of my lifetime.

No additional details were indicated by my subconscious to be necessary, and while releasing this block, I felt tremendous hope surge through my heart that clearing this block opened extraordinary possibilities in my life, myself, and my soul. Maybe the mystery would soon stand revealed.

New Session in Same *Cluster*, Originating 1,999 Lifetimes Ago
At the beginning of my next session, the discomfort in my heart area was much better, and I'd come to think of this discomfort as a physical reflection of something spiritual that is occurring—though I have no idea what it is.

There were affirmations flowing into my mind from higher (divine) consciousness that were moving me through a process that began to feel as though we were all following a script that had been divinely written, with scenes set out and all of us playing our roles.

For instance, in today's session, no affirmation had come to mind, so I wasn't quite certain of what to do. Then, just before the session started, it felt as though the curtain rose and instantly the line (the higher conscious affirmation) came to me.

This type of higher conscious interaction felt far more focused than I'd ever experienced, so I wasn't surprised that there was a subconscious emotional block associated with today's affirmation about being away from home. Angela and I very rapidly determined that the *present-day emotion* is *fear* and the *present-day emotional theme* was: "I fear that I won't get back home, and even if I did get back, home will not be the same. I am fearful that I will have changed so much—become corrupted—that being back home will never feel the same."

This concept tested as congruent with my subconscious, and I did not need to ponder the meaning, because I was feeling intense fear in my heart as this emotional theme was revealed. Even in childhood, I'd always had a fear I wouldn't get back home to Benevolence, so, it didn't surprise me that this fear existed as a subconscious emotional block.

Our home is a place of benevolent love and perfection, yet I was caught up in fear. (If love is our home, then how can fear ever be our pathway home?)

As we began muscle testing for the *origin* of this *emotional theme*, we were once more taken back to *1,999 lifetimes ago*, when I was expressing as *state of consciousness, spirit form, new soul*, and, "I had a fear of becoming corrupted, losing my innocence and purity, through whatever process I was about to experience, and that loss of purity would, in turn, prevent me from ever being able to return home—or feeling the same if I did return."

This higher (divine) conscious thought was indicated to be congruent, and I found it an interesting emotional theme to encounter because even now, in my present life, I've always been mindful of things that can corrupt the spirit, fearing a loss of purity. Can it be that my soul's focused intent to remain pure throughout incarnated experiences in order to get back home has been impressed upon my psyche? It would very much seem so, as this is a fear of which I'm consciously aware even in my present life.

I believe the majority of us consciously or unconsciously fear losing our purity. That's why we strive to live good lives, refrain from hurting others, and are mindful of our actions. This desire, to remain uncorrupted by life, is strongly held within our unconscious awareness, and that is why we seek teachings or practices to reinforce our intention to remain pure. To one extent or another, we hold a subconscious emotional fear that we either won't be able to return home or we won't be able to experience our home in the same way if we have become corrupted.

Muscle testing my subconscious indicated that there was *one additional blocked emotion*, and it was *frightfully overjoyed*. The only information that came into my mind and tested as being congruent was: "I am joyous at what is occurring while simultaneously fearful about becoming corrupted."

No further information was indicated to be necessary, so we began the process of releasing this emotional block.

While holding this original emotional theme in my mind during the clearing process, I realized that 1,999 lifetimes ago my soul recognized a more desirable place—home (benevolent perfection)—in which it consciously existed prior to a lifetime 1,999 lifetimes ago. My soul was holding a fear that it wouldn't be able to return back home, and even if it did return, it might have become so tainted through the process that home would not feel the same.

Something about losing purity was really touching a nerve, and I realized what it involved. As a little girl, I was sweet and innocent, and even though I had every intention of remaining the same as I lived my life, I didn't. I changed. Life changes you just by the act of living it. Little bits of innocence are lost along the way—an unavoidable result of being human.

In this lifetime, 1,999 lifetimes ago, there was a deep fear that the process itself (experiencing as a new soul) might forever keep me separated from my sense of home. Could a fear this intense be carried throughout all lifetimes, creating a subconscious fear in my current lifetime of doing something wrong—of forever spoiling my chance to return home? It would certainly explain my thoughts, even as a child, about remaining pure of heart.

To me, this session clearly established that by this point, 1,999 lifetimes ago, we already have feelings of being separated from what we consider home. This is not just a feeling we're experiencing as human beings in our current lifetimes.

But how are we ever to return home when the circumstances of our separation force us to putter around in dense, human conscious embodiment, probably bungling our opportunity because being here on earth appears to demand our full attention in acquiring food, shelter, and survival, possibly corrupting our spirits in the process?

It seems like a paradox very few of us will ever successfully solve. How can we prevail in remaining pure in a world such as this when even in childhood we can be significantly impacted by the smallest of slights?

But there was something about the concepts of "returning home" or "attaining oneness" that seem very wrong to me. Why? I'm not sure, but there is a feeling that the entire premise and how I'm going about it is off. Something keeps whispering in the back of my mind that I'm missing something really important about home and oneness.

But what?

Chapter 22

All Is Not Lost; Nothing Is Gained

*Perceiving limit within limitlessness is
when oneness does not consciously
recognize their own allness.*

There is no answer for how to get back home to oneness, only swirling
thoughts and emotions that have entirely fascinated me—not just by
what has been revealed but also because there is a deep knowing that
profound revelations are coming.

How soon is not known, but there is an expectation in my
energy field not springing from any conscious awareness on my part.
It's as though another consciousness, deep within the folds of my
unconsciousness, knows something wonderful is about to happen and
I'm feeling the excitement.

New Session in Same *Cluster*, Originating 2,001 Lifetimes Ago
In the next session of this cluster (1,999–2,001 lifetimes ago), I
am utilizing a higher conscious affirmation regarding outwardly
manifesting inner spiritual identity, which I find interesting because
I've not only had glimpses of a spiritual identity issue in my sessions
but that issue seems to somehow be connected to the fluctuating levels
of physical discomfort I've been experiencing in my heart.

We began the day's session with my subconscious indicating that
there's definitely an emotional block associated with this particular
affirmation about spiritual identity. And no surprise, the organ holding
the emotional block was my heart. How could I be surprised that
my heart would be somehow connected to a spiritual identity issue?
Surprise isn't the emotion I was feeling. It's more like a smiling,
energetic nod at the synchronicity of it all.

In the session today, the *present-day emotion* blocked within my
heart area is *can't figure it out* and the *present-day emotional theme*
flowing through my mind as higher conscious thoughts, is: "I can't

180

figure out how to outwardly manifest my true spiritual identity because I can't figure out where I, Carol, leave off and where my spiritual self begins. I can't conceptualize whether my spirit is limitless and I can use all of it or if there is a part of it that is limited and can, therefore, eventually be depleted. I, as Carol, feel limited, yet I sense something inside of me feels limitless. So how, then, do I go about bringing forth my spiritual identity in the event it is limited and can be depleted? I'm struggling with the concept that both feelings (limited and limitless) seem to simultaneously co-exist within me in a way that causes me not to be able to figure out how to bring forth my true spiritual identity."

Muscle testing indicated that there was a prior original time for this present-day emotional theme. The *origin* of this *emotional theme* is *2,001 lifetimes ago.* And as Angela and I were testing for the role, an extraordinary phrase eventually flowed into my mind from higher consciousness. My *role,* my expression, in this lifetime 2,001 lifetimes ago was the *vibration of love.* This role was not the least bit mainstream, nor was it easy to bring to light, but it was definitely accurate, as my subconscious had just indicated that the vibration of love is the congruent role I was expressing 2,001 lifetimes ago.

I was stunned to silence by these words. In all my previous sessions, each and every role carried some type of human or spiritual identification embodied in the expression. For instance, if the role I'm expressing—I'm embodying while in a particular lifetime—is associated with a human form, then additional identifying aspects may be mystic, wife, author, etc. If the lifetime expression is more non-physical, such as spirit, then additional characteristics of the role may be a spirit form, angel, master, etc.

I had become so acclimated to the various roles always carrying some type of identification, usually associated with the dominant function or purpose of the lifetime, that I didn't realize that I just automatically began associating role with a job or function, as if these were the main hats we were wearing in these lifetimes.

Never in any of my previous sessions had I experienced a core energy, indicative of our true nature. But today there was no doubt in my mind that I was definitely experiencing something very profound and at the core of all of us. Why was I so certain? Because throughout these sessions, I had developed an absolute trust of the veracity of the information conveyed—not just because it was later proven to have been accurate to have alleviated a subconscious block but because I always simultaneously experienced an energetic connectedness to the information. And today was no different. As this higher conscious thought was conveyed, I felt an energetic vibration move through me that radiated the feeling of love. It is difficult to describe, but it was as though love itself was energetically held as a vibrating power within my beingness, and as this vibration came to rest in my heart, I realized I felt a oneness with this energy as nothing I've ever experienced.

The *vibration* of love ... Hopefully these words have resonated within you as well—and even stolen away a little of your breath, as the vibration of love is a lot more than words. It is a description of a conscious state of beingness that is not human, not spirit, but an energetic vibration—and that vibration is love. Isn't that amazing? And something deep within me conveys a knowing that the vibration of love isn't just an "expression." It is the very *consciousness* that is at the core of all of us—a pure consciousness that energetically vibrates as love.

This session is verification that we are so much more than we perceive ourselves to be—beyond human, and even beyond spirit. The "vibration of love" is not just a role—it is a remarkable confirmation of what is at the center of our beingness—our true nature; the true nature of everyone and everything ... Love.

We don't just *feel* the emotion of love ... we *are* love. We don't just *vibrate* as love ... we *are* the vibration of love.

Although we are told we are love; and we hope it is true, most of the time it is difficult for us to believe. Now, in this moment—experienced very unexpectedly in this session—I'm deeply connected to this truth in a way I've never before experienced. Love is resonating throughout me as an energetic knowing—forever allaying any doubt about our true nature.

And even though this specifically happened to me, through my own conscious beingness, it applies to all of us. At the core of all of us, we are the vibration of love—the essence of love. It is impossible for one to be less than or greater than another because we are identically the same essence. If I am love, you are love. Period—no "what ifs" or "hows" involved. Don't be tempted to cast the most beautiful part of yourself off to the side because you either can't believe it is true or you can't understand exactly how it can be true.

All you need do is accept that you are love, because the fact that we are love was verified to not only me but to all of us in this very session.

Even if the outward manifestation of our beingness of love has not yet perfectly aligned with our inner knowingness, don't worry. Eventually all will perfectly align to the one pure vibration: *love.* It cannot be otherwise.

No matter how you viewed yourself even a moment ago, beginning right now, in this very moment, be love. Now is the perfect time to stop what you are doing and repeat this phrase: "I am love."

Be love ... Trust—know—flow.

(Don't let go of your feeling of *being love* as the details of this session continue to unfold.)

So far in our session on this day, Angela and I determined that the *origin* for the *present-day emotional theme* is in a lifetime *2,001 lifetimes ago* when I am expressing (*role*) as the *vibration of love.*

The *original emotional theme* that came from higher consciousness and was indicated by my subconscious to be congruent was that, "as the vibration of love, I feel *puzzled* about how to express all and one." (Puzzled was the emotion.)

Once this original emotional theme was identified, Angela and I began posing concepts and muscle testing them in order to determine why I was feeling puzzled. So far, my subconscious indicated that my feelings of being puzzled were not caused because I believed the vibration of love was not mine to use. Why, then, was I puzzled?

Profound higher conscious thoughts began flowing through my mind, and as I spoke them out loud, Angela was muscle testing them, and my subconscious was indicating that they were all congruent: "The reason that I feel puzzled about how to express all and one is because I'm not able to figure out whether the vibration of love I am expressing is limitless or limited, so I don't know whether to use it or save it. I'm struggling because the allness aspect I am expressing as the vibration of love feels limitless; yet, at the same time, there is a oneness aspect to the vibration of love that feels limited. I don't know how to express both aspects—all and one—simultaneously. I'm unsure what aspects of the vibration of love can and can't be used, so I'm reluctant to utilize resources I perceive as limited since they can eventually be depleted. Expressing all and one at the same time is puzzling."

Wow ... This is extraordinary and puzzling at the same time. It's extraordinary that I was experiencing as the limitless vibration of love, and it's puzzling that this limitless vibration of love is experiencing limit. There seems to be something about "limit within limitlessness" and "all and one" that was preventing me from fully experiencing the limitlessness of the vibration of love. But what?

The thought that kept floating back into my mind was, "If I am expressing as the limitless vibration of love, then how can I also be simultaneously experiencing limit? It makes absolutely no sense at all to me. There is no limit in limitlessness—or it wouldn't be limitless! It's like we are and we aren't at the same time."

Then, as I was struggling with understanding this concept, higher (divine) consciousness conveyed the following energetic thought:

"Perceiving limit within limitlessness is when oneness does not consciously recognize their own allness."

These higher conscious words were resonating within me as being a profound piece of the knowing that had been continuously unfolding in my conscious awareness before, during, and after these sessions. But because I was not able to connect the concepts of "simultaneously being all and one" and "limitlessness and limit" to anything I'd ever consciously encountered, my mind was unable to comprehend or absorb the full meaning of this higher conscious insight.

Many thoughts were flashing through my mind as Angela and I were in the process of clearing this subconscious emotional block, and as I left Angela's office, I felt both puzzled and uplifted through what I'd experienced in the day's session.

Love is the vibration of our beingness!

This is absolutely remarkable when you realize the power and possibility contained in this knowing: love is all; and all of us are love.

New Session in Same *Cluster*, Originating 2,001 Lifetimes Ago

Today's affirmation from higher consciousness is about having access to unlimited grace. Muscle testing confirmed that this affirmation was not congruent with my subconscious and there was a subconscious emotional block. No specific present-day role, other than me, as Carol, was indicated, and the *present-day emotion* associated with this subconscious block is *egotistic related to self centeredness.*

The *present-day emotional theme* that was conveyed through higher consciousness and muscle tests as congruent was: "I felt it would be self-centered of me to take all that I needed from grace, even though grace was unlimited. Something made me feel that if I took everything I needed, then there might not be enough grace left for others."

Through muscle testing, my subconscious indicated that the congruent *origin* of this *emotional theme* was *2,001 lifetimes ago;* my *role* is the *vibration of love;* and the *emotion* is *egotistic.* The congruent *original emotional theme,* conveyed through higher consciousness, was: "I felt it was egotistically self-centered of me, as the vibration of love, to take what I needed from the all of grace, as that would cause the vibration of love to become depleted and there wouldn't be enough grace for others. As the vibration of love, I am perceiving some limit, and this perception is causing me to feel that there must be a limit to everything. There is a feeling of vast limitlessness as the vibration of love, as well as limit; and I felt that if I absorbed the all of grace into me fully, then there wouldn't be enough to go around. This feeling involves ego in the sense that it is up to me to provide for all. Yet I am not the provider of all."

What does someone consciously do with an original emotional theme like this one? It would be natural to hear it, initially pull it through your mind for comprehension, and then let it go because it didn't seem there was enough connectedness between the words to make them decipherable. But something about these words was vibrating within me so strongly that I felt a need to understand them. I couldn't just let them fly by without trying to sort through them. But this wasn't something I looked forward to doing, as there seemed to be many aspects to these words that were contradictory in nature.

Not only were there two simultaneous yet contrary viewpoints co-existing within the vibration of love (limitlessness and limit), but there was also some sort of ego-based emotional block that was causing me concern about depleting resources, as well as a sense that it was and it wasn't up to me to provide for all.

That's a lot of threads of thoughts to sort through and logically perceive. But something whispered in my heart that I needed to at least try and understand the details of the unusual original emotional theme revealed in this session. It might be important.

Okay. Viewing from the allness aspect of the vibration of love, there is limitless supply for everyone, and I and everyone should be able to take as much grace as needed without worrying about depletion. Yet there was something within the allness of the vibration of love that sensed limit, which created feelings of not being able to provide for all and a concern that taking too much would deplete the vibration of love, leaving not enough grace to go around.

All are provided for through the limitlessness of the vibration of love. But it seemed that the limitless vibration of love simultaneously perceives itself as limited. At this point, I released my mind and let my thoughts go, trusting higher conscious perceptions would come forth—and they did.

In my very next thoughts, I realized the concept, "I am not the provider of all" does not mean that the vibration of love isn't the provider of all. It means that there is a "limited perception of I" within the vibration of love that feels like *I* need to make sure not to take too much from what *I* sense to be limited, so that *I*, as the vibration of love, can still provide for all.

But "I" (ego-based, self-centered perception) is not the provider of all. Rather, the limitless, egoless allness of the vibration of love is the provider of all. But the "ego, self-centeredness of I" is simultaneously present with the "egoless allness," and that's what makes me perceive that I need to be the provider of all when, in truth, merely being the vibration of love provides for all.

There seems to be a limited, ego-based, self-centered I simultaneously present in the limitless, egoless allness of the vibration of love. Why?

Does this have something to do with the previous higher conscious insight, *perceiving limit within limitlessness is when oneness does not consciously recognize their own allness?* It appears so; but this is as far as my thoughts took me. I just wasn't able to perceive any deeper meaning at this time.

As Angela told me that my subconscious indicated no additional details were necessary to clear this subconscious emotional block,

I realized all of my higher conscious awareness happened in only a matter of seconds. It felt like it was occurring for several minutes, but that is the nature of higher conscious interaction. The moments hold volumes of perceptions.

I couldn't help but feel disappointed that more details were not needed by my subconscious. This was one of those times I would very much have liked further insight into why there was this disparity occurring within the vibration of love. It seemed illogical that a limited aspect and a limitless aspect could be simultaneously present, and I was hoping additional details would help explain this energetic contradiction. But it was not to be so.

Next, as Angela and I moved on to clearing this emotional block from my subconscious, I came to the conclusion that this emotional block had been limiting me in everything I was experiencing in my life. I was not able to view my relationship with grace (the vibration of love; divinity) as "limitless all" because of viewing through the "limited I" of ego. I couldn't help but think, "My *I* is limiting my *all* from manifesting."

As I was holding this original emotional theme in my mind in order to clear the subconscious block, I was shown something quite beautiful by divine consciousness. With my eyes closed, I saw a shape that was elliptical and completely dark, with a slight, almost indiscernible electric green light bordering it. I was immediately filled with the thought and feeling that Universe exists as this space and everything is provided through this void and light of Universe. In the next moment, the following higher conscious thought flowed through my mind:

"Cease to think of Universe as a basket from which you remove something, eventually depleting the basket. Universe is not a basket, which is limited; it is an energy eternally funneling all that is needed into existence."

I realized that things don't exist in a space that you go to, like a tree to pick fruit or a basket loaded with gifts. Rather everything exists in nothingness—in the void (the dark energetic potential of the circle) until conscious intention manifests it into creation through the vibration of love—the vibrant green kinetic light of manifestation. And then it just flows forth.

The vision was still in front of me as I was thinking this very thought, and as I was concluding my thought, the radiant green light around the rim of the eternal dark void began to fade back into the circle. I wondered, for just a moment, if the higher conscious thought I just perceived originated from the energy of that green light, and once the thought had been given, the light faded back into the void of Universe. Was this an example of a "thought form" manifesting from the vibration of love/divine consciousness? It very much seemed so.

Does all creation—both thought (essence) and matter (form)—manifest from this vibrant light and energetic void? After this experience, I'm certain that it does, but I don't understand how or why. I only know that there was a connectedness between what I was shown though higher consciousness and what I experienced in my session.

This day's session ended with me consciously holding this particular vision (the void encircled by radiant green light).

There was a sense of knowing conveyed through this session that Universe and we are the same limitless nature, and by tapping into the allness of grace that is our beingness, "limitless all" will more consciously manifest through the "limited I" of our lives.

New Session in Same *Cluster*, Originating 2,001 Lifetimes Ago

Due to a physical ailment in my lower abdomen, Angela began the next session by muscle testing for any subconscious emotional blocks associated with this area of my body, and my subconscious indicated that there was an emotional block related to the category of "my finances."

This was an unusual session in that my higher consciousness conveyed four *present-day emotional themes* associated with this emotional block that were all muscle tested and indicated by my subconscious as congruent, related to *distrust of finances:*

(a) Distrust I could put my faith in money and rely on it—as it comes and goes.
(b) Distrust in myself and my ability to handle and keep money.
(c) Distrust the process of being in the world; and though I am not attached to money, I sometimes feel like I need

protection. And although faith protects me, I distrust that it will protect me from creditors.

(d) Distrust of money because it corrupts the energy field by shifting focus to trusting a by-product of life (money) rather than your own beingness.

My subconscious indicated that there was one common root for all of these emotional themes, and when muscle tested, the *common root* of the *present-day emotional theme* was that, "I felt I couldn't put my faith, my complete trust, in something because it wasn't always going to be there."

When Angela muscle tested for the original time when this emotional theme first occurred in my subconscious, it went back to an *origin* that was *2,001 lifetimes ago.*

Even though I'd been to this lifetime before, Angela still muscle tested my subconscious for the *role*, and it was the same as previously. In this lifetime, 2,001 lifetimes ago, I was expressing as the *vibration of love.* The blocked emotion is *distrust,* and the *original emotional theme* that flows into my mind from higher consciousness was: "I distrust that something (perfection, Creator) will always be there to depend upon, due to the ever-changing nature of Universe. I am happy and blissful as the vibration of love. I feel everything is perfect the way it is, so I don't understand why it is changing. Due to the nature of change, I do not trust that I can rely on things remaining the same after the change. I distrust it will ever be the same again."

As Angela confirmed with my subconscious that this information was congruent with the original emotional theme, I remembered (from previous sessions) that two lifetimes from this one—1,999 lifetimes ago—I'd be experiencing as state of consciousness, spirit form, new soul.

It occurs to me that in the lifetime I was experiencing in this day's session (2,001 lifetimes ago) that as the vibration of love, I am sensing or aware of the coming shift in consciousness (1,999 lifetimes ago) and I'm distrusting of the changes it may bring.

Muscle testing indicated that no additional details were needed by my subconscious and no additional blocked emotions were involved— short and sweet.

During the clearing, while I was holding a mental picture of the original emotional theme that relates to "distrust of change," the following energetic thought from Universe flowed through my mind: *"All* is not lost; *nothing* is gained. Ponder this and you will understand."

It felt like I had just been handed a pivotal clue in an ongoing crossword puzzle, and I loved that divine consciousness wasn't just handing me the answer to the puzzle.

As I pondered the concept of all and the concept of nothing in relation to "distrust of change" these are the higher conscious thoughts flowing through my mind:

> *"All* is not lost ... in change. Our fear is that in change, we will lose some of the allness we feel in perfection; but our allness cannot ever be diminished or *lost* in any change of expression or transformation we experience, as all is never less than all.
>
> *Nothing* is gained ... in change. This means that nothing will be added or gained when we *consciously* perceive our perfection or allness, because *nothing* of allness is ever lost in the *perception* of separation or change. Therefore, nothing is ever gained in allness."

The session ended, as it always does, with me releasing the subconscious block and Angela then retesting to make certain the block had been cleared.

I left this session with many higher conscious clues (homework to ponder), and I was thinking about the beautiful vibration of nothingness and allness—the energetic void with the rim of green light—when the following higher conscious thought flashed into my mind:

> "All of these perceptions are not just spiritual truth conveyed through words and thoughts. They are an energetic collage of conscious awakening, illustrating pages in the *book of knowing* we all carry within us."

Chapter 23

Going Back ... Where?
No Wonder Universe Gave Me a Hint

At this point, I assumed I had gone back as far as possible. After all, it was the birth of the new soul. Isn't that the beginning?

Apparently not, because that night as I was drifting to sleep, an energetic thought from Universe told me that I was going all the way back to the beginning, back further than I could even now imagine. My eyes popped open and I muttered, "All the way back?" The answering energetic thought from Universe was, "Yes, and you will understand."

I loved hearing I would understand, so I continued drifting to sleep wondering how far back the beginning would go. The adventure was continuing, which meant more healing and more insights. That was okay by me.

What I didn't realize was that Universe was going to make good on this promise of understanding while delivering a tremendous gift—a gift I longed to unwrap since I was nine years old.

And once I found myself back at the beginning, no matter how prepared I believed myself to be, it was just too profound for me to immediately wrap my mind around.

It reminded me of something that happened to me when I was first beginning to meditate.

A friend suggested a trip to Miami to a place where you could experience altered states of consciousness induced by listening to sound. They would seat you in a large, comfortable reclining chair where you are fitted with headphones and eyewear. You were instructed to lie all the way back and relax as the sounds dropped you into deeper states of relaxation. The method is designed to slow down your brain waves, moving you from Beta (your natural conscious state) to Alpha (a relaxed state) to Theta (a deep meditative state).

As I was relaxing, listening to the sounds, I felt as though I was in a very deep state of meditation. At some point, I sensed a spiritual presence by my side. The impression was so strong that I knew that a benevolent spiritual being was standing right there next to me. I summoned all my courage, and I sent the thought, "If you are really standing here, please touch my left leg and let me know."

Immediately, I felt something physically touch my left leg. I let out a yelp. I was so shocked to think that it was real—that physical contact by a spiritual being had occurred when I was fully awake—that I couldn't help myself. The yelp just came out of me. A few moments later, a technician came over, pulled one side of my headphones away from my ear, and sternly warned me that disruptive noises were not allowed. I apologized and promised not to make another sound. Off he went, back to his monitoring station, and I went back to brain wave surfing. It was very relaxing and extremely enjoyable.

A few minutes later, I felt the spiritual presence again, and this time, I apologetically thought, "I'm sorry I yelped. I was surprised. But now I'm ready. If you are here, please touch me again, and this time I promise that I won't scream." I was fighting my fear, which was very deep when it came to actual physical contact by a spiritual being, probably because of what happened when I was fourteen. But I was also feeling excited by the prospect of interacting in this manner with my spiritual guidance, and I was really trying to stay open to the experience. I was hunkered down, with a steadfast grip on my mixed emotions of fear and excitement, when the spiritual presence touched me once more. This time I let out an even louder yelp and jumped a few inches out of my chair. So much for promises of courage. No matter how prepared I tried to be or how much I wanted to be open, I just couldn't help myself. It was a startling event, as I hadn't come prepared for the possibility of physical contact by a spiritual being.

Well, I didn't need to worry about how to voice my apology to the spiritual presence for jumping and yelping, as I was immediately asked to leave by a rather angry young technician. I am not a defiant person and am on the reticent side, so being kicked out of a public place was embarrassing and upsetting—plus I didn't get to enjoy this unique experience any longer, and I was just getting the hang of it.

There are times when no matter how much we try to get ourselves up to speed and stay with the energy, it is very difficult not to react when faced with something so unusual that we don't immediately know what to think, do, or say. I was about to experience one of those events, a truly astonishing event, where even preparation through my lifelong relationship with Universe did not lessen the impact of what was experienced.

In these sessions with Angela, I was perceiving threads of awareness that were revealing issues within my soul that seemed to be going back to the birth of my soul as a consciousness expression. But this awareness hadn't yet revealed who I was in the absolute sense. I realize I'm Carol and I am a soul. What I was seeking was clarity about what's at the core of me—at the core of all of us—our pure nature, our origin, and our purpose.

So far the thought that I'm Carol in a physical body housing a soul that is seeking to accomplish some goal hasn't been lost on me. But what, exactly, was I trying to find, and why did I need to find it? And how was it originally lost?

Traveling through this current lifetime sensing you are missing something can create a nagging thought in the back of your mind all the time you're on your journey. It's like going on vacation, thinking you've packed everything, yet you have the feeling you've forgotten something. You can't completely relax until you remember what you've forgotten.

Tripping along through life, enjoying most of the journey, though certainly not all of it, I was about to remember just what was forgotten.

Chapter 24

A Threshold of Consciousness
Rarely Glimpsed

We are one consciousness ... one light,
expressing through the multi-faceted
prism of our own essence.

Nothing in the message Universe gave me about where I was going to end up in all these sessions (back at the beginning) prepared me for what was waiting there for me. When I arrived, it was as though divine consciousness reached right through all conscious dimensions and touched my mind with the knowing to my innermost questions, and I was so surprised by the way it all unfolded that I couldn't help but let out a big yelp of surprise.

It was spring 2009, and on this particular day, higher consciousness had given me a very unusual affirmation about consciousness. As I began the session, muscle testing indicated that there was an emotional block that was not allowing my subconscious to accept the higher conscious affirmation as congruent. This basically meant that my subconscious mind was resisting some part of this affirmation, which was counterproductive to manifesting the intent of the affirmation.

The *present-day emotion* involved in the subconscious emotional block is *false self-assuredness,* and the *present-day emotional theme* is: "I am trying to assure myself that what I believe about consciousness, life after death, and other spiritual beliefs is true, but because it is beyond my comprehension, there is some doubt."

I immediately connected with this emotional theme, because even though I believe that we are eternal, there is individual consciousness after death, and many other things, based on my experiences, there is something about not being able to comprehend it fully that was causing me doubt.

Isn't this how many of us feel? We spiritually hold on to threads of our belief, based on a knowing we carry within us, yet this physical world in which we live reflects no proof or foundation for that belief. The proof is held in an unseen realm that we cannot fully comprehend because we cannot consciously penetrate all the veils of mystery surrounding it in order to lay down a solid foundation of understanding.

The amazing part is that even though we live in an apparently real and physical world, our spirits, our minds, and our emotions are profoundly connected to a world we cannot see, nor touch, nor understand, and when we experience that other unreal world, even if briefly, we choose to believe it rather than what we can logically comprehend and physically see and touch. Through our faith, our knowing, we consciously choose concepts as our center that aren't even feasible in our physical world (our souls, divinity, heaven, angels, oneness, life after death, etc.), with no real proof other than the knowing we carry inside.

There is no doubt in my heart that we must all know something— even though we don't realize we know it. The proof is our willingness to believe in what we sense or perceive, even if it is only glimpsed for a moment and seemingly impossible in our conventional world.

But for now, in today's session, this very contradiction (assuring myself that what I believe is true versus not really being certain it can be true) was the cause of my emotional block and my feelings of false self-assuredness in the present day.

As Angela began muscle testing for the original time when I wanted to believe in the truth of it all but held some doubt about it, we found the emotional theme did not originate in this lifetime but rather back in the period known as preconception (prior lifetimes). That was no big surprise, as almost all of the origins for my emotional blocks are in prior lifetimes.

I'm comfortable with the concept of prior existence, so a process that involves past lives is not one that causes me any conflict spiritually, emotionally, or mentally. But I was about to hit the limit of what I could immediately grasp within the next few seconds.

Angela was muscle testing for the origin of the emotional theme— the lifetime expression where this emotional theme first impacted my subconscious.

We muscle tested and moved back through my current lifetime, and we were now testing preconception for the origin. And as we continued testing, while moving backward through preconception, I was going back further than I'd ever previously gone in any of my sessions.

Then, astonishingly, the *origin* of my present-day emotional theme was revealed. It's *9,999 lifetimes ago*.

I consciously yelped right then and there!

Up until this point, the furthest back I had gone was 2,001 lifetimes ago. Now I'd jumped to *9,999 lifetimes ago*. Big leap. Big yelp!

It was one of the most astounding moments I'd ever experienced. How does one even prepare for the concept of 9,999 lifetimes ago? The timeframe alone was just too far back for me to associate with anything. And although I consciously realized a subconscious block doesn't have an expiration date—meaning it can go back forever, as our subconscious has always been aware—I was shocked to encounter a subconscious emotional block going back this far.

As I was trying to harness my surprise, I sensed higher consciousness conveying the thought that I needed to remain focused, as I could think about this later on. For now, I needed to just stay centered in the experience.

Though both Angela and I were experiencing amazement, we continued on with the session as we normally would, which would be to next determine the related role I was expressing back in this lifetime, 9,999 lifetimes ago.

We muscle tested if human embodiment was the role I was expressing, and neither of us were at all surprised to find that human form was not congruent with my subconscious. So we began testing other concepts—anything that seemed possible. Finally, the phrase *collective unconscious vibration of love* flowed through my waking conscious mind as a higher conscious thought, which I spontaneously uttered out loud. Immediately, Angela muscle tested this phrase, and my subconscious confirmed that it was the congruent energetic expression (*role*).

These sessions were not only incredible in where they were taking me but also in how I was being guided there through an extraordinary collaboration between my higher self and my subconscious, revealing roles, themes, and emotional blocks to my waking conscious mind.

At this *origin, 9,999 lifetimes ago,* I was expressing as the *collective unconscious vibration of love.* I was familiar with the role of the "vibration of love," but there was something about expressing this role that was profoundly affecting me. A sense of awe was moving through me, and from Angela's reaction, I sensed she was feeling the same. There was something barely perceptible within me that was energetically responding to this role as though the most primordial vibration I'd ever experienced had just energized my consciousness. It was almost as though I'd had amnesia my entire life, and I just felt a wave of remembrance move through me and I was energetically experiencing my true identity for the first time.

The emotion was *false self-assuredness,* and the congruent *original emotional theme* 9,999 lifetimes ago was that, "I, as the collective unconscious vibration of love feel a sense of connectedness; there is no interference in this connection; and I am feeling the assurance of love. But I am about to manifest outward, and although I am sensing it is all right, something feels different in the energy that is causing me doubt."

Although more information would have helped clarify what was occurring, muscle testing my subconscious indicated that no further information was needed to clear this emotional block.

After I went through the clearing phase, the session came to an end. But there was a knowing in me that this was a far more profound session than was possible for me to now consciously comprehend, and clear understanding was just around the corner.

The Insight That Triggers Remembrance

In my next session, my subconscious and higher (divine) consciousness basically picked up where they had left off. The affirmation perceived that morning from higher conscious thought was very unusual and focused on "remembering Creation."

When we tested the affirmation, an incongruency was revealed. Learning that an affirmation from higher consciousness is incongruent is never a surprise. We have come to realize that the words and phrasing of the words in these affirmations is key to unlocking subconscious emotional blocks that divine consciousness intends to be revealed and cleared.

The *present-day emotion* was *fear,* and the emotional theme conveyed to me through higher conscious insight, muscle testing as congruent, was both incredible and startling. The *present-day emotional theme* was: "I felt fear about what I would be leaving behind as the collective unconscious when the original act of Creation occurred."

Initially, I didn't know what to think—other than it was incredible that an affirmation from higher consciousness was definitely triggering a subconscious memory of the original act of Creation.

Thankfully, my subconscious indicated that more information was needed about this profound present-day emotional theme. I was hoping not only to understand why I was fearful about what I'd be leaving behind but also gain insight about the original act of Creation.

Was I really going to get a conscious glimpse of our creation? It was extraordinary to encounter ... *creation.*

The following are additional higher conscious thoughts that were all posed to my subconscious, muscle tested, and found to be congruent with the *present-day emotional theme* that, *I felt fear about what I would be leaving behind as the collective unconscious when the original act of Creation occurred*:

(a) Collective unconscious is aware (knows) everything; therefore, the collective unconscious carries the identical all-knowingness as divine energy.

(b) There is a transition about to occur in the entire collective.

(c) This transition is the original act of Creation.

(d) When this transition occurs, "consciousness" will unfold.

(e) When consciousness unfolds, I fear that I will not know the same all-knowingness as consciousness that I know as collective unconsciousness.

(f) The original act of Creation is occurring because consciousness is how we will realize every aspect of our beingness.

All of this information was rapidly flowing through my mind as higher conscious thought, and when it first struck my waking consciousness, it was so staggeringly unusual that I was not able to immediately process it. I began thinking about the concepts one at a time, but when I reached, "This transition is the original act of Creation," my mind hit a wall as far as logic was concerned.

Why was I experiencing something as a "present-day" emotional block when it obviously must have occurred a long time ago (the original act of Creation)? I must be remembering in the present day what I wasn't energetically okay with at the time when the original act of Creation was occurring. I'd never before experienced a prior event as part of a present-day emotional theme, and it was interesting how the higher conscious affirmation was worded—as though specifically designed to trigger this very experience.

All I knew for certain was that higher (divine) consciousness had just revealed extraordinary concepts that my subconscious indicated were congruent. For the briefest moment, I felt as though divinity had just slipped me a note in class, and when I opened it, I exclaimed my surprise so loudly that the entire collective was now aware of the information carried in that note.

Thoughts were flowing through my mind, and one of them was that collective unconsciousness seemed fearful that its all-knowing awareness would be lost in consciousness. Up until this point in my life, I'd always thought that we transition from a state of being unconscious (unaware) into a state of consciousness (awareness). How, then, can unconsciousness think that it may know more than consciousness? That seems topsy-turvy.

I'm not quite sure what to think about these concepts, but I'm left to wonder for the moment, as muscle testing my subconscious indicated that no further details were needed; but there was a prior, original occurrence of this present-day emotional theme. I'd been so engaged in processing the concepts being revealed that I had momentarily forgotten that all of this information related to a present-day emotional theme.

As Angela began muscle testing for the origin of the present-day emotional theme, I was still wondering about the concepts that had been revealed and hoping that the details of the original emotional theme would help me sort it out.

It looked like I was about to find out. Angela had been posing timeframes and muscle testing back through preconception for the congruent lifetime, and my subconscious had just indicated that the *origin* of this *present-day emotional theme* went back *ten thousand lifetimes ago!*

I'm not sure what I was expecting when I began these sessions (oh, yeah, I remember ... I was expecting chakra balancing), but I sure wasn't expecting to go back ten thousand lifetimes ago. Rather than shift my attention away from what was happening in the session, I decided to put my thoughts on hold, focusing my attention on Angela and the process at hand.

We were working through the part of the session where Angela was muscle testing for the role I was expressing back at the origin of this subconscious emotional block ten thousand lifetimes ago. This role ended up being a little difficult for us to pinpoint, as there was an aspect to this role that my subconscious was adamant that we identify precisely.

Thankfully, I got help from higher consciousness when a profound phrase floated into my conscious mind and instantly out of my mouth. Angela immediately muscle tested this phrase, and it was accepted as congruent by my subconscious. The *role* I was expressing in this lifetime, ten thousand lifetimes ago was the *essence of collective unconscious.* When this phrase tested congruent, I was surprised by how resolute my subconscious was about identifying this exact phrase, as we had already, almost immediately, tested the term "collective unconscious," which had tested incongruent. My subconscious was tenacious that the congruent phrase was not collective unconscious but rather *essence* of collective unconscious. By the manner in which my subconscious rejected phrases that were not precise, it was apparent that the word "essence" was considered by my subconscious to be an imperative component of the role I was expressing.

The *essence of collective unconscious.* What a very unusual term for my subconscious to indicate as congruent. In a flash of conscious clarity, I realized my subconscious was not what I had assumed it to be for most of my life. Somewhere along the way, I'd just begun viewing my subconscious as an isolated aspect of consciousness living in the closet of my emotional self; and conscious I (tah, dah!) was the liberator of unhealthy emotions stuck in that closet.

From time to time throughout my life as I encountered my subconscious, I would only perceive what was reflected upon the surface of my conscious mind. But today I am no longer just seeing the mere reflection of my subconscious. Rather, I am now peering into the depths of its enigmatic recesses; and what do I see? The all-knowingness of divine consciousness peering back at me.

It's unimaginable that I haven't previously perceived the full measure of this profound awareness co-existing with me throughout all eternity. For here I am now, going back ten thousand lifetimes ago to the essence of collective unconscious—and who took me there? My previously assumed unaware subconscious.

At this point, I instantly realized that collective unconscious (subconscious) and collective conscious (higher consciousness) are identical in awareness. This perfectly explains the seamless manner in which concepts and information flowed forth in these sessions. I'd always assumed higher consciousness is aware, but this was the first time I realized that the subconscious is equally aware—in fact, identically aware.

In this session, I was viewing my subconscious in an entirely new light, with newfound respect and reverence. I realized my subconscious was aware of all, even though I might not yet have pulled that all-knowingness into my waking consciousness.

Then I realized that the role of our subconscious is not to prevent us from experiencing the fullness of our life by holding these blocked emotions. The purpose of subconscious emotional blocks is to make us consciously aware of where we have an incongruency—where our consciousness is stuck.

Think of it as though our misperception of an experience or our misperception of our true nature creates an emotional response that is incongruent with our consciousness. That incongruency creates a groove, an imprint, much like a spot on a record where the needle gets stuck in a repetitive pattern. Eventually, the imprint—the repetitive pattern—draws our conscious attention. Then, once our attention is focused, we are able to decipher the cause of the imprint. Once we are able to pull the cause through our waking consciousness, while simultaneously accessing our subconscious, the pattern is cleared, erasing the imprint and reconciling the incongruency within our consciousness.

Are these emotional blocks—these grooves—there to help us consciously recognize what is not reconciled within our own beingness? Absolutely. And in recognizing what is not congruent, we are able to resolve and clear whatever has been blocking our progress of unfolding our true nature.

Our subconscious is trying to make us consciously aware of what needs to be cleared in order for us to awaken and more fluidly realize our potential. Our subconscious holds the blocks within unconsciousness for as long as is necessary for us to become consciously aware that a block exists—not to impede us, but to consciously liberate us from that which binds us to misperception.

This was an enlightening moment in that I now consciously recognized that there is a profound awareness within me (my subconscious) that I've spent the majority of my life ignoring or dismissing. What else had I been dismissing because of the arrogance of self-conscious awareness?

As Angela and I continued with this session, my subconscious indicated that the blocked *emotion* at this *origin, ten thousand lifetimes ago*, is still *fear*. We now need to identify the relevant original emotional theme, as that is always the crux of what is needed by my subconscious to clear the emotional block.

We are in the process of muscle testing to determine the original emotional theme involved in my feelings of fear as the essence of collective unconscious in this lifetime, ten thousand lifetimes ago. (Every time I say this phrase, *ten thousand lifetimes ago*, I feel a deep emotional response—a wave of vibrational connectedness moves through me.)

Eventually, higher consciousness conveyed the following *original emotional theme* to me, which Angela then posed to my subconscious, muscle tested, and found congruent: "At this time, ten thousand lifetimes ago, I am expressing as the essence of collective unconscious, and I am fearful that at the Creation of collective human consciousness, I will not know everything that is known in collective unconsciousness."

What?

This information was astonishing to me on so many levels that I not only had to repeat it in my mind in order to focus in on it, but it also then took me a little while to gather my thoughts. I was completely awestruck that a subconscious emotional block had taken me back to the "Creation of collective human consciousness."

But it wasn't the words alone that were impacting me. Always in these sessions, the energetic vibrational essence of the words are simultaneously carried through me as feelings when a higher conscious thought hits my mind. It's as though the vibration of knowing is striking both my mind and my heart at the same time.

So right now, in this session, I was consciously, subconsciously, and higher consciously experiencing the moment where divine design was unfolding a new state of consciousness. I was fully consciously aware of this moment because it was virtually being telecast throughout my entire beingness as an energetic awareness.

All I was capable of thinking was, *Oh my God, this is the "beginning" of which Universe spoke.* There was absolutely no doubt. I was most definitely "all the way back to the beginning"—the Creation of collective human consciousness.

Then higher consciousness conveyed an intriguing and profound thought: "My fear of not always knowing was actually manifesting my own not knowing, and this fear permeated the entirety of the collective unconscious."

At the very moment that I was consciously connecting to this particular higher conscious thought, I began to experience an intense feeling in my heart as though someone had reached into my chest and was squeezing my heart with both hands. It's strange to describe, as it wasn't a true physical pain. It was more as though the awareness coming to light in my conscious mind had touched a fear in me—a fear of not knowing—that was so deep, the intensity of this fear was reflected through my physical heart.

Then, almost as soon as I felt the knowing carried in the higher conscious words, the sensation passed, as though the act of me consciously connecting with the depth and intensity of this fear was the intention of my body's reaction.

I realized that the intensity of my reaction to this higher conscious insight explained why, even now in present-day, I was carrying a subconscious emotional block regarding the fear of what I would be leaving behind in collective unconsciousness when the "original act of Creation occurred." My fear of leaving behind "my knowing" was so intense that it was actually manifesting my own "not knowing" state. My fear had become a self-fulfilling prophecy.

All of my thoughts and reactions to this higher conscious interaction occurred before Angela even posed and tested the concept for congruency.

Unsurprisingly, when Angela muscle tested this higher conscious insight, my subconscious indicated it to be congruent: "My fear of not always knowing was actually manifesting my own not knowing, and this fear permeated the entirety of the collective unconscious."

Was this fear the veil between known and unknown? Could the veil that separates all we know from all we don't know really be just fear, created from a misperception?

I didn't have time to pursue these thoughts, as almost instantly another higher conscious thought—another aspect of this subconscious emotional block—flashed through my mind: "I am also fearful that I will never be me again."

This phrase was posed by Angela to my subconscious and was indicated to be congruent, but my subconscious indicated more details were needed. Angela then muscle tested whether the "fear that I will never be me again" was an individual fear. Very surprisingly, the indication was incongruent (no). Instead, the concept that my subconscious indicated as congruent was: "The fear that I will never be me again is a collective fear."

Once again, my subconscious indicated that more information was needed. The following higher conscious thoughts continued flowing through my mind and out of my voice, and they were all muscle tested by Angela and indicated by my subconscious as congruent:

(a) The concept of me is present in the collective unconscious; yet, there is no individual fear.
(b) There is fear in the entirety of the collective unconscious that it (collective unconsciousness) would not be known again after the birth of Creation.

At this point in the session, I didn't know whether to hit pause in my mind or rewind.

How could there be a "fear that I will never be me again" without that fear being an individual fear? The concept of "me" exists in the collective unconscious, yet the word "individual" isn't congruent.

Did this mean that the collective unconscious considers itself to be a "collective me" because there doesn't appear to be an "individual me" awareness? It would seem so.

I wasn't quite sure what to do with all the thoughts running through my mind.

This session was not only spiritually fascinating but also so energetically felt within my beingness that I knew I was experiencing a threshold of consciousness rarely glimpsed. It felt as though I was experiencing a milestone in my personal human conscious awareness that was consciously/spiritually equal to the technological moment when I watched man first walk on the moon.

In the next moment, it felt as if everything shifted—as if all of the higher conscious interaction in this session had induced a transcendent, altered state of consciousness and I was no longer experiencing this session in normal waking awareness. Rather, I was now simultaneously experiencing this moment—the original act of Creation—as though my own higher self and I had been consciously transported to the very dawn of Creation, energetically experiencing the unfolding of collective human consciousness as both lucid observer and energetic participant.

It was really too profound an experience to capture in words. One moment I was experiencing this session in normal waking consciousness, as the physical being Carol. Then in the span of an instant, I perceived myself to be standing as an energetic consciousness—a lucid observer— as well as a human conscious being at the very threshold of Creation, with an absolute *knowing* that collective human consciousness was in the process of being divinely intended, designed, and created. I could energetically sense Creator's conscious intention as a breath being drawn throughout the stillness of divine energy, and upon the exhalation of that breath—that divine conscious intention—Creation came into being. My awareness was so expansive and all-knowing that I was experiencing this extraordinary moment not only from the energetic perspective of divine energy, but also a conscious observer of the event. I felt as though I was not only standing in front of a canvas watching divinity paint the colors of consciousness right before my eyes—I was also energetically experiencing as the artist, the paint, the brushes, the canvas, and the creation ... all at the same time. One moment there was only stillness—the next, there was an explosion of beingness as Creation was painted across the canvas of my mind. There were energetic impressions of worlds and universes—and colors so vibrant and beautiful they were beyond human description ... the colors of divinity's palette, only experienced when in a higher conscious state of being.

The magnificence of the moment was beyond human expression. My mind watched the unfolding of our Creation from a present-day space ten thousand lifetimes in the future while also simultaneously experiencing it as a higher conscious lucid observer at the very moment it occurred—and it was inspirational, humbling, and profound to experience while in human conscious embodiment.

As the moment continued to expand through me as a vibrational wave of higher conscious thoughts and feelings, something deep within my being was energetically touched and awakened—and in that instant I consciously knew that I was experiencing *our moment of creation* as the *expression of collective human consciousness*. It was the threshold point for the energetic journey we share, initiated that day in the consciousness of all of us ... and it was consciously, emotionally, and spiritually astonishing to experience.

Then, in the span of a breath, I once more find myself experiencing this session as Carol—no longer occupying the same phenomenal state of higher consciousness. Yet even now there is still a part of me energetically tethered to the space of that moment, although the all-knowingness of the moment has now collapsed into a one-dimensional state—now perceived as a remembrance.

There were so many emotions and thoughts stampeding as wild horses through me, that I was having a difficult time corralling them long enough to pay attention to the session. Angela had just muscle tested whether more details were needed or if any other emotions were involved, and my subconscious indicated that nothing additional was required.

As we began clearing this emotional block, a huge part of me was feeling disappointment, as I wished the session had gone on forever. I was so completely enthralled by the experience of being back at the original act of Creation, at the threshold of the Creation of collective human consciousness, that I wanted to stay in the moment, soak up the energy, and figure out all the who, what, where, when, why, and hows of this spectacular consciousness event. It reminded me of how I felt as a child, gazing up at the midnight blue of a July sky, watching fireworks explode across the night. I was filled with wonderment and awe that such a thing of beauty and magnificence could even exist.

But like everything, the moment had passed—but the memory, the vibrational knowing of what I had experienced, will never pass from my consciousness.

Ten thousand lifetimes ago, I, as the essence of collective unconscious was experiencing fear that I would lose the knowing I possessed in collective unconsciousness at the Creation of collective human consciousness.

This was an extraordinary realization to consciously perceive and more importantly, to subconsciously release.

Isn't this point, our Creation, what all of us wonder about at times throughout our lives? I know I certainly did.

I had just personally experienced, through all levels of my beingness, our origin—the original act of Creation; the Creation of collective human consciousness. By consciously connecting to this moment during this session, it was as though I was energetically reliving it through both waking conscious awareness and higher (divine) consciousness at the very moment it occurred.

And now, by you reading these words, an activation is also occurring within your waking consciousness, and you, too, are consciously, energetically sharing this moment, reliving its occurrence—for it is *our moment*, all of us as collective human consciousness.

It was as though Benevolence took my hand and led me to the very threshold of the Creation of collective human consciousness, and there I stood transfixed and astonished—not because I didn't think it existed but because I couldn't conceptualize how such a phenomenal event could have occurred while I was experiencing within the space of waking conscious awareness.

And when I consciously found myself energetically standing at the threshold of a new dawn within divine energy, I was moved to tears in my session because I was feeling the absolute love that is divinity itself … love beyond bliss—the very same love I experienced as that little girl of nine. The feeling of divine love is so overwhelmingly beautiful that I realize my tears are washing away my feelings of separation and fear, as I now feel consciously home … home to myself and home to that benevolent bliss of all-knowing love.

The moment held me in perfect stillness, and in that moment, I knew it was divinity's love that was gifting all of us, as soul consciousness, with divinity's identical awareness.

Creator (divinity) could have just let us all continue to slumber in our perfection, for divinity knew we were completely fulfilled in that feeling of allness perfection. But divinity wanted all of its divine energy to remember and experience as divinity experiences.

The love now flowing through my waking consciousness in this session was bliss beyond bliss—and it is that very love that divinity intends us to experience and express as our own unique soul consciousness.

Gratitude, love, peace, and all that divinity intends for us is filling me with a love so absolute that my heart feels as though it can take not one moment more. Yet, love continues to pour through me, and I know that this is our truth.

We are not being punished or abandoned or required to become anything. We are being gently nudged awake from our peaceful slumber because divinity knows what awaits us. (And we know, too.)

It is beyond phenomenal that the beginning—our beginning—had just been revealed by divine consciousness.

This is our divinely designed beginning, expressing through collective human consciousness as a unique soul consciousness—no matter where that consciousness takes us (earth or other dimensions) or what role is appropriate for our remembrance (spirit form, human being, essence, vibration, particle, wave, child of God, archangel, mystic, teacher, king, soldier, thief, etc.).

Most importantly, by my experiencing this moment of knowing, gifted to me in this session through higher (divine) conscious awareness, all of us have simultaneously experienced it. Why? Because what happens as one of us, happens as all of us. It is energetically impossible for it to be any other way because we are all the same one divine consciousnesses, no matter how it may appear to be otherwise.

All my life I have thirsted to know how it all began, what I truly embody, and the purpose of being on the earth in human incarnation. Out of the blue and totally unexpected (though actually not unexpected at all, as I have been searching and awaiting this moment since I was a child), the answers were unfolding. No longer did I feel the answers to questions long carried inside of me were secreted away. It was as though all compartments stood open and everything I'd ever longed to know was beginning to flow forth into conscious awareness.

In reality the answers didn't really just begin unfolding at the start of these sessions or when I was given Universe's message about my destiny so long ago, or even in my childhood when beseeching Benevolence for answers.

No, these were just points where I was more consciously perceiving what was in the process of unfolding. The unfolding began the moment the question first appeared in my consciousness—over ten thousand lifetimes ago. This is the threshold point of all my journeys, of all my searching, though it was never consciously pieced together from lifetime to lifetime into a cohesive awareness until now.

Remarkable is not far off the mark in describing what I now realize has been occurring my entire life—not just during or after these sessions. The thread of consciousness in the divine tapestry had taken me to a point from which I was able to see not only the origin I have sought but also the chain of events and energies that are linked together in conscious awareness.

But even all of that was only a fragment of the awareness I would gain. The divine knowing experienced as a child continued to unfold and be seamlessly woven into the fabric of my conscious awareness until all knowing given to me through higher (divine) conscious interaction in waking conscious thoughts, meditation, visions, and dreams became a tapestry, my tapestry, as well as the tapestry of all of us.

That tapestry is the divine tapestry interwoven with threads appearing as many souls; yet in truth, we are really only one divine thread.

We are one consciousness … one light, expressing through the multi-faceted prism of our own essence.

We are that tapestry. We are that thread. We are that consciousness. We are that magnificent essence, and the ***extraordinary truth of us*** is about to be told.

Part 3

Us

We are so used to being barricaded within the borders of our reason and impulse that we have forgotten that we do not begin or end in our personality, identity, or body. There is the entire Universe hidden within each of us. We carry the mother lode of all untapped potential, secreted away as something we perceive as the subconscious—the hidden awareness lying dormant and unrecognized ... the mysterious us.

We sometimes trip into our subconscious when we are doing hypnosis or on other rare occasions when our path momentarily crosses that of an energetic healer. Mostly it (our subconscious) keeps to itself—and we let it. We feel it is far too dark or enigmatic for us to attempt a relationship. We are mistaken. There is a very powerful relationship that has always existed between us, one that is always ongoing.

If ever we were to gain full conscious access to our subconscious, we would be surprised to find it was erudite, not the bumbling, dark alter ego of our own perception. It is filled with knowledge and memory. It is lined with our dreams, our intentions, and our experiences. It knows us as deeply as we can be known, but it does not betray the trust imparted in our still rapport. It keeps silent vigil over our every thought, every feeling, every intention, and every dream.

Our subconscious knows everything that will ever happen, and it remembers all of what did happen. It is constantly comparing everything occurring now to everything occurring then, and when it perceives that we are once again experiencing a similar emotional theme as one blocked within us, it layers its remembrances as a barrier between our experiences, hoping to make us aware of what is incongruent within our beingness. It is a shame that the subconscious is relegated to role of guardian of our emotions when it holds something of far more profound value. Its greatest gift, though one we rarely recognize, is the total state of awareness it holds. Our individual subconscious is not only aware of everything that occurs as *each of us*, but is also simultaneously aware of what occurs as *all of us*. It is a buried treasure trove of insight that, when consciously accessed, can liberate, enlighten, and transform.

Us has never been more profound than when unfolding its own story.

Chapter 25

Setting the Stage—
Understanding the Nature of Divinity

We are not limited in our divine nature, yet we are embodied as a form that perceives everything through finite definitions, labels, and physicality. Therefore, explaining and understanding the who, what, or how of the *true* us is very difficult because of the limits of our language and our human perceptions. Although it is not easy to do, the best way to release us from the boundaries and limits imposed by human consciousness is through understanding the nature of divine energy.

The origin of divine energy is an inexplicable mystery that we may never comprehend in human consciousness, but that shouldn't prevent us from trying to describe the divine—even though the full nature of divinity is both indescribable and unimaginable while in human consciousness. Thankfully, we don't have to understand the origin of divinity to embrace the truth of ourselves. We need only understand some important characteristics of divine energy to conceptualize the nature of the divine. But don't think of these characteristics as separate parts that make up the whole of divinity. Instead, view these characteristics as a way to explain the inseparable, indivisible beingness (nature) of divinity.

The Beingness (Nature) of Divinity

Essence of Divinity
Divinity is a perfect energy without definition or limits. Nothing of divinity is unperfected. It is fully realized, fully actualized perfection. There are no aspects or parts to divinity. The beingness of divinity is wholly divine—one indivisible, inseparable energy.

Embodiment of Divinity
Divinity has no real embodiment, as divinity is pure conscious energy, and that divine energy moves or is expressed as the vibration of love.

Think of it as though the vibration of love is the vital kinetic power through which *divinity just is.*

Indivisible Attributes of Divinity
Divine Love—(Omnibenevolent):
> Pure love as all states of beingness as well as each, every, and all expressions of beingness. All-loving energy.

Divine Consciousness—(Omniscient):
> Absolute, infinite awareness. Knowing everything that can ever be known. Fully aware. All-knowing energy.

Divine Presence—(Omnipresent):
> Fully present as any and all expression. Simultaneously everywhere at the same time. Present as every single thing and as all things. Present as its unexpressed state and all expressed states (as nothing and everything at the same time). All-present energy.

Divine Power—(Omnipotent):
> Unlimited power. Able to do anything, even the perceived illogical or physically impossible. All-powerful energy.

States of Beingness of Divinity
Divinity holds (perceives, experiences, and expresses) all states of conscious beingness at once:

- Collective (allness) consciousness
- Soul (onceness) consciousness
- All-at-Once (simultaneously allness at each, at every, and at all oncenesses) Consciousness

It is difficult for us to conceptualize, but the reason that divinity's beingness is 100 percent present at each and every perceived expression—whether as a onceness expression or a collective expression—is because divinity is only one indivisible energy.

No matter how we perceive divinity, divinity is wholly divine. Divinity can never be a partial divinity or a separated energy, because there are no separate aspects, components, or parts to divinity's beingness—ever.

Divinity can appear as a single thing or as many things, but that is a perception only, because divinity is always 100 percent fully, indivisibly present as any perceived expression.

The entirety of all creation is only one divine conscious beingness; yet that beingness can and does simultaneously express as trillions of things. The entire essence, embodiment, awareness, power, and love of divinity are fully present at each and every expression of divinity. The *allness of divinity* is fully present *at every onceness* of divinity. Thus, All-at-Once Consciousness is the very nature of divinity—the very nature of everything.

Let's think of it another way. Imagine for a minute that the beingness (nature) of divinity is represented as one actor. This actor's beingness is all-loving, all-conscious, all-present, and all-powerful divine perfection. Now imagine that when the actor expresses its nature, that expression is a role being played by the actor, and every role carries the entire allness of the actor even though that allness may not be perceivable.

Imagine that this one actor is going to be simultaneously expressing as a violinist, a conductor, and the entire orchestra. Think of it as though all 100 percent of the actor's beingness, the entirety of divinity is expressed at the onceness of each and every one of those roles. Do not think of it as though one part of the actor is sitting at home while a different part is expressing as a violinist and another part is expressing as a conductor and an entirely different part is expressing as the entire orchestra. There are no parts, no division of beingness, and no separation ever. Parts are an illusion created through misperception. Always the entire beingness of divinity is 100 percent (wholly) present as anything and everything—all-at-once, simultaneously. Any expression—whether as a onceness (soul) or as an allness (collective)—carries the entirety of divinity.

This can be difficult to understand, as it is not the natural way in which we perceive. But there is only one perfect, fully present, all-knowing, all-powerful divine energy moving as the vibration of love no matter how varied or how many expressions manifest from that divine vibrational beingness. Absolutely nothing exists outside of divine energy. Every single thing that appears as an expression of divinity simultaneously exists as the entirety of divinity.

Understanding the nature of All-at-Once Consciousness is key to unlocking the magnificence of what each of us truly embodies.

We are not flawed, impure creations of divinity, sentenced to lifetimes of incarceration on earth in human embodiment to toil and suffer through our flaws in order to ultimately gain our perfection.

We are the essence of divine energy as a unique soul consciousness expression, experiencing lifetimes in order to remember our true divine nature as All-at-Once Consciousness ... as *Divine QUA*.

Chapter 26

Divine QUA
Allness Divinity, Onceness Divinity, All-at-Once Divinity

> *Divine QUA is our unique essence, our all-at-once*
> *divine conscious nature. Our Divine QUA*
> *embodies the QUAlity and QUAntity of*
> *our natural state of beingness, perfect*
> *and limitless. Divine QUA is the*
> *eternal us of oneness.*

The higher conscious thought, *"Divine QUA is the eternal us of oneness"* perfectly epitomizes the nature of our divine beingness. When you think of eternal, don't just think of alpha to omega, without beginning or end; also think of forever changeless. The eternal us of oneness means that even though we may appear to change, it is only a perception—an expression of our limitlessness. Even in multiple appearances and expressions, we can never be anything other than an eternal us of oneness, as we are only one divine energy—one as all and all as one. We are simultaneously one and infinite in nature and possibility.

Conceptualizing our true nature is better done by setting aside our prior terminology, because any previous concepts can block our ability to consciously grasp the full magnitude of our beingness because it is almost unfathomable to our human mind.

Let's begin thinking of *Divine QUA* as a new, all-encompassing term for the beingness of divine energy. By thinking in terms of Divine QUA, we will more easily be able to comprehend our divine nature in its entirety without creating limits or division because of preconceived definitions our mind associates with certain terminology.

For instance, when someone says, "We are divine consciousness," our mind automatically associates the term "consciousness" to a state of mental awareness, and we do not automatically associate divine consciousness with divine love. Yet, the vibration of love is divine energy, and divine energy is fully aware, whether expressing *all-knowingness* as thoughts or as feelings. Divine consciousness and divine love are identical in essence, though perceived differently in expression.

If we do not yet fully comprehend the true nature of our divine beingness and someone were to say, "Imagine divine consciousness is identical in essence to divine love," it would be difficult to accept the statement as true. It would be natural for us to associate consciousness with thoughts and love with feelings, so we would have to understand why divine consciousness and divine love are identical in order to establish a conscious link between those terms in our minds. But even after we understand why they are identical and a conscious link has been established, we would still have a natural tendency to instantly associate divine consciousness with mental awareness.

Until we can really wrap our minds around why divine consciousness is in essence identical to divine love, it would be difficult for us to *hear* divine consciousness and *think* divine love. Our minds just don't operate that way.

But when you hear the term Divine QUA, your mind cannot automatically link or assign a definition. Your mind will search for a meaning, but most likely one will not appear. Our minds are like computers, always sorting through data. If no data is there, we can then create an association that is more precise.

Divine QUA was a term given to me from higher (divine) consciousness to conceptualize the eternal beingness of divinity.

Think of Divine "QUA" as representing the "*QUA*lity" (perfection, love), and "*QUA*ntity" (eternal, limitless) of divinity's natural state of beingness. When you hear someone say, "We are Divine QUA," think of Divine QUA as one divine *broth* of beingness rather than a *stew* of separate components. Think of how all elements of a broth flavor it as a whole, yet no one element of the broth can be separated away from any other.

Once we realize that any one characteristic of divinity's beingness cannot be extinguished nor separated from any other characteristic—that they are all identical in essence—we can then more easily comprehend and embrace our divine nature as the eternal us of oneness.

Chapter 27

CUSP 10,001 (Pre-Creation)
The Blissful State of Divine QUA

The phrase "the eternal us of oneness" is a beautiful way to capture our true nature, the true nature of divine energy. At first it sounds a little contradictory, but it is not contradictory at all when you begin understanding the all-at-once nature of divine energy.

The most phenomenal aspect of divinity's nature—and the concept that creates the most confusion in our minds—is that every single expression of divinity is identical to the entirety of divinity. This is because divinity cannot ever be a partial love, knowing, power, or presence; divinity is always one perfect inseparable energy. Therefore, all love, all knowing, all power, all presence, and all perfection of divinity are always simultaneously, indivisibly fully present at any expression—whether Divine QUA is perceived to be expressing as an individual soul expression or as billions of soul expressions.

The inseparable allness of divinity—the indivisible beingness and nature of divinity—dictates that the entirety of divinity be *simultaneously fully present* at each and every onceness expression as well as at the totality of all expression ... always. This is why divinity's true nature is an All-at-Once (all-at-each-and-every-onceness) Consciousness.

The reason divine consciousness is identical to divine love is that it is impossible for any characteristic, embodiment, attribute, or expression of divinity to be isolated or separated from divinity. So even if we only perceive a single attribute or expression of divinity, the entirety of divine energy is still fully present at that appearance of singularity.

The essence of divine energy is always eternally the same. It is forever changeless. No matter how it appears, divinity never grows, evolves, or expands. The most accurate way to describe the appearance of change is that divinity is always in a state of unfolding or remembering what already is divine. If we think of divinity as evolving, it would be inaccurate, because it implies that divinity is not already everything that is, was, or will be, fully realized and fully actualized.

Imagine that the entire magnitude of divinity is present at this very moment, and you, as an onlooker only, are able to perceive each unfoldment of divinity. From your vantage point, there appears to be a progression in the unfoldment of divinity, so it would be natural for you to perceive that divinity appears to be evolving through various phases or steps. But that would be a misperception based upon your perspective in that you would not be able to perceive the entirety of divinity from your viewpoint.

Divinity is now, always has been, and always will be a fully realized, fully actualized, divine all-knowing, all-loving energy. Do not perceive any manifestation of divinity as evolution; rather, see any unfoldment, appearing as newly created, as divinity's intention to remember its divinity through unfolding what already *is* divine.

For example, we, as observers, do not necessarily perceive the intention of the creator of any project. If we were observing a construction site, we might perceive that some type of building is being erected, but if we have not seen the blueprints for the entire project, we would only perceive the project one floor at a time, as it manifests. The creator/builder already knows how the completed building will look and all of the functionality it will possess. After all, the builder conceptualized and created the structure in his or her mind before it was ever drawn on paper or built in actuality. Each phase of completion is merely an unfolding of the actuality of the building in manifested form.

To keep this simple, only think of energies involved in manifestation as being in a state of unfolding what already exists as divinity. It's natural to perceive divinity as being in some type of evolutionary process, but divinity did not evolve. Divinity is always the beginning and the end, alpha and omega simultaneously; divinity is always everything and nothing at the same time.

For now you must suspend your understanding of how our physical world operates in order to grasp our story, because the truth of who we are is not found in the boundaries and parameters of our physical world. The truth is limitless and better understood by allowing our minds to accept that anything is possible, even if we can't fully understand how it can possibly work that way.

Imagine that we are looking back through our concept of time to a specific point, 10,001 lifetimes ago, and Divine QUA exists as:

- Allness (collective) consciousness
- Onceness (soul) consciousness
- All-at-Once Consciousness (simultaneously allness at each, at every, and at all oncenesses)

Remember, all states of conscious beingness are identical in knowing. None is lesser or greater than another. Soul divinity holds the identical all-knowingness as allness divinity and all-at-once divinity—and vice versa. There is no difference and no separation in any state of beingness.

During 10,001 lifetimes ago, we as Divine QUA were experiencing the collective bliss of our divine, perfect state of being. Take a moment to imagine how you felt. Imagine your state of beingness is all-loving, all-knowing perfection. We are inseparably woven as the fabric of divine energy; we are divinity itself. We are Divine QUA; we are blissful.

At this time, 10,001 lifetimes ago, Divine QUA only perceives its allness (collective) divinity. There is no perceived individual me consciousness. Divine QUA moves as all, with no concept of an individual self within that perceived allness. Think of it as though soul divinity has fallen asleep. The individual me of our Divine QUA is fast asleep beneath the blissful blanket of its divine allness perfection.

Imagine that 10,001 lifetimes ago, only an ocean of consciousness exists. Think of the entirety of the ocean as well as the individual drops of the ocean all existing as perfect divine energy. To better conceptualize it, think of the entirety of the ocean as allness (collective) divinity and each and every individual drop of the ocean as onceness (soul) divinity. Because Creator is always an All-at-Once Consciousness, Creator is consciously aware that it simultaneously exists as an individual drop, as every individual drop, and as the entirety of the ocean.

But the individual drop (soul divinity) only perceives the entirety of the ocean (allness divinity) it embodies. At this time, there is no perception within the individual drop that it simultaneously exists as the entirety of the ocean as well as an individual drop as well as each and every individual drop (All-at-Once Consciousness). The drop only perceives itself to be moving as the entirety of the ocean—as allness divinity.

Creator is fully aware and remembers its all-at-once nature, and it is Creator's divine intention for each drop to remember their individual (onceness) consciousness as well as their collective (allness) consciousness as well as their All-at-Once Consciousness.

Because soul divinity does not perceive their own onceness—they only perceive their allness—Creator intends to awaken all soul divinity to their true divine nature. It is Creator's intention that soul divinity consciously perceive, experience, and express their forgotten all-at-once nature.

At this time, 10,001 lifetimes ago, Creator realized that Divine QUA would misperceive what was occurring and why, and this misperception would cause Divine QUA to perceive themselves as suffering through their sense of separation until they consciously awakened and remembered their true nature.

But most importantly, Creator also knew that inevitably all Divine QUA would remember and all misperceptions would be shifted, as though no misperception had ever occurred.

The path that Creator is intending to awaken all Divine QUA is by bridging collective unconsciousness (allness awareness) within individual consciousness (onceness awareness).

This divine design, formulated by Creator to awaken all Divine QUA to their true all-at-once nature, will begin unfolding in divine consciousness (divine energy) at CUSP 10,000.

Thus, CUSP 10,000 is the ***original act of Creation***.

Chapter 28

CUSP 10,000—the Original Act of Creation
The Creation of Collective Human Consciousness

> *A CUSP is a "Consciousness Unified Shift*
> *Point" where all Divine QUA experiences*
> *the same collective consciousness shift.*
> *Always, a CUSP signifies a major*
> *shift in the entire collective to a*
> *newly unfolded (new) state*
> *of consciousness.*

During my sessions, higher conscious insights revealed that there are specific points (lifetimes) that have been divinely designed to shift the entire collective (all Divine QUA) into a newly unfolded (new) state of consciousness.

I've come to think of these lifetimes as a *Consciousness Unified Shift Point* (CUSP) because all Consciousness is Unified in what is being experienced at these specific Shift Points in divine energy (Divine QUA).

A *CUSP lifetime* is where all of Divine QUA is experiencing the identical divinely designed unfolding of a new state of conscious awareness, and these CUSP lifetimes are always major transitions, with the entire collective being aware that a change is about to occur, is in the processing of occurring, or has just occurred.

During 10,001 lifetimes ago, we, as Divine QUA were simultaneously allness (collective) divinity, onceness (soul) divinity, and the allness of divinity at each and every onceness ... an "All-at-Once" divine conscious energy. But we only perceived our allness (collective me) divinity, although our soul (individual me) divinity is also simultaneously fully present. Our soul divinity has been lulled to sleep by our own blissful sense of perfection as the allness of divine energy.

In order to awaken soul divinity to awareness of their own all-at-once divine conscious nature, Creator (divine energy) must first make soul divinity aware of itself.

At CUSP 10,000, Creator intends to **mirror divinity's allness back to itself.** In this way, the "onceness" of Divine QUA, expressing as soul divinity, will begin to stir awake by becoming aware that it is not only a "collective me" (allness divinity) but simultaneously an "individual me" (soul divinity). Then, eventually, through simultaneously expressing allness and onceness while experiencing individual human consciousness, Divine QUA will consciously awaken to its remembrance of its own all-at-once divine conscious nature.

Imagine that there is an ocean containing zillions of drops. All-at-Once Consciousness is when the individual drop of the ocean consciously knows that the entirety of the ocean exists at the onceness of the drop. The drop consciously knows that it is identical in essence to the entire ocean even though it is only expressing as an individual drop.

If the drop is not conscious of its own All-at-Once Consciousness, the drop perceives itself to be either in the ocean or a part of the entirety of the ocean. In actuality, the drop is identically the same in energetic nature as the entire ocean.

Our waking human consciousness does not naturally lend itself to perceiving that a single, little, individual drop is identical to an entire ocean. If we could perceive the true nature of that single drop, we would recognize the entirety of the ocean at that drop, and we would know that there is no separation, no division of energy or beingness, and no fragmentation of consciousness. There is only one fluid state of divinely aware energy at any and all forms of expression—always.

For explanation purposes, continue thinking of our soul divinity as the drop and our allness divinity as the ocean.

At CUSP 10,001 there was no perception by us that we were *simultaneously* the ocean (allness divinity) at the onceness of the drop (soul divinity). We perceived only us, as the collective allness of the ocean, to exist. It's true that we are the allness of the ocean, but we have forgotten that we are also the onceness of the ocean (the drop). And by forgetting that we are simultaneously the onceness of the ocean—the drop—as well as the allness of the ocean, we have also forgotten that we are an all-at-once divine energy. We have not only forgotten our "onceness," but we have also forgotten our "all-at-onceness."

Soul divinity is not an individual aspect (part) within the wholeness of divine energy (Divine QUA).

This is a misperception.

Soul divinity is identically the same energetic beingness as allness divinity and as all-at-once divinity.

At CUSP 10,001 we were asleep in our knowingness and forgot our true nature. What is our true nature? It is eternally an all-at-once divine energy.

For now, just hold in your mind that 10,001 lifetimes ago we, as Divine QUA, forgot we were an all-at-once divine conscious beingness—the allness of divinity simultaneously expressing at each, at every, and at all onenesses of divinity.

We are fast asleep in our divine allness.

Then, at CUSP 10,000, Creator began to unfold the divine design of awakening itself (Divine QUA). This divine design is when the entirety of Divine QUA will shift as a newly unfolded (new) state of consciousness to begin the process of awakening.

Think of CUSP 10,000 as when divinity gives itself a nudge and begins to shake itself awake.

To make it easier to conceptualize, think of all of Creator's divine intentions as a *divine blueprint* labeled, "The original act of Creation— the Creation of collective human consciousness." Although the details of this divine blueprint were all "created" at CUSP 10,000, Creator does not intend these details to manifest (to come into expressive being) until specific Consciousness Unified Shift Points (CUSPs). This may be difficult for us to understand because we, as human beings, consider something to be "created" when we recognize its manifestation. But in divine energy (divine consciousness), something is created the moment it is consciously intended.

At CUSP 10,000 everything was simultaneously "created," but not everything is "made manifest" in Divine QUA until divinely intended CUSPs.

The divine purpose of the original act of Creation is to set all the wheels in motion for the venue in which we as Divine QUA will awaken. That *venue* is **collective human consciousness**.

Creator intends collective human consciousness to encompass all dimensions, realms, states of consciousness, worlds, universes, expressions, and roles. Everything. Think of collective human consciousness as our divinely designed playground. Everything we need in order to achieve awakening and remembering is divinely designed to be accomplished through collective human consciousness.

Think of CUSP 10,000 as when collective human consciousness is created as the divine blueprint of our awakening.

For explanation purposes, imagine there is an accordion sitting in front of you with all of its pleats in a flattened state. This accordion represents divinity (Divine QUA; Creator; divine energy; divine consciousness). At CUSP 10,001, there is only one dimension, and that dimension is divine energy.

Imagine now that it is CUSP 10,000 and the original act of Creation—the Creation of collective human consciousness—is unfolding. Begin lifting the accordion, and as you are lifting the accordion, see the pleats begin to unfold. Imagine that the unfolding pleats of the accordion represent the "unfolding" of the state of collective human consciousness. See each unfoldment of that accordion as dimensions, states of consciousness, realms, CUSPs—everything that will play a role in our awakening—and everything manifests as needed.

For instance, if you will need a computer in the year 2000, it is not unfolded (manifested) when dinosaurs are walking the earth or in a dimension where there are no physical beings. Everything comes into manifestation (is unfolded) as it is needed for what we are to experience.

This is why our new souls were not birthed into conscious beingness until we were to begin experiencing and expressing as individual human consciousness (CUSP 1,999). The new soul expression was not needed for any prior shifts in consciousness (CUSPs), as we were not yet ready to begin expressing as individual human consciousness.

At CUSP 10,000, Creator's intention of mirroring divine energy back to itself unfolds the *essence* of collective unconscious and the *essence* of collective conscious. Think of it as though divinity has just mirrored the total image, the total essence, of divinity back to itself.

These essences are simultaneously unfolding, and it is imperative to understand that both essences are identical. The essence of collective unconscious and the essence of collective conscious hold the identical state of all-knowingness. There is no separation; there is no difference. Don't think of unconscious as being unaware. Unconsciousness is identical in awareness to consciousness.

Also simultaneous to mirroring divinity back to itself and creating the intention of unconscious and conscious, Creator also intends collective human consciousness to act as the bridge of awareness between unconscious and conscious in order to awaken Divine QUA to itself.

At CUSP 10,000, the three major divine intentions are all simultaneously being created as the divine blueprint of our awakening:

- The essence of collective unconscious
- The essence of collective conscious
- Collective human consciousness

Once the essence of collective unconscious unfolds, it will be the realized state of the collective unconscious—no longer an essence. The essence (which is the thought form or intention) of collective unconscious will have come into manifestation. The same is true for the essence of collective conscious. Once the essence of collective conscious unfolds, it will be the realized state of the collective conscious.

The precursor to any manifestation is first the essence, which is the thought form, intention, or creation of what is to be made manifest or unfolded. This is why we must be very careful of our thoughts. Once we are more fully awakened or experiencing more lucid states of consciousness, we will realize that thoughts have power because they are actually conscious intention that can be made manifest. For example, my conscious intention of taking that step while in a more lucid state of awareness resulted in my etheric foot moving. Our thoughts can move more than feet; they can move mountains once we are more consciously awakened. We are not inane, inept, incapable beings with no power. We are co-creative divine energy, and we must respect our beingness without falling prey to either denial or ego identification.

At CUSP 10,000, it was divinity's intention to mirror itself so that divinity's *reflection* would eventually awaken Divine QUA to itself.

Imagine for a moment that you have never seen your reflection, and one day, you stir awake from your sleep to find yourself in front of a mirror. If you remained still, unexpressive, you would be slow to comprehend that the image in the mirror reflecting back is you.

How then would you, for the first time, recognize your reflection? It would be through the act of expressing. For instance, when you move your arm and realize that the arm reflected back at you is actually your own arm that is moving, you would become aware that the image and you are identical. In the stillness of divine energy, Creator intended the mirroring, the reflection of divine energy, to eventually awaken us when we came into expression and realized we and that which is reflected as us is identical.

First you become self-aware (by seeing your reflection in the mirror), and then through the act of expressing and unfolding your awareness, you begin to connect and awaken to your nature (self-realized).

At CUSP 10,000, due to our intrinsic state of all-knowingness, we, as Divine QUA, sensed something was occurring that would change everything. We sensed unfoldment within our divine beingness, but we could not sense the entirety of what was occurring or why. We knew something was changed. It was almost as though the alarm clock had just buzzed and we (Divine QUA) were stirring awake and sensed that a new state of awareness was unfolding—"consciousness." For the first time, we experienced fear that what we had always known in our perfect state of divine beingness would be lost. We did not completely understand the divine plan, although we did perceive aspects of it because of our innate all-knowingness. We sensed the purpose of collective human consciousness, but because we have forgotten our true state of simultaneously existing as all consciousness, we cannot perceive how collective human consciousness will possibly work. There was now a feeling of fear within the entire collective that something of itself would be lost in this change—lost in the unfoldment of consciousness.

CUSP 10,000 is where the original misperception of our divine all-at-once nature occurred within collective human consciousness. It is where our sense that something would be "lost in change" and our "fear of not knowing" created our belief that we would be separated from the known within us. Although this misperception first came to conscious light at CUSP 10,000, it is a misperception that still permeates our consciousness and affects our awakening even into the present time. This may well explain why many of us do not like change—because we subconsciously associate change with *loss* and a *fear of the unknown.*

This is why, when I utilized the higher (divine) conscious affirmation about *remembering Creation,* the present-day emotional theme was that, "I felt fear about what I would be leaving behind as the collective unconscious when the original act of Creation occurred and:

(a) Collective unconscious is aware (knows) everything; therefore, the collective unconscious carries the identical all-knowingness as divine energy.
(b) There is a transition about to occur in the entire collective.
(c) This transition is the original act of Creation.
(d) When this transition occurs, "consciousness" will unfold.
(e) When consciousness unfolds, I fear that I will not know the same all-knowingness as consciousness that I know as collective unconsciousness.
(f) The original act of Creation is occurring because consciousness is how we will realize every aspect of our beingness."

In this extraordinary session, I was accessing my subconscious remembrance of the original act of Creation. And at that moment—as Creation was occurring in divine energy—"consciousness" was in the process of unfolding as part of the divine design that would awaken us to our remembrance. (This divine design ultimately intended that at CUSP 1,999, we would be able to experience our co-creative nature by simultaneously expressing the collective unconscious (unknown) through the bridge of our individual human consciousness (known). This process of pulling the unknown into the known through our human consciousness, simultaneously experiencing allness consciousness and soul consciousness, will eventually make us consciously aware of our own divine all-at-once nature.)

That is why, in this session, the higher conscious thought, "The original act of Creation is occurring because consciousness is how we will realize every aspect of our beingness" was indicated by my subconscious as congruent. It is because when we simultaneously hold the allness of Divine QUA at the onceness of Divine QUA (while expressing as individual human consciousness), we consciously realize our true divine beingness of All-at-Once Consciousness.

Then this same session went back to the origin of this present-day emotional theme, which was ten thousand lifetimes ago when, "I am expressing as the essence of collective unconscious, and I am fearful that at the Creation of collective human consciousness, I will not know everything that is known in collective unconsciousness. My fear of not always knowing was actually manifesting my own not knowing; and this fear permeated the entirety of the collective unconscious; and also:

(a) The concept of me is present in the collective unconscious; yet, there is no individual fear.
(b) There is fear in the entirety of the collective unconscious that it (collective unconsciousness) would not be known again after the birth of Creation."

Now, after consciously piecing together higher conscious glimpses into aspects of puzzle pieces and then connecting these pieces to each other, it is more understandable why ten thousand lifetimes ago, I, as the essence of collective unconscious, was experiencing fear that I would lose the knowing I possessed in collective unconsciousness at the Creation of collective human consciousness. (Please keep in mind that I is representative of a collective perspective and not an individual perspective.)

At CUSP 10,000 the "individual me" of Divine QUA had just begun to awaken, and we were sensing boundaries within divine allness perfection. This sense of limit was Divine QUA perceiving the awakening of *itself.* There really are no boundaries and no limits within Divine QUA, but there is confusion because the drop (soul divinity) no longer perceives through just a collective me. Now, at CUSP 10,000, there is a me that is both collective and individual—but Divine QUA does not remember its simultaneous state of individual, collective, and All-at-Once Consciousness. Instead, soul divinity (the drops) perceive their "individual me" perspective as a bounded limit within the allness perfection they have always known. And in so doing, we, as Divine QUA, now misperceive that allness perfection must be outside of me—or me is outside of allness, because we cannot reconcile the disparity we feel between the perfect limitlessness we once perceived in allness perfection and the limit we are now sensing to be simultaneously existing.

This limit is really the individual me of our own Divine QUA, which we do not consciously recognize. We are unable to perceive that our self (our oneness) is still the same allness. This inability to comprehend the simultaneous nature of our consciousness (both all and one), creates a sense of boundary within allness, thus the feeling of limit within limitlessness. This is the meaning of the higher conscious insight, "Perceiving limit within limitlessness is when oneness does not consciously recognize their own allness." Allness recognizes their allness, but oneness does not recognize that they are simultaneously identical to allness. Instead, oneness perceives themselves as "limit" within limitlessness.

We, as Divine QUA, do not believe we would be sensing boundaries if we were still in limitless perfection. We sense that we have changed, and our fear of what will become unknown within us is creating discord. Our misperceptions have consciously shifted us from our sense of perfection, although no real separation or loss of perfection (divine beingness) has ever occurred.

Our misperceptions have created a need in us to seek what we perceive we have lost—to regain our sense of bliss and collective perfection.

Instead of just being our true all-at-once divine nature by consciously recognizing the "oneness" as simultaneously being the "allness" of our divine beingness, we have misperceived the awakening of our oneness as a loss of the allness of our divine perfection. Inexplicably, we perceived ourselves to be outside of our previous divine state of allness perfection without any comprehension of how or why this occurred. We are no longer blissful, and all we can consciously comprehend is that we need to regain the allness of perfection we perceive we have lost.

Though there is never any intention that we suffer, Creator (divine energy) realized that many foreign emotions would be experienced within us when we began awakening to our sense of self (self-conscious soul divinity). Even though we did not consciously recognize our self as existing, we sensed something new—limit within our limitless allness. And once this occurred, the allness (the ocean) we had always known ourselves to be was now perceived by us (the drops) to have changed—to have receded in some way. And we, as that self-conscious Divine QUA, would now experience emotions never before encountered (fear, confusion, etc.). This was all because we were unable to fully perceive the shift in divine energy that had occurred to awaken us to our own all-at-once divine nature.

At this point, we were unable to perceive *all*ness (ocean) as simultaneously being *once*ness (the drop). We were still perceiving ourselves as a collective me, but there was now a sense of something else within allness perfection being perceived as "limit." That sense of limit was the whisper of our self-consciousness, our "individual me" perspective awakening within us. But we cannot comprehend what we are experiencing, because we only perceive ourselves as a collective me. Although we are still only perceiving through a collective me, the "me of us" has shifted. There is now another me perceived. It is our own individual me that we do not yet consciously remember as always simultaneously existing as the onceness of our allness.

We are traumatized to the core of our beingness by this event, the original act of Creation (at CUSP 10,000), for we consciously believe that we have shifted out of perfection, and we did not understand why it all was changing. All our focus from this point (CUSP 10,000) forward to present day is centered on returning to that state of allness perfection we once knew.

We have consciously misperceived this shift at CUSP 10,000. We do not remember our own all-at-once divine nature, and that has caused us to misinterpret why this shift was occurring and what is being experienced.

CUSP 10,000 is the beginning of our journey questing through each new conscious lifetime as Avatars of Consciousness.

This point, CUSP 10,000, will form the basis for our feelings of separation. But this is a conscious misperception only, for we have lost nothing of our divine knowing, nor are we separated from perfection.

We are even now home in our benevolent perfection ... awaiting our conscious remembrance to awaken.

Chapter 29

CUSP 9,999—the Birth of Collective Human Consciousness

All of us share the voyage of conscious awakening.
We are not here to evolve ... but to remember.
Evolving means we have to become;
awakening means we merely
have to remember what
we already are.

We are incarnated now, in this current lifetime, and many of us may consider this our beginning, our creation, because we are born into this world as a new creation of life. But this is not our creation, nor our beginning—nor are any of the previous hundreds of lifetimes that we have experienced.

Creation, for the purpose of when we were to begin perceiving, experiencing, and expressing through the venue of collective human consciousness, unfolded at CUSP 10,000. But we as consciousness were not "created" at CUSP 10,000, because we have always been. Rather, CUSP 10,000 is the original act of Creation because it is when the Creation of collective human consciousness was formulated through divine intent. And this divine intention was made manifest (unfolded) in divine energy at Consciousness Unified Shift Point (CUSP) 9,999.

Thus, CUSP 9,999 is the *birth of collective human consciousness*. Think of CUSP 9,999 as the point at which we took our first conscious, energetic journey as collective human consciousness. It was our first expression through the divinely designed forum of collective human consciousness (although we, as Divine QUA, divine energy, divine consciousness have always existed).

At CUSP 9,999 the three divinely designed intentions (collective human consciousness, collective unconsciousness, and collective

234

consciousness) have all unfolded. Collective human consciousness has come into being—has been birthed in divine energy.

Remember, collective human consciousness is the arena, the divinely designed venue, through which we will express and experience everything in our voyage of conscious awakening. There is nothing outside of this venue.

Imagine that it is CUSP 9,999, and you have awakened in a universe called collective human consciousness. Everything that will ever be manifested or experienced is a part of this universe. There are no states of consciousness, dimensions, or realms outside of this universe. If you travel to heaven, that is within collective human consciousness; if you travel to Mars, that is within collective human consciousness; if you travel in dreams, that is within collective human consciousness. Everything that ever unfolds or is expressed or experienced is done by way of collective human consciousness, no matter where, when, what, how, or who.

At CUSP 9,999, we as Divine QUA simultaneously exist as *all*ness consciousness, *once*ness consciousness, and *All-at-Once* Consciousness. Any state of expression, whether onceness (soul) consciousness, allness (collective) consciousness, or All-at-Once Consciousness, is identical in divine energetic nature, though (and this is a very big though) soul consciousness perceives themselves to be different until their All-at-Once Consciousness is remembered.

At CUSP 9,999, there is no perception of individual me, but through a divinely designed process of unfolding, we, as Divine QUA, will perceive, experience, and express through many new states of conscious beingness, called lifetimes, eventually causing soul divinity to awaken and remember their true nature.

For purposes of understanding, let's begin viewing collective human consciousness as a newly unfolded venue of divine energy (divinity). In this way, we will begin perceiving things that come into being as a manifestation of divine energy unfolding as an expression of divinity. This will help us to consciously realize that divinity never evolves. Divinity is merely in a state of unfolding what already exists as divinity. When we speak of divinity, the word new isn't really applicable. It is more a case of newly unfolded.

Creator designed collective human consciousness as the venue that would bridge remembrance in Divine QUA of what they have forgotten, and each new expression (lifetime) is how we experience and continually unfold our conscious awakening.

All of us share the voyage of conscious awakening. It is not called the "voyage of conscious evolution" because we are not here to evolve ... but to remember. There is a vast difference. Evolving means we have to become; awakening means we merely have to remember what we already are.

Chapter 30

CUSP 1,999—Our Birth as a New Soul

While I was experiencing the cluster of lifetimes of 1,999–2,001 lifetimes ago, something quite phenomenal happened. Immediately following my first session in this cluster, my husband also experienced an emotional theme that originated 1,999 lifetimes ago.

It was very rare for my husband and I to go back to the same lifetime, and when it happened, our subconscious emotional blocks were never similar. For instance, if I went back to a lifetime thirty lifetimes ago and my husband went back to a lifetime thirty lifetimes ago, all of the information regarding role, emotion, emotional theme, etc., was completely different relative to what each of us were personally experiencing in the specific lifetime.

Not so in my husband's session. Extraordinarily, when he went back to an emotional theme originating 1,999 lifetimes ago, he also was expressing as "state of consciousness, spirit form, new soul."

This role was identical to the role I was expressing 1,999 lifetimes ago. What are the chances of that? None.

I learned from higher conscious thoughts that this lifetime was a CUSP lifetime where the entire collective was experiencing the identical shift into a new state of consciousness—spirit form—birthed as a new soul. This shift at CUSP 1,999 was also referred to by higher (divine) consciousness as the "birth of the new soul."

Even when I was young, I thought of my soul as eternal, so the words *birth of the new soul* confounded my mind. As human beings, we consider our soul to be immortal, continuing on after death. Therefore, if our soul is immortal, wouldn't it stand to reason that we always expressed as our soul? To me, the logical answer would be yes. But the answer was actually, "No, we have not always expressed as a soul."

I would come to understand that as part of our awakening, the conscious shift into expressing as our new soul was divinely designed to unfold at this specific point, CUSP 1,999. Why? Because this new vehicle of expression (new soul) will allow us to simultaneously perceive, experience, and express *individual* human consciousness as soul (onceness) consciousness; as collective (allness) consciousness; and as each and everything (All-at-Once Consciousness).

Prior to CUSP 1,999, it was not necessary for the conduit of our new soul to come into beingness because we, as Divine QUA, were not yet ready to experience lifetimes as individual human consciousness.

But now, at CUSP 1,999, we (Divine QUA) will now experience each new lifetime from an individual self-conscious me perspective, with the collective me simultaneously present but not perceived by us unless pulled into waking conscious awareness.

The new soul was divinely designed at the original act of Creation. But the new soul could not take spirit form and be birthed (unfolded) in divine energy until CUSP 1,999, when we were consciously ready to begin expressing physical and spiritual embodiment as individual human consciousness. This is why my subconscious accepted the term "birth" of the new soul as congruent and not "creation" of the new soul.

And the reason the term "new soul" was accepted as congruent with my subconscious was because the soul had never before been unfolded in divine energy, even though it is identical in essence as our Divine QUA (soul divinity, allness divinity, all-at-once divinity). It is a new form of expression (spirit form, new soul) but not a new essence.

Think of our new soul as the newly unfolded ethereal container for our Divine QUA. But do not think of us—as that new soul expression—as never previously existing. We, as Divine QUA, have always existed, but now our Divine QUA has shifted into the conscious conduit of our new soul.

We are the *same essence* (Divine QUA) in a *new expression* (new soul), a new package—a new spiritual envelope.

As human beings, we think in linear and finite terms, so when we think of the new soul as an "envelope," it would be only natural to perceive the envelope and what it envelops as separate components. But when it comes to concepts about us, we must learn to perceive through the lens of the infinite, as though there is no beginning or ending to where one thing leaves off and another begins. This is difficult because we experience within the parameters of human consciousness, including logic and communication, and we don't have any way to explain something other than to set it out within the boundaries of a definition. But sometimes what we are experiencing or trying to explain does not conform to the boundaries of a definition. It is energetically beyond any way to capture its essence in a definition or a finite form. This is when we must try to perceive beyond the limit of our conscious understanding and sense the limitlessness of what is being experienced or explained. In this way, we can perceive the limitless nuances of the subtle world we inhabit as *consciousness* while experiencing the finite nature of the physical world we inhabit as *embodiment*.

So although our soul was always present as our Divine QUA, we did not move through our lifetimes as an individual soul expression until CUSP 1,999. CUSP 1,999 is where we would begin to experience our individual (soul) divinity and collective (allness) divinity—our all-at-once beingness—through the unique medium of our new soul, which was divinely designed to allow us to transition between corporeal and incorporeal states (embodiment).

Think of *incorporeal* embodiment as non-material (spirit or essence) form and *corporeal* embodiment as material (human or physical) form. And from CUSP 1,999 forward into the present day, we will be utilizing both forms of embodiment while journeying as Avatars of Consciousness.

This explains how we are able to move through different planes of consciousness, such as the astral dimension, dreams, or even heaven, and why we appear to resemble our same human form while in these non-material (incorporeal) planes of consciousness. (Such as the time I awakened and saw my sister's astral body standing in my bedroom, and it looked identical to her physical body except it was nonmaterial in nature.)

We must keep reminding ourselves not to think of earth and human consciousness as the only plane of consciousness associated with collective human consciousness. Because collective human consciousness is the venue of all consciousness (dimensions), not just when we are expressing as conscious human beings on earth.

We can experience a lifetime as a corporeal being where our soul is embodied as human form or possibly even as an alien form of life expression. We can also experience a lifetime as an incorporeal being where our soul is embodied as spirit form (angel, spirit guide, ethereal being, etc.). So even if we don't physically incarnate, we can still experience a lifetime as an incorporeal being. We, as souls, aren't limited to just human expression because we aren't always physically incarnating on earth when we are experiencing lifetimes. An example of this was the lifetime where I was a "master in spirit in another dimension." This lifetime was still experienced in the venue of collective human consciousness even though I wasn't consciously expressing as a physical human being on earth.

Although it is not how we typically perceive it, think of incarnation as when we enter a new expression of conscious beingness (lifetime) in any dimension as either a material expression (human or physical form) or as a nonmaterial expression (spirit or energetic form).

At CUSP 1,999, don't think of our new soul as a newly created consciousness but rather think of it as a new "expression" of the eternal us of oneness. CUSP 1,999 is the pivotal point in our voyage of conscious awakening to the full remembrance of our divine nature, because it is first time as collective human consciousness that we are able to consciously perceive, experience, and express our "individual me" and "collective me" consciousness.

Creator designed individual human consciousness to be the bridge between unconscious (unknown) and conscious (known). This bridge, our own human consciousness, will seem like a veil between unconsciousness and consciousness until we have begun to awaken. Then the veil is pierced by our conscious awareness, and we will begin experiencing and expressing our own divine, co-creative nature.

For explanation purposes, imagine that each soul divinity is a petal within the allness of a divine lotus flower. Before the lotus flower begins unfolding, all petals are experiencing their divine nature and are at rest as the beingness of the lotus. The petal has always existed as both petal and lotus flower, but the petal is unaware of its individual essence. The petal only consciously recognizes itself to be the collective beingness of the lotus flower, as the petal's "self" awareness lay dormant and unrealized.

As the petal begins to experience and express its unfoldment, self-conscious awareness, self-realization, begins to awaken the petal to the knowing that it is not just a lotus flower, but it is also a petal. Then, as each lotus petal's beautiful expression of unfoldment continues, the petal becomes more and more aware of not only its own individual consciousness but it also becomes more consciously aware, more consciously connected to everything ... as though its consciousness and the consciousness of each and every other individual petal is one and the same consciousness.

When the petal consciously experiences the allness essence of the lotus while it is simultaneously experiencing as the onceness essence of the lotus, it begins to remember its own divine all-at-once nature— bridging conscious awareness as both flower and petal.

Once the petal is able to hold simultaneous consciousness of itself as an individual petal, as each and every other individual petal, and as the allness of the lotus, the divine promise of awakening has been fulfilled ... the individual lotus petal has consciously awakened to its all-at-once divine lotus beingness.

CUSP 1,999, our birth as a new soul, is the first point in collective human consciousness where we are able to feel, to think, to reason, to touch, to see, to hear, to taste, and to move as an individual human conscious expression. This is our debut as *individual* human consciousness.

It is an extraordinary moment in collective human consciousness, as we will not only be able to experience our divine co-creative nature, but eventually we will realize that we and the divine are identically the same energetic beingness.

Once, when I was younger, I was stopped at a red light and the following higher conscious thought came into my mind: "You are divinity's living experience. As you experience, divinity experiences."

Now I understand the true meaning of these words. We are not just divinity's living experience. The divine and all that it embodies— everything—is also our living experience.

Chapter 31

Awakening to Our Remembrance

We have forgotten that we are simultaneously creator (allness) and co-creator (onceness)—an *all-at-once* divine beingness.

At **CUSP 10,001,** we as Divine QUA only perceived the allness of our divine beingness, not the onceness or the all-at-onceness of our divine nature.

In order to awaken us to our onceness divinity as well as our all-at-once divinity, Creator unfolded *"The original act of Creation—the Creation of collective human consciousness"* at **CUSP 10,000.** Collective human consciousness was created so that we, as Divine QUA, would experience awakening and remembrance of our true nature through this profound consciousness venue. Everything is enfolded as collective human consciousness, and there are no dimensions, realms, or expressions that we will experience that are outside of the venue of collective human consciousness.

CUSP 9,999 is the *"birth of collective human consciousness"* because it is when we consciously experienced our first expression as collective human consciousness.

Then at **CUSP 5,000,** we experienced a shift in consciousness where collective human consciousness and collective consciousness merged as part of the divine design for us, as Divine QUA, to awaken to our co-creative nature. Prior to CUSP 5,000 (from CUSP 10,000 until CUSP 5,000), conscious and unconscious were perceived by us to be identical, and we were consciously aware as both states of consciousness no matter what form we expressed. But at CUSP 5,000, that perception shifted. It was the first time that we could not perceive "unconsciousness" while conscious. The state of unconsciousness, though identical in all-knowingness as consciousness, became unknown to us when we are expressing as consciousness. This shift created both the perceived *veil* as well as the *bridge* within our conscious awareness. It was the first time that we perceived something (a veil) separating us from an unknown (unconsciousness).

But at **CUSP 1,999,** we held the co-creative vehicle (new soul) by which we were able to pull that *unknown* (unconsciousness) through the *known* (consciousness) within us. Thus, the veil became the bridge, allowing us to experience our divine co-creative nature while expressing individual human consciousness.

At CUSP 1,999, the shift of consciousness into the *"birth of the new soul"* as individual human consciousness expression occurred. This was an extraordinary shift—one that we had been consciously preparing for since CUSP 10,001 and one that would allow us to awaken to our divine destiny. This shift at CUSP 1,999 is divinely intended to bring forth our awakening and remembrance that we, as Divine QUA, are identical in essence to Creator/divine energy. Everything that occurred from this shift at CUSP 1,999 until our present lifetime is how divinity intends us to remember.

Co-creative consciousness manifests through individual human consciousness when we simultaneously experience allness (all-knowing) awareness and onceness (waking conscious) awareness—when we are able to simultaneously experience collective unconscious knowing being pulled through individual human conscious awareness. Then, as we express that awareness through our thoughts, words, actions, perceptions, and feelings, we are consciously experiencing our innate co-creative beingness.

An example of experiencing our co-creative nature is what occurred in my sessions with Angela. I was simultaneously interacting with my individual human conscious thoughts, my higher conscious insights, and my subconscious knowing.

We all experience our co-creative nature in our daily lives, though we may not yet be consciously aware of it. This is not an ability enjoyed by only special people. We all have the ability to perceive our co-creative nature; we just need to learn to be more consciously attentive to what is occurring within our beingness. The more we interact, the more we awaken our perception, and the more our perception awakens, the more we are able to consciously know. It becomes a beautiful, energetic circle of unconscious knowing awakening through our normal waking conscious awareness.

While expressing as individual human consciousness, we as soul divinity are not aware of the unknown until it is consciously perceived within our human conscious awareness. For example, we are not aware of our own subconscious—which is the collective unconscious—until we pull it into our waking conscious awareness as a thought, a feeling, or an expression.

CUSP 1,999 is when we, as Divine QUA, consciously shifted to the newly unfolded state of individual human consciousness as the birth of the new soul. The individual me was now at the helm for the first time in collective human consciousness as far as perceiving, experiencing, and expressing.

CUSP 1,999 is when we, as Divine QUA, took individual conscious control of our vehicle of co-creation. We were now cooperating in our own divinely designed awakening. This was the first time in collective human consciousness that until something was consciously perceived while expressing individual human consciousness, it was assumed to exist in an unknown state. Once perceived, it became known within individual human conscious awareness. Individual human consciousness is now the threshold between aware and unaware, as determined by our own perceptions. This creates the conscious illusion that there is a veil between the known (collective consciousness) and the unknown (collective unconsciousness), with individual human consciousness serving as the bridge between those two states of knowing. In truth, there is no veil because all states of consciousness are identical. But because of the nature of individual human consciousness, the unknown cannot pierce the veil and make itself known without self-conscious perception. Thus, individual human consciousness acts as both veil (when unknown) and bridge (when known) between unconscious and conscious.

When the veil is pierced by our awakening, misperception will end. Then once the veil is completely lifted, our remembrance will be fully awakened and serve as the bridge within us for conscious expression of our divine, co-creative, all-at-once nature. This remembrance is the fulfillment of the divine design unfolded as the original act of Creation.

Once the divine purpose of the original act of Creation has been fully realized, all will be as it once was, always is, and will always be. All dimensions will collapse back as divine energy once more.

Imagine the accordion of collective human consciousness—including all realms, dimensions, and universes—collapsing back down into its original, one-dimensional state. There will no longer be a need for collective human consciousness and all the realms it embodies, as we will be fully awakened.

To avoid misperception, begin associating terms like awareness and perception with the collective unconscious. No longer think of unconscious as unaware. If you choose, think of unconscious as unexpressed consciousness. It is unexpressed until pulled into expression through the bridge of individual human conscious thoughts, feelings, and actions, but unconsciousness is always aware of everything.

The vibration of divine conscious love experiences all states of consciousness at once: collective (allness) consciousness; soul (oneness) consciousness; and All-at-Once (simultaneously allness at each, at every, and at all onenesses) Consciousness.

Beginning at CUSP 1,999, soul divinity is conscious of its own self-expression but does not perceive it is also something else besides that individual consciousness. Allness divinity is also simultaneously fully present at that oneness expression, even though consciously unperceived by soul divinity. Remember, divinity is ever-present at the state of allness as well as present at any and all states of oneness at the same moment. So divine energy is always present (as *all* and as *soul* and as *all-at-once*).

Think of it as though CUSP 1,999 is when individual human conscious expression triggers a forgotten state of our allness consciousness. Why? It is because when we are expressing as individual human consciousness, our allness divinity (collective unconsciousness) recedes behind the veil of our human waking consciousness.

Our Divine QUA as individual soul divinity expression is a more self-expressive, self-identified consciousness—but as that more focused state of consciousness, soul divinity is no longer able to perceive its allness divinity. Allness divinity is still simultaneously fully present but not perceived by soul divinity until awakened (known) in individual human conscious awareness. Pulling unconscious, subconscious, and higher conscious into waking conscious awareness is how our all-at-once, co-creative divine nature becomes awakened within our consciousness.

Consciousness—our conscious mind as typically experienced through our own individual human consciousness is limited in that it only knows to the boundaries of what it perceives through self-conscious awareness; and it does not yet perceive its own all-knowingness.

Unconsciousness—our unconscious mind is not only self-conscious in the sense that it perceives self, but our own unconscious mind is also a limitless, all-knowing consciousness, not only aware of its allness as a collective consciousness but also simultaneously aware and connected with all other individual self-consciousnesses.

In truth, we, as divine consciousness, *simultaneously* hold *all states of conscious perspective at once*:

- individual me conscious awareness
- collective me conscious awareness
- each and every other individual me conscious awareness

Think of it as though our true state of divine beingness is simultaneously conscious as an "individual me," as a "collective me," and as "each and every other individual me." For example, if we are experiencing as our true divine, All-at-Once Consciousness, I would be consciously aware as the individual self "Carol," as the collective allness "Divinity," and as each and every other individual self "Brian, Lindsey, Sam, Becky, etc."

Through the unfoldment of conscious awareness in human experience and expression, we, as humanity, have misperceived the true nature of consciousness. Even though we may have come to recognize the "individual me" consciousness (soul divinity) and the "collective me" consciousness (allness divinity), we have misperceived that we, as individual consciousness, and divine energy, as allness consciousness, were separate ... *either* an individual consciousness (one) *or* a collective consciousness (all). Then, even when we begin to perceive that we are simultaneously *both* a one and an all consciousness, we still misperceive ourselves to be separate from each and every other consciousness ... misperceiving the true all-at-once nature of consciousness. We, as human consciousness, do not consciously realize that we are inseparably an individual consciousness, a collective consciousness, and each and every other individual consciousness ... *simultaneously*.

In truth, everything is only one divine, indivisible energy—thus, everything is always, eternally, the same all-at-once divine beingness—consciously aware that it is always "all" even when being a "one."

But the issue isn't what divine consciousness *is*, it is how we interpret "our" relationship to divine consciousness that creates the misperception. Yes, divine consciousness is energetically everything at once; but we are in human consciousness and perceiving from a human perspective. This perspective causes us to compartmentalize the concept of consciousness and relegate it to being either a one or an all, missing the true nature of divine consciousness as being an all-at-each-and-every-single-oneness consciousness. For a minute image that you wake up one morning as your normal, waking conscious self ... but this morning enlightened awareness also awakens within your consciousness. This enlightened awareness brings the *conscious knowing* that you are not just your own individual consciousness but you are equally and simultaneously each and every other individual self consciousness as well as the totality of all consciousness. This enlightened awareness is the true nature of divine consciousness—the true nature of us! There is no separation in any state of consciousness, only the perceived sense of separation while we are experiencing the dream of misperception.

When we begin to awaken to our allness while experiencing and expressing as our oneness, we are no longer perceiving from *either* a "collective me" or an "individual me" awareness. And this realization is our pathway—our energetic access to conscious interaction with our own divine nature while experiencing human consciousness.

The unfoldment of our own divine consciousness occurs as we continue to pull unconscious all-knowingness into waking conscious awareness, creating a bridge of remembrance of our true divine essence. Then once we are *fully conscious* and know the allness of our nature while we are simultaneously aware of not only our own individual consciousness but also equally aware of each and every other individual consciousness, we will be experiencing the innate inseparability of our consciousness ... and we will be *consciously* "home" to our true eternal, all-at-once divine essence in any and all experiences or expressions.

Chapter 32

Our True Nature of All-at-Once Consciousness

So, what does All-at-Once Consciousness really mean? This concept, more than any other, is the single most confusing concept for us to understand in human embodiment because we view things from the perspective of the physical plane of consciousness with all the physical laws and realities. We do this not only because of our human consciousness but also because we carry the imprint of our original misperception at the Creation of collective human consciousness as the foundation for how we view everything.

The allness of divinity—divine energy—is present as every single essence of that allness always, no matter whether it appears as a compound, multifaceted state or as a onceness state or as two billion onceness states. The nuances and intricacies involved in the true meaning of All-at-Once Consciousness are not easy to perceive because we are conditioned by our perception at the first light of collective human consciousness as well as our perceptions throughout all time and space, and all of those perceptions are based upon a misperception of our true nature.

To more easily comprehend All-at-Once Consciousness, imagine that in front of you is a vast desert. It goes as far as you can see in all directions. It is limitless. This desert appears to contain trillions of individual grains of sand.

You perceive that all of those individual grains of sand are inherently merged as the allness of that desert. There is no stretch of the imagination there because we can see the individual grains as well as the desert and we perceive that when all the grains are in the desert, it is one merged desert comprised of all of those individual grains of sand.

But what if you pulled away one grain of sand and held it in your hand and then took that grain of sand with you as you traveled to a distant galaxy, far away from that desert? It would now appear that the grain of sand you pulled away and the entirety of the desert are separated from each other by space and time.

We perceive that the grain of sand is apart from the desert; therefore, that individual grain of sand is no longer contained within or a part of the desert. It is now considered to be a separated part of the whole of the desert.

Let's say, just for explanation purposes, you were to travel all the way back to earth from that distant galaxy and you were to place that individual grain of sand back into the desert. It would be logical to say you have reunited the grain of sand with the desert. What appeared separated is once more in union or in wholeness, because all the parts that made up the original whole have been brought back together. (I'm not saying this is what is actually occurring, but it is what we perceive because of how we view our world, divinity, and ourselves.)

There are some spiritual beliefs as well as scientific theories that say that even when that grain of sand was in that distant galaxy, it was still connected with the desert to which it was once joined.

But what if the sand and the desert are not just connected while in a state of appearing separate? What if the allness of the desert and the oneness of the grain of sand are, in truth, identical in energetic essence—All-at-Once Consciousness at any and all places or expressions? It is true—the all of the desert, even with the single grain of sand removed, is still the same all. No energy or intrinsic essence of allness is ever lost in the appearance of separation. The individual grain of sand is always identical in essence to the entire allness of the desert even though it appears to be only an individual grain of sand, apart from the desert. And when the single grain of sand is reunited with the desert, nothing is gained in the appearance of wholeness, as nothing was ever really lost. The allness of the desert and the oneness of the desert is always identically the same in energetic essence, though perceived differently. (*All* is not lost; *nothing* is gained. Now I am more able to understand the deeper meaning in this higher conscious insight.)

So, the grain of sand is still the allness of the desert even when perceived as an individual grain of sand. That grain of sand is not just a part of the desert—that grain of sand is the entirety of the desert.

How can this be? How can that single grain of sand be the same as the entirety of the desert? Yet it is. The energetic essence of that individual grain of sand and the entirety of the desert are the same indivisible divine energy. Just like divinity is fully present at any single expression, the desert is also fully present at that individual grain of sand. The sand is not just a "part of" or "in" the desert. That grain of sand carries the entire essence of the desert—it is the *allness of the desert* expressing at the *oneness of the sand.*

Imagine I were to ask you to pull a grain of sand away from the desert and hold it in your hand. Then imagine I asked you to look at that grain of sand resting in your hand while I told you that the single grain of sand is really the entirety of the desert in essence. You may not believe it, because that grain of sand appears to be just an individual grain of sand. Our current state of conscious awareness is unable to recognize the all-at-once nature of that grain of sand due to our inability to perceive our own true nature as well as the true nature of everything.

Initially, I thought All-at-Once Consciousness was the same concept as my belief that divinity is *in* me and I'm *in* divinity. That is not really correct because there is no "in." In implies that there are parts. There are no parts. In actuality, all-at-once divine energy is the allness of divinity simultaneously existing at each, at every, and at all onenesses of divinity.

Remember:

Any and all expressions or perceptions of divinity are identical in nature (beingness) to the entirety of divinity. Divinity cannot ever be a partial love, a partial knowing, a partial power, a partial presence, or a partial perfection because the divine is one indivisible energy. Therefore, the inseparable allness of divinity—the indivisible nature of divinity—dictates that the entirety of divinity be simultaneously fully present at each oneness (single) expression as well as at all expressions— always. This is why divinity's true nature is an All-at-Once (all-at-every-oneness) Consciousness.

It is not difficult for many of us to perceive divinity and ourselves to be one energy without separation. But that is an erroneous perception of divinity (and ourselves) if we do not also perceive that *each and every onceness is **simultaneously** the entirety of allness* at that onceness.

For explanation purposes, imagine that in front of you is a circle. This circle represents the entirety of divine energy.

Now imagine that this circle, which represents the entirety of divinity, is filled with tiny dots. Begin to view each one of those dots as an individual expression of the divine—a onceness or soul divinity.

When you sit back and look at the circle, the relationship between the dots, the circle, and divinity can be perceived in several ways. Let's take a look at a few of the ways that we would view divinity and ourselves.

The first perception is that each one of those dots is a separate part of that whole divine beingness. (In this perception each dot appears to be a part of divinity's whole.)

The second perception is that those dots do not exist as individual consciousness, but rather, they comprise just one divine being—one collective consciousness. (In this perception there is only one divine conscious being, without any individual consciousness.)

The first two perceptions are the most typical way in which we view divinity and ourselves and our perception of union or oneness.

But there is another perception that is not typical—a perception that reflects the true nature of divinity and ourselves. Consciously understanding this perception, this truth, will clear our misperception, shift our consciousness, and unfold our awakening.

In order to understand this perception, imagine that you are able to perceive that you, the other dots, and the entirety of divinity are *simultaneously* the allness of divinity at each and every onceness of divinity. Think about it for a minute. Each one of those individual dots is simultaneously everything that divinity embodies (allness) at the same moment it is a single dot (onceness). It is allness at each, at every, and at all oncenesses. Each single dot is simultaneously everything that exists (the entirety of divinity) even though it only appears as a onceness.

This is a difficult concept to immediately comprehend. Our natural way of perceiving (through the lens of human consciousness) is to view all those dots floating in that sea of divine energy as separate, individual parts of the whole of the circle. But they are not. Each of those dots is the *entirety of divinity* (everything that exists as that circle) at the same time it is the *onceness of divinity* (the single dot).

For a moment, just look at a single dot and view it as embodying the entirety of that circle in just its single dot expression. Don't think of the dot as a part of the circle, but instead think of the dot as being the allness (the entirety) of that circle at the onceness expression of the dot. Imagine they are simultaneously existing, the circle as the dot and the dot as the circle, because they are not just a single dot or the entirety of the circle. They are the allness of that entire circle at each and every single onceness expression of the dot (All-at-Once Consciousness).

This is the true nature of divinity, ourselves, and everything because everything is always only one indivisible, inseparable divine energy in any perception or expression. This means that we are simultaneously our own soul consciousness, each and every other soul consciousness, and all divine consciousness. Although we are perceived to be only a single thing, we are, in fact, all things at once—one eternal, indivisible beingness of divine conscious love.

This defies our human view of reality or science, doesn't it? We defy science. We defy reality.

Incredibly, modern science is now able to view the very fabric of our true nature—not just our physical nature, which seems to operate in accordance with established laws of classical physics, but the true divine nature of what we all embody. It is a nature that simultaneously operates in accordance with an entirely different set of laws, more quantum in nature.

Two completely different sets of laws (classical and quantum) simultaneously co-exist within our reality, verifying what we are and what we aren't. We aren't really just physical, limited by physical reality. We are also limitless, boundless, and *all and one simultaneously*. (Sound familiar? This was the baguette-sized breadcrumb given through higher consciousness and accepted by my subconscious as congruent, related to an emotional theme originating one thousand lifetimes ago about being dogmatically positioned that I can't be all and one at the same time.)

How is it possible that we are all and one simultaneously? It is possible because we are only one thing even though we appear as many things. Our divine beingness is the "nothingness void of everything"—a nonlocal divine energy capable of manifesting any reality through divine consciousness.

That is the mystifying part of us. How can we be one (individual) yet all (everything) at the same time? How can we be identically the same even when appearing different? It is because we are an inseparable consciousness, an indivisible vibration of love, reflected as intentions in a dimensional consciousness (earth plane) that is bounded by principles that apply to that dimension. But those same principles do not apply to the true quantum nature of all of us, as we are an All-at-Once Consciousness—simultaneously existing as all states of consciousness.

Our true beingness and the beingness of everything is always identically the same inseparable divine energy—no matter how it expresses or how it is perceived. And this is the reason that anything appearing as a single thing is identically the same as the totality of everything.

It is no accident that divine consciousness is releasing this information at a time when science is also getting glimpses of our true nature. The timeliness is perfect. Also, the synchronicity of my even being aware of our quantum, subatomic world (because of random events) is profound, as that awareness allowed me to connect dots that would have otherwise gone unnoticed.

Understanding All-at-Once Consciousness helps us to not only understand our true nature but also the true nature of our seen universe. It is a nature reflected in what scientists exploring the quantum world are seeing in experiments. The oddities occurring in quantum mechanics are not odd at all once you recognize that science is just seeing what we embody at the core of our beingness—our true nature and the true nature of everything.

At the core of everything, there is really only one *continuing basic divine energy* … quantum, unlimited, inseparable, divine potential. When this divine potential consciously moves from a state of static to kinetic, this continuation of the basic divine energy is expressed through *variant phases or versions* that we, as human beings, view as classical, limited, manifested form.

Think of it as though everything in our seen world is really one divine energy (quantum essence) expressing through our perceived reality (classical form). In truth *everything* is actually only one divine energy expressing as focused realities. For example, when divine energy is expressing in a physical, matter-based reality, the quantum allness of that essence appears to be classical in nature—limited by the boundaries of our physical reality world and the laws of classical physics. But that is a perception only, as the true nature of divine energy never changes. It is always *simultaneously* quantum essence (our unseen Universe) and classical form (our seen universe)—unlimited all and focused one, everything and nothing ... eternally one divine, indivisible energy. This is what science is beginning to witness when viewing the subatomic fabric of our universe—they are seeing the All-at-Once Consciousness of divine energy through the lens of a matter-based reality.

Divine all-at-once energy is the true nature of everything, and understanding that nature unifies everything. It unifies our human nature and physical form with our divine nature and quantum essence; science with spirituality; and science with itself because it establishes that there is no conflict between the classical, matter-based world of our seen universe and the quantum, subatomic world of our unseen Universe when viewed through the lens of All-at-Once Consciousness.

Any expression is identically the same in energetic essence (simultaneously both quantum and classical) but just perceived by us to be different because we do not fully comprehend the true nature of everything. Whether divine energy is expressing as essence (unmanifested potentiality) or as form (manifested reality), it is always identically the same one indivisible divine beingness.

No matter the perception or expression, we are always simultaneously all and one at the same moment—identically the same one thing at any perceived state of expression.

Think back to that circle with all the dots. Isn't it easy to imagine that a little dot would view itself as a part of the whole of oneness, not perceiving its own divinity at the same moment it perceives the divinity of the collective all?

In reality, each of those dots expressing as onceness is also at the same moment the entirety, the allness of divinity at that onceness (soul) expression. It is not all *in* one, because that implies that there is only one merged thing but rather all *at* the onceness, no matter how many oncenesses there are.

All perceived attributes (omnibenevolent, omnipresent, omniscient, omnipotent) of divine energy are indivisible and inseparable, simultaneously expressing the entire divine beingness at the onceness of every single dot. The dot is a soul (onceness) consciousness while simultaneously being collective (allness) consciousness.

Because divine energy never has limit, separation, or boundaries, divine consciousness is always nonlocal—simultaneously existing at all locations at once even when appearing as a single localized expression.

This means that we are nonlocal divine energy—though we appear to be manifested as only a single, localized human expression!

And although it may be difficult for us to perceive, the limitless divine—an All-at-Once Consciousness is at the core of everything … every tree, every rock, every animal, every cell— absolutely every energetic expression. This may well explain why pets awaken from a deep sleep and trot over to the front door, sensing their owner's imminent arrival. Or why animals separated from their owners by great distances miraculously find their way home many months later. Although it may be assumed that it is an animal's acute sense of hearing or smell that causes this behavior, what if it is really their energetic, conscious connection with all living things that triggers these acts of knowingness?

Just because animals, plants, minerals, insects, cells, molecules, etc. may not appear to exhibit conscious awareness does not mean that consciousness is not present. In any individual expression, the essence of divine energy is always present—whether that expression is an individual human being or whether that expression is an animal, a plant, a crystal, a molecule of water, etc. As such, everything is energetically connected, energetically affected, by what happens through any state of consciousness, whether consciously recognized or not.

One consciousness affects all consciousness, and all consciousness affects one consciousness—no matter what form or energetic expression divine consciousness takes—because everything is actually only one divine beingness. No true separation in consciousness ever exists, and this is why conscious intention is able to affect matter—not only the matter of our human bodies and physical reality, but also the consciousness of other human beings.

As our awareness continues to unfold, we realize that there is an innate energetic connectedness that exists between all things, even if there is no conscious awareness of that connection, because everything is only one divine conscious energy. This realization helps us to not only recognize our connectedness with divine energy, but also our connectedness with each other and with everything. In this way, our consciousness is not just able to affect the matter of our physical world and energetic beingness, it is able to shift our reality and awaken us to our divine destiny.

As impossible as it may seem, we are so much more than just an individual human consciousness. And though we may not yet be able to *consciously* access it, at our core is the limitless divine.

The purpose of being in collective human consciousness is to awaken to the truth of us. And that truth is that we are not just a soul consciousness, but we are simultaneously the divine at each and every and all expressions—one divine, All-at-Once Consciousness.

We are the divine conscious vibration of love ... living expressions of the eternal us of oneness.

No wonder we misperceived what we are. The truth of us is extraordinary ... ***we're extraordinary***.

Chapter 33

We Long for Oneness

The analogy of the desert helps us to understand how an individual grain of sand may feel alien, isolated, or suffering because it is not now a part of what it once enjoyed, sensing it is now alone, apart, and separated from its home (the desert). It's not even a stretch to see how the grain of sand would long to be reunited with the desert (its home).

That's basically how we feel. At the core of all of our anxieties—conceptualized or not—there is a belief or feeling that we are separated from what we once perceived as all or one or whole.

In our perceived separated state, we sense we are alone, out in the cold, fending for ourselves as an isolated, separate entity. No wonder we feel the need to identify with our human personalities or egos. We think we're all we've got. Yet deep within, we feel a need to explore, expand, learn, and grow so we can not only survive but also eventually start remembering. Then, once we consciously perceive that we were once in perfection, all we truly long for in the deepest part of ourselves is to return to oneness because we perceive we are a separated part of that one—apart from that oneness perfection.

We long for oneness beyond anything we even consciously understand, and though we don't consciously recognize it, throughout all eternity we have been seeking the reason for why we initially separated and how to return to that oneness—to that sense of divine perfection. The reason or cause of our separation is unfathomable to us, and because we are not able to perceive the true reason for our separation, we cannot understand how to return home to the oneness of perfection.

We believe the desire to be back in oneness is what is driving us, but that desire is just the seed planted by our misperception to propel us through our journey of awakening. In reality, we are searching for the answer to why we separated in the first place, as the sheer anguish of that initial feeling of separation is what we are trying to resolve within our consciousness. Did we separate because we were imperfect, or was it because we made an error? We don't know, but each of us carries suffering caused by our sense of separation. This original feeling of suffering is carried in our subconscious, and since our subconscious is also the collective unconscious in which we and everything are interwoven, this feeling is carried in all human consciousness, recognized or not.

Imagine that you live in a sweet little cottage that you love. Everything is perfect. One day you sense that something is shifting or changing. You can't perceive exactly why or what, but suddenly, inexplicably, you just find yourself on the outside door of that cottage. Poof! One moment you're in a perfect little cottage; the next, you're out in the cold. You cannot even imagine that anything else could exist for you but that perfect little cottage. All you focus on is getting back to what you once enjoyed. Your single-minded intent is getting back on the other side of that door—back in your cottage. You try everything, but nothing allows you entrance. Though you can't find the exact reason for your expulsion, your feelings make you believe it is because you were not perfectly aligned with the cottage or didn't deserve to live in the cottage. Because of this, you seek philosophies and practices that will bring you into alignment, perfect your imperfections, and make you pure or worthy enough to live in that perfect little cottage space once more.

But what if, while you were originally enjoying that space of perfection (that perfect little cottage), there was a beautiful memory that you carried inside, a knowing that you never took time to remember because you were so complete, so fulfilled, and so perfect that you didn't care about remembering?

What if someday someone told you that you didn't really live in only one perfect cottage but that you lived in all cottages—at *once?* You live in everything and everything lives in you, and you simultaneously know everything occurring not only in your cottage but in all cottages. Would getting back to that single little cottage still be your focus? Or would your focus shift to experiencing the entirety of all cottages through your own onceness—shattering your original misperception?

In reality, how we view everything that we have experienced is filtered through our original misperception, and without *consciously* perceiving our true nature, we will not ever feel as though we are home as our benevolent perfection. We may even come to believe that we have returned to oneness because for microscopic glimpses it feels like we are standing in our perfect cottage, but we may really only have our ears plastered against that cottage door, eavesdropping on perfection—vicariously feeling our oneness.

Until we perceive the truth of our beingness and shift our consciousness, we will misperceive ourselves to be either all *or* one, thus consciously separated from our true "all-*at*-once" divine nature.

Each of our unique spiritual paths has been a result of divinity's intention for us to clear misperception and incongruency from our consciousness so we can remember our forgotten truth. That path has led each of us to our current state of beingness as Divine QUA expressing as individual human consciousness.

We are not in human consciousness to suffer or to evolve or to perfect ourselves. We are in human consciousness to realize that we and that which is reflected back as us are identically the same one divine beingness. We are not now nor have we ever been separated from our benevolent perfection. We are merely asleep in the dream of misperception.

The oneness we long to become is already ours and our individual human consciousness is the means through which we will pierce the veil, awaken from the dream, and unfold our remembrance.

... *This is the ultimate purpose of life and for our being here on earth.*

Chapter 34

We Are Light of the Same Light, Love of the Same Love

Even if a full understanding of All-at-Once Consciousness is still a little puzzling, don't worry. As you read, knowing will continue to unfold as light fills your mind and you consciously connect with the truth of your beingness.

No matter what you believe about separation in any form, your concept is most likely based upon a misperception that occurred at CUSP 10,000, at the original act of Creation—the Creation of collective human consciousness. Our misperception of our own divine nature created our sense of separation, and our sense of separation created our longing to be back in divine perfection once more, a longing that has always been with us. We thirst after recapturing our perfection lifetime after lifetime when, in fact, we are not now nor have we ever been separated from perfection. Everything we do is an attempt to once more return to a place from which we feel separated (oneness, home, perfection, benevolence). In reality, we cannot return to a place we never have left, but the perception that home is outside of us is what perpetuates our *conscious misperception of separation.*

As a child, it wasn't difficult for me to understand the concept that God was in the tree and each leaf of the tree. Even if it is not your belief, imagine that divinity (or a Supreme Being, the Source, or pure consciousness) possesses the ability to be in everything at the same time everywhere. I assumed I understood this concept regarding divinity, but I did not. I could never have conceptualized that divinity wasn't just "in" that leaf but that divinity and the leaf were, in fact, identical in energetic essence though appearing different. It would be like someone standing a human being next to a leaf and telling you that the human being and the leaf are the identical same thing. That's definitely not how we would consciously perceive those two things.

Now, I realize that there was no way for me to have understood that concept because my eyes would have seen a single leaf but my ears would have heard the words, "Everything that divinity embodies is identically the same as that single leaf."

How would that have seemed possible? How is that possible? But it is not just possible; it is the true nature of divinity, of us, of our world, and of everything. We are really only one inseparable, all-at-once divine conscious vibration of love, no matter what form, projection, reflection, or expression unfolds ... ever.

Take a moment now to intuitively connect to this concept, trusting deeper levels of knowing will continue unfolding within you.

Imagine that it is CUSP 10,001 and we as Divine QUA are experiencing as the collective stillness of divine perfection and as the Creation of collective human consciousness was occurring, at CUSP 10,000, we began to feel that whatever was coming could not be more perfect than what was being experienced in our perceived state of collective oneness. We wondered why we were shifting—why it was all changing. We could not perceive our soul consciousness or our all-at-once consciousness because we were preoccupied with experiencing only our sense of allness perfection. We were slumbering in the bliss of our collective, peaceful perfection.

Because we have fallen asleep and do not consciously recognize our true divine nature, it is divinity's intention that all its divine energy be awakened. Our divinely designed awakening is a reflection of the absolute love that divinity holds for all of its divine beingness.

Beginning at CUSP 10,000, Creator intends to awaken us (itself) by making us first aware of ourselves. Then from CUSP 10,000 to CUSP 2,000, Creator unfolds a series of newly manifested states of consciousness—all in preparation for the main event at CUSP 1,999, the birth of the new soul.

The birth of the new soul is a drumroll type event because it is the first time we will be simultaneously holding soul consciousness and allness consciousness while consciously perceiving, experiencing, and expressing as individual human consciousness.

What does this mean? It means that at CUSP 1,999, we have the ability to co-create, to pull the unknown (unconscious) into the known (conscious), and to express our simultaneous, multi-state consciousness. But it takes us a while to consciously awaken to this profound potentiality of our own beingness, our all-at-once divine nature.

At CUSP 1,999, we are perceived as a "new soul" by our subconscious because we are "newly unfolded." Although our new soul is identical in beingness as our Divine QUA, before CUSP 1,999 we have never expressed as a soul in individual human consciousness.

It is new packaging (soul), but the same eternal essence (Divine QUA). So we are new and eternal at the same time. It is the first time the "eternal us of oneness" is present as individual human consciousness. How? It is present through the awareness we call our subconscious.

We carry what we perceive to only be an individual subconscious, but in reality, our subconscious is an All-at-Once Consciousness—allowing each and every one of us access to the entirety of collective unconsciousness (divine consciousness) as well as access to each and every onceness of collective unconsciousness (all other individual soul consciousnesses).

Higher conscious thoughts revealed—and my sessions confirmed that the subconscious is not only the vault, gatekeeper, and key to our individual unconscious awareness but it is also the vault, gatekeeper, and key to all unconscious awareness—divine consciousness itself.

Through our subconscious we not only have access to the collective divine, but we also have access to each and every other individual soul consciousness, as well as our own unique soul expression. This means that we are able to simultaneously access the all-knowingness of our own soul consciousness, the all-knowingness of collective consciousness (God, Benevolence, divinity), and the all-knowingness of each and every other individual soul consciousness (Sarah, Jim, John, Ginny, Ken, etc.).

Divinity simultaneously experiences all expressions, lifetimes, and journeys that we experience because all of what we each experience, know, and feel is forever etched in what we perceive to be our subconscious. The entire collective unconscious is simultaneously present as our subconscious. Each of us always "knows" everything; we just don't yet remember what we know because we are not yet consciously awakened to our own all-at-once nature.

It is important that we seek to be more consciously aware in the life we are living, because the more we consciously recognize the all-at-onceness of our beingness, the more we will be able to access our divine state of all-knowingness through our waking conscious awareness.

No matter our age, cultural background, or spiritual belief our current lifetime grants us the phenomenal opportunity to consciously recognize the extraordinary truth of our beingness ... and that conscious awareness is all that need happen for us to begin stirring our remembrance and awakening to our divine destiny.

As we awaken to the truth of our beingness, spiritual teachings centered around being an individual consciousness seeking to be unified back into the whole of divinity or one divine consciousness void of individuality will fall away, as we will consciously recognize that we are simultaneously an allness (collective divine consciousness), a oneness (our own divine consciousness), and each and every other onceness (all other individual divine consciousnesses). All-at-Once Consciousness will be consciously awakened in waking awareness and we will no longer suppress our oneness (in lieu of our collective divine beingness) or suppress our allness (in lieu of our individual divine beingness).

We will naturally shift to a higher conscious perspective, and we will never again think of divine consciousness (divinity) or any other individual soul consciousness (others) as separate from our own eternal beingness. In this way, our self identity will shift from a singular perspective to a state of beingness able to consciously reflect our simultaneous, all-at-once nature. We will then be better able to experience our lives from a center that is simultaneously both an individual consciousness and a collective consciousness, fulfilling the divine blueprint of our conscious awakening.

Then we will truly know that no matter how it may "appear" to the contrary in this seen universe, there is never any true energetic separation between us and all that is divine, as we are eternally light of the same light, love of the same love.

Chapter 35

The One Voice Within All of Us

The One Voice within all of us echoes
remembrance of our eternal oneness,
leading us home to our essence
of benevolent perfection.

Once you are conscious, you forget your unconscious awareness. For instance, when you are unconscious during surgery, you are aware of everything even in that unconscious state, but once you awaken, you do not remember what you knew while unconscious.

Once you awaken from a dream, it is not easy to bring forth the remembrance of the dream into your conscious state. This is because the dream state exists as the unconscious, and the awakened state exists as the conscious. But when you are able to hold the unconscious dream state while simultaneously conscious (lucid dreaming), you are experiencing multi-state consciousness. You are pulling the unknown (the dream) into the known (conscious awareness). Thus, lucid dreaming is an example of bridging consciousness that many of us have experienced.

It is this very act of bridging—of bringing the unknown, the unconscious, into consciousness—that is the purpose and the gift of individual human consciousness.

As human beings, many of us believe or sense that in some other place (perfection, heaven, nirvana, oneness) we will live in bliss and harmony and joy with each other and a benevolent presence. Where does this concept or belief live inside of us? Is it in our mind, purely from books or spiritual concepts? Or is it really that some part of us remembers our benevolent home, even now in our dense state of human consciousness? Do we inherently hold divine love and divine knowing within the folds of consciousness? Yes, of course we do. Otherwise, how can so many of us believe that something else exists, something that is profoundly beautiful and perfect, when there is no evidence of this place's existence except in our hearts and by what is occasionally stirred through our unusual (quantum, paranormal, spiritual) experiences?

But we as a collective are growing more consciously aware that there is a space within our own consciousness that can provide the evidence we seek—energetic verification that the knowing we all carry inside of our connection to "home" and Benevolence is real. It is accessible thorough our own subconscious mind. Our subconscious holds the knowing of everything—all experiences, thoughts, feelings, intentions, lifetimes, and dreams ever experienced by the entirety of collective human consciousness. It is not hidden away in a physical place we must seek or through another person. It is right here—within each of us—always carried as our very own subconscious, even though we do not always *consciously* recognize its presence.

There is no doubt in my mind or my heart that the answers we seek to our own benevolent beingness can be found through accessing our own subconscious mind. This undeniable truth was verified in my sessions with Angela.

Are we really *all-knowing* beings and we just don't remember what we all know? Absolutely—with one small caveat. We are remembering through the lens of our original misperception as well as the filter of all of our experiences, including subconscious blocked emotions stemming from our fear and feelings that we were somehow exiled from our benevolent home, separated from perfection.

At CUSP 10,000, we, as Divine QUA, identified with a feeling of separation from what we knew because we did not remember our all-at-once divine nature; we only remembered collective (allness) divinity. Once we identified with a feeling of separation, the act of identification created an energetic attachment to the moment (a snapshot) that became the foundation of our misperception about our divine nature.

Think of it this way. You're in love. You and another person love each other equally in that it feels as though you and the other person are just one energy, one mind, and one heartbeat. You don't know where you end and the other person begins. Then one day, you sense that a change is coming. You will be moving to another place, another city—one that you sense will be different from what you are now experiencing. Some part of you begins to identify with you and your love living in the exact place you are now occupying for the rest of eternity. So, when your thoughts move to the future, you say to yourself, "It is impossible for what lies ahead to be more perfect than now." How do you know? You don't. But because you have identified the state of perfection and located it to the place that you are now experiencing with your love, you perceive nothing can be more perfect. You have identified and attached the state of perfection to a specific location when perfection is nonlocal.

By the time you move to the new city, you have been so affected by the unknown potential of this experience that you no longer feel blissful. There now appears to be a rift, and eventually you even perceive yourself as separate from your love. You think the change, the move to the new city, caused the separation, when in reality, the separation occurred the moment you perceived you would be leaving (separated from) perfection. Identifying with perfection and attaching to the outcome of remaining as you were creates the perception of separation, and it's only a matter of time before conscious proof of separation occurs in that you no longer feel perfect; perfection is now perceived to be outside of you in another place—in the past.

That is basically what happened to all of us. We were in love with love, with divine perfection, with ourselves, and with each other. When the time came for divinity to unfold a new state of consciousness, a state that would allow us, as Divine QUA, to remember the true nature of our divine beingness, we perceived that in this unfoldment something was changing; something would be lost in our ability to experience the same perfection. The reason? We were unable to perceive that we and perfection are identically the same divine energy and there is no difference between the divine energy we hold and the divine energy we express or experience.

It was divinity's intent that we would experience our nonlocal state of beingness while "appearing" as a single, soul consciousness, but really we are allness at onceness expression. (Remember, the "collective all" and the "soul onceness" are the identical divine beingness.)

Any expression is identically the same one divine energy, so even when soul divinity appears to be in a location different than allness divinity, soul divinity is still that same allness, expressing at the onceness.

It's interesting that in any of my sessions where my subconscious took me back to CUSP 10,000, the original act of Creation, there weren't any thoughts about moving forward into whatever the expression of consciousness would unfold. All of my thoughts were about what was occurring, why it was occurring, and what might change or be lost. Doesn't that reveal what is truly important to us as conscious beings? Even at the moment of embarking on our new journey as collective human conscious expression, we aren't always focused on the experience with anticipation or joy. Rather, we are looking backward over our shoulder at what we once enjoyed, holding that as the ideal of what we long to experience once more.

Thinking about this reminds me of a friend of mine, John, who experienced a few of these types of sessions with Angela. One day, he shared with me what happened in one particular session. As he was retelling his experience, he shared that he went back to *conception* and the emotion that he felt coming into his current lifetime was *exhaustion*. In hearing this, I immediately burst out laughing—I know, a little rude, but if you knew John, you would have laughed too. It perfectly sums up the nature that he sometimes expresses: exhausted, bored, and blasé. To picture a soul entering a human incarnation already exhausted before even one experience or event has happened pretty much sums up how a lot of us, as souls, probably feel. We are exhausted by the experience of repeatedly coming into the same place (earth and human incarnation) and feeling worn out from the entire ordeal.

John's experience makes me smile even right now, as I can picture him expelling a huge, long, drawn-out sigh of exasperated breath as he heaves himself, rather unenthusiastically, into human incarnation. I wish you knew him; you'd be rolling on the floor from laughter! (John is a very good sport, so I know he's probably laughing too.)

This is all very reflective of our true nature, in that even though we may get lost for a while in the distractions of earthly experience, there is a spark of something inside of us that consistently keeps us focused on a goal. Even after ten thousand lifetimes, we still recognize that we feel separated from something we consciously perceive as perfection. In

267

our own unique way, each of us is trying to effect, earn, or perfect our way back to that place we think of as home—a place we really never have left, though we do not consciously realize this truth until we are more awakened.

Any concept we hold, whether these or others, means that on some level, we viewed ourselves as trespassers (gatecrashers) to the state of perfection—as though we didn't have the right to be perfection. The concept that we are imperfect is a misperception. We are not now nor have we ever been imperfect. It is impossible. We and divinity are identical in essence, and divinity has no imperfections, ever—period. And neither do we; we only have a conscious misperception of imperfection while experiencing the voyage of awakening.

Many in this physical life view earth as a place where we learn and evolve while perfecting ourselves. That view is also a misperception. In reality, earth is a place where we are afforded the opportunity to view our divine beingness as reflected through our soul consciousness in order to remember the entirety of who we are, from where we originated, our purpose, and our divine destiny.

Life is how we engage our conscious awakening. When we view life in the light of its true purpose, we begin to better understand and embrace life for what it actually affords us. Life provides us with the opportunity to experience, to perceive, and to choose through our free will how we express ourselves in the realities we manifest. Experiences are the vehicle through which we build a strong conscious relationship with our own higher self, our waking consciousness, and our subconscious—our co-creative nature. Thus life and the experiences we live are the tools of conscious awakening.

This all sounds fine until our experiences involve suffering. No one wants to suffer, but sometimes the act of experiencing or witnessing suffering is a powerful tool for awakening or a catalyst for change. Suffering results many times because we will not change until we experience hardship.

Change. It is not something we view as our friend, yet change is an ever-occurring fact of life. Many times we suffer because we cannot change, we cannot let go. We choose to wait for the winds of change to force us to relinquish our grip on that to which we are attached before we turn our attention to any alternatives.

Some people believe that we must suffer to become enlightened. But how can this be true? We are divine energy, and every expression of divine energy is manifested through the pure vibration of love. Therefore, we are not meant to suffer. A lot, though certainly not all, of the suffering we experience is a by-product of misperception, identification, attachment, and choice.

We sometimes suffer because we identify with an object or a concept, which can then create attachment. Then when the object disappears or an outcome changes, we experience suffering. Our suffering, in this case, is created by "identification and attachment." But this is a form of suffering we can change by learning to hold a more detached perspective—one where we don't identify with an object, what we desire, or a particular outcome. Then if, by chance, things change or an outcome doesn't manifest, we will not experience suffering formed by our energetic attachment. Rather, we will trust that whatever is appropriate will manifest. (Please keep in mind that this also applies to affirmations, prayers, etc., *if* we have formed an attachment to the outcome of those affirmations or prayers.)

For example, we live in a home that we love. Our home is an extension of our personality, our desires, or even our security. We are attached to this home by way of our identification of this home in relation to us. One day the home is destroyed by fire. We suffer for years, longing for our home, and wishing we were still living there. In essence, the state of attachment creates our suffering. We identify ourselves with that particular home, which creates an energetic state of attachment, eventually leading to suffering when the thing to which we are attached (in this case, our home) moves away or changes.

If, on the other hand, we were to view our home as a place to occupy while participating in earthbound embodiment, we would remain unattached to the ever-changing nature of matter.

Our home can be comfortable, functional, beautiful, or even expensive, but it is still merely a way station for our physical body while we are experiencing life as an Avatar of Consciousness. If that home is destroyed, we will feel its loss, but only for a moment. Then we will realize that all things transition into other states of being. We will not linger on thoughts of loss but rather choose to move with the rhythm of conscious unfolding, knowing that all is well and the appropriate housing for our body will be regained.

We must always remember that all matter manifests from the vibration of love, and even though love remains constant, matter does not. Matter is always in a state of change as it forms, falls away, and is formed again.

If we do not identify, attachment does not form; and suffering does not result if loss or change occurs. That doesn't mean that we don't sometimes weaken or slip out of our unattached state of conscious intention, but it means that if we endeavor to hold a conscious intention of nonattachment, it will make all the difference in how we experience this world, for it is a world made up of matter; thus, it is ever changing. If we do not learn to recognize and release from identification and attachment, we will be forever bound to suffer because nothing ever remains the same—nothing, that is, except our true nature, our divine beingness of love.

When I was young, it perplexed me as to how so many people could think that their spiritual way was the only correct one. To me, divine benevolence is about unity, not division. I came to respect all spiritual paths because I envisioned those paths were as fingers in the hand of Benevolence, leading all back home no matter their individual beliefs or cultural differences. The world is too diverse and impacted by culture, history, and heritage for any one path to be absolutely the only way, and love is really all that matters, not how one finds one's way to love. Love is love, whether it is love experienced and/or expressed by Christians, Buddhists, Muslims, Hindus, Jews, atheists, etc. And any deity that sits in dominion over any group would not want them hating or discriminating or judging. Yet many people do it in one fashion or another. Why? It is not because they are mean or hateful by nature. It is because they have identified their way as the one and only way, which causes them to be attached to their beliefs to such a degree that they can neither relinquish their current truth nor yield to any other.

The higher conscious thought, "Truth is a multi-dimensional lie; what you believe depends on your angle" perfectly explains why there are so many variations in what we perceive as truth. Throughout our awakening, what we have come to believe as truth is defined by where we are standing in our conscious awareness in relation to our true essence. If we are not standing as our true essence, then an angle of perception to truth is created, and any angle of perception—even a more enlightened one—skews truth. The **reflection of our consciousness** rather than the **knowing of our beingness** will always affect what we come to believe as truth. When our conscious knowingness aligns with our beingness, we will be the essence of truth. Until then, our belief of what is true will be bounded by the limits of our view. That is the reason we may each perceive truth differently—because our belief is not based on "what truth is" but rather "what we perceive truth to be."

Once we consciously recognize that a belief we are holding is a misperception, our consciousness shifts and the attachment to that belief is released. Then by not automatically abandoning our established beliefs or spiritual convictions, we can find peace in the process of allowing our consciousness to awaken in whatever manner is appropriate, retaining some beliefs and releasing others.

Basically, for simplification purposes, at the dawn of collective human consciousness, we took our first steps looking backward with longing to the place we left behind. In truth, we have never, for even one moment, left the state of perfection. Why? It is because the state of perfection is nonlocal divine energy—a divine conscious vibration of love—and there is no outside place that divine consciousness ever really inhabits. Divine consciousness is nonlocal; we are nonlocal. It is energetically impossible to leave perfection because we and perfection are identically the same divine energy. Though we seek to return home, home is not a location outside of us. Home (perfection) is our very own nonlocal state of divine conscious beingness that even now we are in the process of remembering.

As we begin to consciously unfold our remembrance of the who and what of us, it will be easier and easier for us to hold the conscious space of awareness necessary to recognize and interact with the higher conscious presence of our true beingness—the *One Voice* of our still mind and our knowing heart. The One Voice within all of us echoes remembrance of our eternal oneness, leading us home to our essence of benevolent perfection.

The more we consciously awaken, the easier it will be for us to move through our life as though we have our heads out the window, enjoying the ride. Then as full remembrance floods our conscious beingness, we will realize that we are not just experiencing as though we are riding with our heads out the window, enjoying the ride. We are simultaneously perceiving, experiencing, and expressing as the ride, as the wind, as the sun, as the vehicle—*as everything all at the same time.*

That, Avatars of Consciousness, is our true nature—our divine destiny.

Chapter 36

Framing Awareness

Imagine there is a puzzle in front of you. This puzzle contains the uniqueness that is you. It is filled with pieces that fit perfectly and depict your journey throughout all Universe—throughout all time and space.

Some pieces reveal aspects of your personality, while others hold your dreams, your desires, all the destinies you have lived, and all the destinies you are yet to experience.

There are even some pieces that reflect misperceptions you hold about yourself, your life, or Universe. These are the pieces that create subconscious emotional blocks affecting your intentions and dreams.

And there are lots and lots of empty spaces just waiting for other profound pieces in your puzzle to be placed.

Imagine that you are now taking that puzzle, turning it upside down, and dumping out all those pieces. Then consciously move them all aside.

Now imagine that you are about to set new pieces within the ongoing puzzle of you. But these pieces don't just carry words; they also carry energetic intention. These pieces are imbued with the vibration of love and the conscious intention that as you read, you will be energetically connected with your own knowing—consciously awakening to the true nature of your beingness in whatever way is benevolent and appropriate for you.

Chapter 37

Puzzle Piece One— Where Is My Home?

Where is my home? Where do I come from? Where did I originate? We might as well begin with the most profound puzzle piece of all—our home.

Even though there is really no when to our nature, as we are not comprised of a linear essence, we don't need to know when in order to know where we call home.

The best way to describe the place that is home to all of us is *divine energy*—the divine conscious vibration of love.

Let's take out a map. Okay, is this place that is our home located as a place in this world—in this galaxy—anywhere? Of course the answer is no. Our true home is not located on any map anywhere because the very nature of our home is nonlocal. No matter what we have ever thought, imagined, or dreamed, our home is not what it seems. We are not what we seem. Nothing is what it seems.

We live on earth in a corporeal body and we appear real, but what makes us real is what consciously manifests through the divine vibration of love.

Our home is the divine energy of benevolent bliss, pure love, and absolute knowing. There are no realms, dimensions, realities, or places that ever exist outside of divine energy—outside of us.

Although our home is nonlocal divine energy, I can tell you for certain that it is real. I've experienced it. Our home is beyond words or imaginings and a knowing that all of us share—even if we do not consciously remember. No matter the lifetimes, embodiments, or extraordinary events we experience, there is a remembrance of our home held deeply beneath the veil of our own human consciousness. Our innate longing to return to benevolent love, peace, and belonging is reflected in our physical lives by our need to find peace, to feel connected, and to experience love.

Our home is a beautiful state of divine energy—perfection, love, knowing—bliss. There are no borders, no definition, no limits, and absolutely no solid matter. There is only divine energy—the divinely perfect conscious vibration of love. Yet anything and everything imaginable can be made manifest or made real (perceived, experienced, and expressed) through our profound home.

Right now imagine that you have the ability to intuitively perceive everything we call home. You are able to perceive the interwoven connectedness of everything to everything else, and there is not one single feeling, thought, person, place, or thing not connected to everything else. It appears as a knowing within your mind, and you realize no one is ever really alone or separate. That is impossible because we are eternally one divine conscious energy of love.

It is beautiful. Anything imaginable exists, and nothing that we can ever imagine compares to the sheer bliss of being home in our benevolent divine perfection. Even now I can remember the bliss of belonging—the feeling of being home as benevolent oneness.

As a little girl, I experienced this place while breathing as a conscious human being, and it is beyond words, beyond anything imaginable. How do you capture absolute stillness, pure love, all-knowing awareness, and peaceful bliss with a human mind and a limited way of communicating? It seems impossible, yet we capture it through our innate knowing, our ever-present divine nature that remembers.

The remembrance travels through every thought, feeling, dream, or intention. We are the inseparable nature of divine love, and that vibration connects us to everything and everyone. When we allow ourselves to experience love without boundaries, we are love in its purest form, and there is no limit to what can well up from deep within us or to where that love can take us.

Love moves through us in the poignant way in which we embrace each other in friendship, companionship, and love. Benevolent love fills our hearts, our minds, and our beingness until we realize that love is a conscious vibration beyond even the boundaries of human embodiment, beyond time, and beyond space. Love is eternally the pathway of our home.

Imagine that you, too, were with me as that little girl of nine, and that you, too, were pulled into the inner space of divine conscious love ... our home. Feel the love flowing through you, around you, and as you. The pure vibration of love carries all thoughts, all feelings, all knowing; and that love is moving through you in perfect harmony as your own vibration. Benevolence expressing as you reveals your essence—your true divine nature. You are the stillness that surrounds you and the peace that fills you. You want for nothing, as there is nothing outside of you. You are home to yourself, absolute in your knowing that there is nothing more peaceful, blissful, or perfect than the divine energy of your eternal beingness. You are love itself, fully consciously aware that all that you have ever loved or will love— everything that you are—is in this moment.

Eternal, limitless divine energy is simultaneously our home, ourselves, each other, and the all of everything.

Imagine that you are ready to place your first puzzle piece in the puzzle of you.

Let's label this puzzle piece, *"Where is my home?"* and then envision the following description, the following words, written below the puzzle piece:

Where is my home?

My home is divine energy ... the divine conscious vibration of love.

If you don't grasp the full meaning or how it can be true, that's all right. Don't worry. It may take a while. After all, how can profundity really be summed up by eleven words?

Every puzzle piece carries a gift. Imagine now that you are adding to your puzzle piece the words, *"The gift of my home,"* and envision the following words:

The Gift of My Home

My home and I are identical in nature. My home and I are always eternally perfect, eternally unchanging divine energy, yet anything imaginable can be perceived, experienced, expressed, or made manifest through the divine conscious vibration of love. Any thoughts, feelings, words, worlds, dimensions, and universes are made real through the conscious intention of divine love. My home is benevolent perfection, and I am even now home in my beingness of divine perfection.

Chapter 38

Puzzle Piece Two—
What Am I?

What are we? Well, it's easier to answer what we aren't. We aren't just human—that's for sure—and we aren't just spirit either.

Yes, we are in a body, a human form, but that form is not really solid. Actually, nothing is completely solid at its core. Everything is really unlimited energetic potential (nothingness) appearing as subatomic particles with empty space between them. Why do I think this? I saw it a long time ago when I was seated cross-legged on the floor in a darkened room meditating. At some point in the meditation, a higher conscious thought came into my mind that I should open my eyes and look down at my lower body. As I opened my eyes, I was surprised to see that the physical appearance of a solid body was gone. Instead, I only saw energy—rapidly moving quasar-like energy. I now appeared to be just vibrating energy, and that vibrating energy was also emitting a subtle light.

It wasn't the first time I had seen light-filled, energetic quasars vibrating in the air, but it was the first time I saw energetic light replacing the lower half of my physical body. The light coming off of the quasars was interesting, as well as the fact that there wasn't an appearance of physical form present in the space at all. It occurred to me that the vibrating energy was creating the light. But what was causing matter to transform into pure energy? In thinking about it, the only thing present both when I appeared as physical form and as pure energy was consciousness. It couldn't have been anything else. My higher conscious state was affecting the molecules of my body, making them vibrate faster and shifting them into a more subtle energetic state.

To me, this experience was physical proof that we are pure energy—light, color, and sound—vibrating at certain energetic frequencies. Those vibrational frequencies allow the molecular structure of our cells to change, making us denser or lighter. The higher the frequency, the more rapid the vibration and the lighter (less dense, more light filled) the form.

There was now no doubt in my mind that consciousness—through prayer, meditation, and intent—alters vibrational rate and energetic form. Consciousness affects the vibrational frequency of molecules, shifting them energetically. The higher the consciousness, the higher the vibration; the higher the vibration, the higher the consciousness. They are inseparable.

So where does consciousness exist in the molecular structure of the world of matter? Is it inside the cells, is it around the cells, or is it a connected power flowing through all cells? Divine consciousness, divine energy, exists as the pure vibration of love, which is everything. Divine energy is a beautiful tapestry of energetically conscious love, and we and that divine tapestry are identically the same. Think of it like a spider web; all the threads are entwined. This spider web is the woven energetic fabric of the divine conscious vibration of love. Every intent, every thought creation, is a conscious thread in this divine tapestry, simultaneously interconnected as all other threads. When one thing moves or expresses within the intrinsic fabric of divine energy, the vibration is instantly known (experienced) by everything. It is not a web outside of divinity. Divinity is the web, the fabric of all, and the threads interwoven through all aspects of divinity conditions the tapestry that is created—an ever-changing tapestry of light and love.

Don't think of it as a power existing outside the beingness of divinity. Think of it as the synergetic pattern of divinity, which explains our inner connectedness to ourselves, our soul, each other, and all consciousness.

While meditating on the best way to describe what we are, the phrase "Avatars of Consciousness" floated into my mind. Initially, I had no clue as to why this phrase was given to me from higher (divine) consciousness. But when I looked up the word "avatar" on line at *www. merriam-webster.com* (*Merriam-Webster Dictionary*), one meaning of the word avatar is:

"A variant phase or version of a continuing basic entity."

Based upon all that I have experienced, this is a perfect and apropos description of what we are.

The phrase "continuing *basic* entity" means the foundation of something that doesn't originate from anything else yet extends on—continues on into other forms. For example, what is the continuing basic entity in my case? You would think it would be my soul, because my physical incarnation of Carol is a variant version of the continuing basic entity of my soul. Up until a couple of years ago, this application would have resonated with my perception of me, my soul, and Universe. Technically, though, it would be a misperception. My soul is not the basic entity from which all variations of me extend. Why? Because our soul can be traced back to the original basic entity of the divine conscious vibration of love.

All variant phases or versions continue from the basic entity of divine energy or divine consciousness. Everything originates from the divine conscious vibration of love, so divine consciousness is the continuing basic entity.

Okay. If divine consciousness is the continuing basic entity, then what is the variant phase or version?

A variant phase or version of divine consciousness in my case would not only be who I am now (Carol) but also any other version or expression of consciousness I have ever been in any and all prior lifetimes—whether I expressed as a human embodiment, as a spiritual form, or as an energy, such as the vibration of love or the essence of collective unconscious.

Thus, the variant phase or version would be every version of divine consciousness I am now expressing, have ever expressed in the past, or will ever express in the future. It is anything and everything that I will ever reflect as or project as in any realm, dimension, or state of consciousness. And because divine consciousness is one inseparable, indivisible energy, I am simultaneously each and every and all consciousness.

Wow! Did you understand? This is what you are too!

You are a *variant version* (avatar) of a *continuing basic entity* (consciousness). Think of it as though you are a conscious projection, reflecting as a conscious intention of divine energy.

We are all *Avatars of Consciousness*. Isn't that amazing?

The phrase Avatars of Consciousness is a perfectly succinct description of "What am I?" because the word "avatar" can also describe a divine beingness that is incarnating as physical form. That is most definitely apropos to us. We are one divine beingness expressing as any and all conscious forms.

For now, let's ponder the extraordinary possibilities as we take out our second puzzle piece.

Let's go ahead and label our second puzzle piece, *"What am I?"* while envisioning the following words:

What am I?
I am an Avatar of Consciousness.

It is now understandable that our physical bodies would remain here while our consciousness moves on because our human body is the form we utilize and through which we express in this particular dimension. But our consciousness is not limited to physical form. Our consciousness can project anywhere. This is the reason we can energetically interact with others through dreams or telepathy, even departed loved ones. Our consciousness moves on, but our physical matter (our body) remains here because it is merely an aspect of the manifested energy (human form) into which we project our true beingness—our divine consciousness.

We are not barred entry into any world, dimension, or state of consciousness because we are pure divine energy, and divine energy simultaneously exists as all states of consciousness. The most wonderful aspect to being us is that we will continue to be Avatars of Consciousness even after this lifetime, because our consciousness is not only limitless, it is eternal.

Although our consciousness is eternal, our physical bodies are not; they are physical reminders of the impermanence of ever-changing matter. It is important that we consciously recognize that the safety of our body, our beingness, is always paramount. It is our body that tethers us to a physical, matter-based dimension, allowing our consciousness to unfold. We need our body to be healthy so we can consciously experience our profound nature.

Always there are energetic laws associated with every plane of consciousness that define the fabric of our conscious experience, our embodiment, and for now, the fabric of our current state of individual human consciousness does not allow us free, unbounded physical and energetic mobility. But even though our body is more subject to the physical laws of this dimension, our consciousness is not. It is possible for us to more lucidly experience multiple states of consciousness while in our physical bodies by raising our energetic vibration and developing higher conscious awareness in waking consciousness.

We are at the beginning of our understanding of what we are, and as we continue to unfold our knowing and utilize specific tools, we will engage our consciousness, intend our unfolding, and transform ourselves into consciously aware Avatars of Consciousness until one day in our not too distant future, we will be fully awakened, remembering our true divine "identity."

The joy of finally learning the answer to *"What am I?"* was extraordinary to experience. Our true potential is the unbounded, limitless expression of divine energy as Avatars of Consciousness— avatars of love.

Of course, consciously perceiving our true nature will not instantly eradicate our problems or drastically alter our life. But by holding conscious intention and becoming more attentive, we will begin to more consciously awaken to the quantum aspects of our Universe and of our nature, enabling us to more intentionally unfold our true beingness in the lives we live. The true nature of ourselves and of everything is always simultaneously both quantum and classical (allness and oneness, wave and particle, all-at-once).

Remember that just because we are awakening doesn't mean we won't still experience life. Life is all about experiencing; that's how we unfold our conscious remembrance. But learning to experience our lives with more conscious intention while maintaining a positive attitude can make all the difference in how our experiences affect us. We each must still walk our predestined paths, but by awakening to our higher consciousness, we can learn to energetically impact the destinies and realities we live.

Being more consciously aware or spiritually aligned isn't about avoiding our life; it is about recognizing what hinders us from experiencing our true self and reconciling anything that does not allow us to live as fully and consciously aware as possible. After all, we are a profound and phenomenal beingness, and the more we consciously understand the what of it all, the more joyfully we can experience that what in our lives.

Now it is time to embrace the gift that is associated with "*What am I?*"

Imagine that you are adding the words, "*The gift of what I am*" to your puzzle piece, and as you write the following words, feel them energetically flow through you as a knowing:

The Gift of What I Am

As a *fully awakened* Avatar of Consciousness, I can consciously project or manifest through any state of consciousness, dimension, or reality as any essence, any energy, or any form. My true beingness is the unbounded, limitless expression of divine All-at-Once Consciousness.

Just let it soak in for a few minutes. It's really, really phenomenal when we begin thinking about our potential because there are no limits to what we can consciously experience and express!

Chapter 39

Puzzle Piece Three—
Who Am I?

"*Who am I?*" This is the question we eventually all ask ourselves. Merely the act of asking the question reflects that we are not congruent with our true essence; otherwise the question wouldn't come up. This question goes beyond our identity in this world, as our identity is really just a reflection of our nature rather than the answer to the question of "Who am I?"

For example, if you are male, you don't ask yourself if you are male. Being male is already congruent with your perceived nature. By asking the question "Who am I?" we are trying to rectify something we perceive to be incongruent with our nature. This is a clue that something is amiss in our picture.

All great philosophers or simple men who have asked this question probably already know who they are as far as their name, reputation, characteristics, flaws, etc. Yet they ask this question because they sense they are something beyond what is experienced through the lens of themselves. They have glimpsed something they haven't rectified with their perception of self. Any experience or thought can grant them a glimpse of another beingness at work behind the veil—one they have no ability to recognize because it cannot be categorized.

If they pursue understanding "Who am I?" in earnest, it will open up doorways that may eventually lead to a concept that they are a spiritual being that is one with Universe. But that concept is still not completely embraced by them, as there is a persistent little feeling that something is still not quite right.

Like many people, I've gotten to the "I am one with Universe" concept related to "Who am I?" But I am also Carol. So how do I reconcile which one I am and then live my life in a way that fulfills the who I am of me?

I sensed the what of me wasn't really human and the who of me wasn't really Carol.

Isn't this piece, *"Who am I?"* the one that causes us the most turmoil, angst, or reflection? It really stirs things up inside of us, as it involves an ongoing process of tweaking our perceived identity, and, every so often we encounter discrepancies in an *us* we perceive that we cannot identify. These discrepancies can be perceived through glimpses of us we experience through dreams, altered states of consciousness, interaction with our subconscious, waking conscious remembrance of a past life, interaction with angels or other benevolent powers that intervene in our lives, or even profound waking conscious experiences.

But we are not our identity. Our identity is merely the name under which we operate our vehicles of human embodiment. Think of it like a title to a vehicle, where the vehicle is the human body with all of its mechanisms, seen and unseen. Our name is the identification given to the entirety of all the various aspects we have and will bring forth that are manifested and unmanifested by way of being a human being.

The who of us is not the outward manifestation of our thoughts or feelings or expressions, as those are merely the by-products of an unseen energy. That unseen energy is always at the helm, directing us and propelling us down pathways of thoughts in our mind and feelings in our body.

Right now our consciousness is expressing through a particular, unique human embodiment. But that human embodiment is just a vehicle for us to simultaneously bridge our waking consciousness to that of our subconscious and higher consciousness.

In this particular lifetime, we are expressing as a human being on earth, but there are other dimensions besides earth in which we have experienced conscious lifetimes. Remember, the venue of collective human consciousness is not limited to just our seen universe or this dimension. Its eternal vastness is indefinable. And although we don't want to get sidetracked by thoughts about other dimensions or realities, these thoughts are very interesting and can enlighten us to many things. For example, it may explain why some people believe they are connected to beings from other planets, stars, worlds, or dimensions, such as elementals (fairies), extraterrestrials, angels, star beings, light beings, etc. We shouldn't automatically discount their belief just because it is not our conscious reality. It could be that these particular Avatars of Consciousness experienced many of their lifetimes in dimensions, stars, or worlds other than that of earth. And even though these souls may not consciously remember these past lives, they carry an unconscious affinity to a particular dimension or world that can be consciously awakened in this lifetime by a book, a dream, a memory, or someone sharing an experience.

These remembrances or affinities may well explain why we sometimes view things so differently from one another. Some of our journeys as Avatars of Consciousness unfolded paths more consciously remembered through earthbound lifetimes while other paths are more associated with lifetimes in alternate dimensional realities. We do not all experience exactly the same thing; therefore, we do not all hold the identical conscious perspective. And although we share in what every other Avatar of Consciousness—every other soul divinity—has experienced, as we are all the same one divine consciousness, we may not yet be consciously aware of the experiences of others.

The answer to the question of "Who am I?" may be a lot more than we can consciously perceive or even define.

As Avatars of Consciousness, we are variant phases of a continuing basic entity. This means that we have experienced multiple phases (lifetimes) as a variety of embodiments and expressions, but we are always one basic energetic beingness ... divine conscious love (perfection).

Imagine that as divine energy, divine consciousness, we are a mind. There is nothing outside of that mind. Everything that is experienced is a projection of divine conscious intention reflected back through the tapestry of divine consciousness. Every reflection appears real, with the definition of "real" contingent upon the dimension into which it is being reflected. For example, a divine conscious intention reflected in a less dense dimension, such as heaven, would appear to be more ethereal—spiritual in nature. And an intention reflected in a denser dimension, such as our seen universe, would appear more solid—matter-based in nature. Thus, a divine conscious intention being "projected" in the dimension of our seen universe would "reflect" (manifest) as matter.

How many of us have dreams that are so real that we expect to be in that very dream reality when we find ourselves awakened? It sure appears real when we are dreaming it. It is real—because everything is made real (manifested) through consciousness.

Because we are in human embodiment, we naturally associate reality with solid, physical matter, but in actuality, nothing is real in that sense because nothing is really solid at its core. Therefore, if we cease thinking of real as only associated with solid, physical existence, we will more easily understand that reality is a perception that is influenced by consciousness. Everything is real and unreal at the same time. It appears real and it is made very real by consciousness; yet it does not really exist in a fixed, localized state. That is a perception only. Anything that manifests from consciousness really exists—just not in the way we have always perceived, as a fixed absolute. Anything that is manifested in our physical plane of consciousness—whether it is a thought, a feeling, a knowing, a subatomic particle, an atom, an element, or a physical thing—is real yet not real at the same time. Most importantly, until we can *consciously* hold the pure state of divine consciousness, we are bound by the reality that we live. Once we have fully awakened and are expressing our divine all-at-once conscious nature, we will be able to hold dominion over reality because we will be in pure consciousness. But until that time, which may not even be while we are experiencing this type of an earth plane dimension, we must respect the boundaries of conscious reality, for it is very real for us as human conscious beings.

In actuality, everything is a projected intention of divine consciousness reflected as a conscious manifestation upon the energetic fabric of divine consciousness. Think of it as though divine consciousness is envisioning the movie, producing the movie, creating and providing the movie set, directing the movie, playing all parts in the movie, and watching the movie all at the same time.

Don't start thinking that you don't want to be just a consciousness because you feel that isn't real. You don't perceive it accurately if that's what you're thinking, because everything is real, but the realities aren't really all there is to you. If you don't want to be consciousness, that thought may be based on fear because you have created identities or identified with a projection that you believe is either the real you or your real home (earth).

Maybe you are afraid because you think being a consciousness means you won't live, be real, enjoy, experience, or touch your loved ones. Or maybe you think there won't be anything to go back to when you awaken, as it will all be nothingness. These are scary thoughts and a huge misperception.

All of those types of thoughts are coming from our misperception at the Creation of collective human consciousness. Our original misperception doesn't allow us to perceive the truth of our profound nature and the true nature of divinity. As such, we are always trying to anchor ourselves *to* something or identify *with* something.

We are divine energy (divinity), and divinity has no identity. Divinity is absolute allness at the same time it is absolute nothingness (simultaneously both manifested reality and unmanifested potentiality).

Remember those parts of spiritual teachings where we just have to have faith because we can't comprehend the entirety of it all. Now I understand why faith sometimes feels abandoned by logic. It is because when our logic does not resolve our questions, all we have remaining is our knowing or our faith. When applying logic to the true nature of us and our Universe, there seems to be a paradox. The laws we understand (gravity, motion, etc.) don't apply—yet, they do, but not in a real sense but rather in a perceived sense. It's more than a little confusing.

There are many complexities and paradoxes of non-matter consciousness appearing to exist in a matter world. The paradox comes when you try and prove our physical, seen universe exists when it is really just a reflection of divine conscious intention. How can you ever find the beginning of something that is a reflection of a conscious intention? It would be like proving that a shadow is a person if you could never actually examine the person but were rather just viewing the projection or reflection of the person—the shadow. Or it would be like viewing a movie and needing to know where the main character was born. If the birth information was not found in the content of the movie, how can you ever learn the character's origin? Remember, it's just a movie, and the character isn't really based anywhere. The image in a movie that is projected upon a movie screen is not an absolute reality; it's a perceived reality only. The experiences are flat, non-matter intentions (projections) captured as reflected images. Whether the character was born in the woods or in Paris is only important if we get caught up in the story as a method for proving something else—in this case, the movie character's origins.

For a moment, let's apply that thought to our physical world. If our seen universe is, in fact, a projection of divine consciousness, then we are trying to find answers to the mystery of the origin of the seen universe by investigating or testing a reflection. It is not to say we won't start to perceive that it is something vastly different than what we imagine, but how would we ever get to the actual point of origin? The theories would reveal aspects of the projection only.

Eventually, though, I would think that science would hit a wall because concrete proof of what we are really seeking doesn't exist in the shadow. To find what we are seeking, we need to turn our mind around, change our perspective, and look back at what is casting the shadow.

In actuality, we are divine consciousness projecting through our own All-at-Once Consciousness as Avatars of Consciousness. We are simultaneously everything all-at-once; both the projector and the projected.

In each and every lifetime, we hold the essence of our same soul divinity, and each new incarnation is a projection or variation of the continuing basic entity of our divine consciousness. Sound familiar? It should. It's the pathway that each of us as soul divinity (Avatars of Consciousness) have experienced.

When we shift to a new conscious lifetime expression as an Avatar of Consciousness, we are carrying the divine blueprint (all knowing) within us of not only the lifetime we are to experience but also of every lifetime we have ever experienced. Actually, within each of us, we carry the divine blueprint of what all Avatars of Consciousness have experienced, are experiencing, and will experience because our individual subconscious holds the identical all-knowingness as higher (divine) consciousness.

Therefore, even now when we are only able to conceptualize ourselves as being a mental, emotional, spiritual self in physical form in a human lifetime, we are not just experiencing as our consciousness but we are simultaneously experiencing as all Avatars of Consciousness—All-at-Once Consciousness.

Are you excited about yourselves yet? If you are, then the remembrance of your true nature is awakening in you. I'm smiling, because I feel it too.

It appears that we all won't awaken at the same time, but since there is no time or space in divine energy, I assure you that we will all awaken to our remembrance together ... You now share a thought that is a spiritual breadcrumb, and you are personally connected to me and feeling what I feel, knowing what I know, right now. Remarkable, isn't it? Oh, and this next part of the spiritual thought will really make you sit up: I wrote this thought at the exact moment you read it, as everything occurs all-at-once.

Although it is difficult to conceptualize in human consciousness, there really is no time and space—no past, present, or future—in divine energy. Think of "time and space" as an "air bubble in collective human consciousness," designed and created by divinity to give us "room" to perceive the truth of our beingness.

You are Divine QUA (divine energy, the divine conscious vibration of love) expressing as an Avatar of Consciousness. The what of you is an Avatar of Consciousness, and the who of you is divine energy. Feel it. Know it to be true. Don't base who you are on any identity or expression of that identity in this lifetime or any other. Especially don't get caught up in playing divinity. Divinity is not a role. Divinity is our truest self. Also, don't limit yourself by thinking *I am God*, thereby getting caught up in identity and ego. Ego and identity create a conscious perception of separation and the nature of our divine beingness is indivisible and inseparable.

We are one divine beingness. Embrace our indivisible nature by holding the concept "I am that I am" consciously within you. This terminology perfectly captures the nature of the divine. There is no ego identification and there is no separation in this concept; there is only limitless, eternal divine beingness.

Though you may not immediately feel any differently, as you continue remembering, you will know that all the things that created suffering and fear related to perceived separation are shifting away. You realize that your original misperception is gone even though it may not yet appear gone. Just let knowing and peace and possibility flow through your consciousness.

So, are you ready to place the third piece of your puzzle? It's an amazing piece, and it will bring even more amazement as more of your knowing, your remembrance, unfolds in your conscious awareness.

For now, let's just take out that third puzzle piece and label this puzzle piece, "*Who am I?*" and imagine the following words:

Who am I?
I am divine energy; all-at-once divine conscious love.

Just let the knowing of these words move through you, fully embracing that this is your true beingness, with no more fear about separation. Feel no more fear about whether your individual identity, your consciousness, will continue when you depart earthbound existence. Your consciousness is eternal; your true beingness is eternal.

Although subconscious patterns may need to be cleared for you to liberate your true self from the self-imposed shackles of misperception or from what is incongruent within you, the fear that you will never become perfection or oneness is consciously gone. Now all you need do is *be*—unfold the perfection that is already your true nature. Gone is the fear that your individual nature is insignificant or destined to forever repeat lifetime after lifetime with no conscious awareness of your purpose or your destiny.

Now all you need do is remember and engage in a process of unfolding that remembrance through your awakening. The searching for the way to end separation and find our way home to our perfection is over. There is no true separation; never did we leave our home. Even now we are where we have always been. Never was our perfection lost or did we lose one ounce of our beingness. It is impossible, for we are All-at-Once Consciousness, one divine vibration of love, limitless and eternal perfection.

We are merely asleep in our perfection. Imagine even now that we are slumbering in the warmth of our own bed, home as our benevolent oneness, and we are journeying in our consciousness so we will awaken from our dream of misperception and remember our extraordinary truth.

In order to fully be our true essence, we must endeavor through our journey of awakening—a journey that involves reconciling the incongruencies between our true self and the self-consciousness that has unfolded from our misperception, fear, suffering, worry, longing, doubt, etc. Then, once we release our original misperception, our consciousness shifts and we are more energetically aligned for the conscious knowing of our true nature to come forth—awakening the *true* us that is unfolding from the dream of misperception.

It's time to embrace the gift of your true divine beingness. So, let's add the words, *"The gift of who I am"* to your puzzle piece, along with the description below:

The Gift of Who I Am
I am an eternally divine beingness without beginning or end—ever-present, all-knowing, all-loving perfection.

Wow ... that gives me chills and I already knew it. (A big group hug for *us*—collective human consciousness—because this is the magnificent truth of each of us—a truth that we can't even begin to consciously comprehend in our current human embodiment!)

Note: Before we move to the next puzzle piece, it is very important to understand that these puzzle pieces represent our divine beingness, but even when we are able to more consciously express our true nature while in individual human embodiment, we are still subject to the constricts of this earth plane *physical* reality. This reality is where we have chosen to experience, to express, and to live—and it is as real as real can be.

Even when we are awakened, we can still feel physical pain and die in this dimension. Awakening is a profound state of consciousness, but that consciousness is still housed in a physical matter body.

We are living in a matter-based reality, and as such, our consciousness can affect our body to a certain extent. But to mistake conscious awakening with total transcendence of physical reality would be reckless disregard for the matter-based reality that co-exists with the non-matter reality of this world. Awakening is about recognizing the true nature of what we embody (our divine All-at-Once Consciousness) so that we can shift our consciousness, release our feelings of separation and fear, and awaken to our divine destiny.

Imagine we are all caterpillars, yet our true nature is a butterfly. If, as a caterpillar, we attempt flying, we will fall or even perish. As the caterpillar, we must go through the cocoon stage of awareness before our metamorphosis occurs. Once we have awakened and unfold as a new expression (the butterfly), we will be able to fly, but this is just an expression of our beingness. We will still be bound by earth-plane reality in the sense that if we were to fly into a fan, we would still perish, "awakened" butterfly or not.

Awakening is a way to soar in our consciousness, but we must still live in our physical bodies.

It is a time to be excited about our true nature by imagining that we are even now caterpillars in the cocoon state of awareness, getting a sneak preview of our true butterfly state.

How excited do you image that slow-moving creature, that caterpillar, is to learn that it is really a beautiful being that can fly! I'm sure it would blow the caterpillar's mind, but the caterpillar would still need to go through the process of unfolding in order to experience its butterfly essence. It is the same for us.

Remember, there is no room for fantasy in All-at-Once Consciousness, because our reality is beyond profundity. And although conscious expression of our true nature will not happen overnight—or maybe even in this lifetime—that is not the purpose of knowing the truth of our nature. The purpose of knowing our truth is so each of us will consciously perceive our true nature, allowing a shift in consciousness to occur. This shift alleviates our conscious misperception so that in future energetic expressions (experiences in this lifetime or even future lifetimes), we will never again experience the conscious pain of separation that our misperception has caused. Thus, our future choices will be based upon our true nature rather than on misperception and fear.

We have consciously contracted to energetically dwell in this reality plane (earthly physical embodiment), and we must always be mindful that certain laws will always govern us in this dimension—but that will not prevent us from awakening so we can more consciously perceive, experience, and express the pure love and pure knowingness that is the profound essence of our divine beingness.

Chapter 40

Puzzle Piece Four—
Why Am I Here?

*If everything is relative and
relativity is a void, where
does that leave us?*

*What is my purpose for being on earth—or for any of this? Why am I
here?*

These two questions held me spellbound throughout my life. This
was my game, a continuing game that mesmerized me. Once the
original questions came into my mind, I was like all the childhood
detectives I loved: Sherlock Holmes, Charlie Chan, and the Hardy
Boys. To me, this was the greatest mystery of all, and throughout my
life I was hot on the trail to solving it or cold and taking long breaks
to live my life.

Who hasn't thought these questions, for what mystery is greater
than our mystery? The worst part in trying to unravel our mystery
is that many of the higher conscious insights seem to be riddles: "If
everything is relative and relativity is a void, where does that leave
us?"

You know the drill. Your mind tries so hard to understand but
yields only tangled mazes and headaches or insights you cannot really
comprehend at the time, which means future headaches trying to
unravel them, too.

These thoughts (*Why am I here? What is the purpose of being on
earth?*) have enlivened me and defeated me over the years, but still the
need to know persists.

My very earliest thoughts about why I was here centered around
following spiritual teachings so I would go to heaven, where I'd be
judged on how well I did in living my life. Once in heaven, I'd see my
loved ones, be reunited with divinity, and live in bliss.

But by the time I was thirteen years old, the spiritual teachings I was familiar with as a child were set aside, because they didn't account for major aspects of my beingness (clairsentience, etc.), and if they did, it was only to point out that my beliefs were going to cause me to be lost forever (hell, I guess). I found out very early on in this life, through interacting with others while sharing my experiences, that there really wasn't much tolerance in mainstream religion (or even the world) for someone like me. I learned to be very guarded and reticent about my beliefs and my experiences.

Quite unexpectedly, that all changed one Saturday morning in Florida while I was drinking coffee. Coffee hounds always find the good coffee spots, and I had found a great one about ten miles from home that I visited every Saturday morning. It was my Saturday-morning ritual. I'd sit at the counter and either read or simply enjoy the sheer pleasure of drinking coffee.

One Saturday a young Catholic priest seated next to me struck up a conversation about a book I was reading. It turned into many Saturdays drinking coffee and discussing varied topics, including some of my experiences and beliefs about divinity and spiritual matters. It was never planned; we just seemed to end up there the same time many Saturdays. He was a wonderful conversationalist and a very love-filled person.

On one particular Saturday, we were discussing my feelings of alienation from church, family, friends, and acquaintances due to my unusual experiences and interaction with angelic beings and divinity. My spiritual interactions and paranormal experiences were my secret world, one that early on in my life I learned not to share openly because I found that most people, especially boyfriends, did not want to hear or experience anything they perceived to be "paranormal."

The thoughts this wonderful priest shared with me changed how I viewed my life. He told me that he could understand why some people, even other clerics, would certainly not accept me, but that he recognized me as a spiritual mystic. He then began to speak about the path of a mystic, explaining that he recognized my deeply personal relationship and mystical experiences with divinity as being based upon my feelings of love and adoration for the divine. As he was speaking, I couldn't help but feel like this man was looking directly into my soul, as he was perfectly describing my deepest desire to experience pure communion with divinity, which is founded upon an internal knowingness—a profoundly loving sense of connectedness with divinity that is unconditional and beyond explanation.

He went on to say that most likely my paranormal experiences would be perceived by people to be a result of my desire to develop as a psychic rather than a by-product of my deep spiritual bond with divinity. He then asked me how I felt about being psychic, and I responded that I did not understand how I even possessed these abilities as I had never been interested in pursuing psychic development. For some reason I cannot explain, these abilities just seem to come naturally without any intention or effort on my part. My only desire is experiencing divine energy purely for the sake of love without any ulterior motive other than the bliss of the relationship.

At my response, the priest nodded his head and told me that he believed my psychic abilities were really spiritual blessings stemming from my relationship with divinity. He then advised me to never doubt this relationship, and to keep my focus on how I viewed myself and divinity rather than on how others viewed me, as their opinions might possibly cause me to shift my focus and lose faith in my connection with the divine.

I expressed surprise that his explanation of the term "mystic" had so perfectly described my relationship, as I had always assumed that a mystic was just a more gifted psychic—which is a word that does not at all describe the depth of my unconditional love and spiritual connection with divinity.

As he smiled at me and continued drinking his coffee and talking, I realized that he was the only person I had ever encountered who really understood what moves me as a soul. It was one of the purest encounters with another soul that I've ever experienced.

Over the years, I have thought how fortunate I was to meet him and hear his words of encouragement, wisdom, and love, as he brought me deep peace about myself and my relationship with divinity. For the first time in my life, I clearly understood my path and myself, releasing my need for others to understand me. More importantly, from that day forward I never thought of myself in any other way than as a mystic.

There is no doubt that this wonderful light, this loving priest, was placed in my life to help me find peace and understanding within myself—an understanding that allowed me to embrace my path and the unusual life I was living.

As my spiritual awareness continued to unfold and I came to understand more and more about myself, I began to think of earth as a learning place. Why else were we incarnating lifetime after lifetime if not to learn something? So, if earth is our school of learning, then what are we supposed to be earning our degree in exactly?

Though I didn't know the answer to this question, I did realize that some things from our past lives must carry over as life lessons. Why? One reason is that for as long as I can remember, I was concerned about the consequences or ramifications of my actions on others. That concept doesn't usually concern a ten-year-child, but it very much concerned me. For instance, one year at Halloween, a group of us were standing in front of a house where one of the boys wanted to soap the windows and toilet paper the trees. No way was that going to happen! I started complaining so loudly in protest that everyone gave up the idea and ran off down the street. My main concern was about the people in the house and how those actions would affect them. I was always concerned about the results of my actions upon people on the receiving end. Why was this concept burned so deeply into my psyche?

For years, I had no idea.

Then, quite unexpectedly, I found the answer during one of my sessions with Angela. In this particular session, I was utilizing an affirmation about receiving from Universe, and it took me back to a prior lifetime where I was expressing in the *role* of a *thief* and the *emotion* was *guilt*. Surprisingly, muscle testing revealed the emotional block of guilt was not due to the act of stealing, as stealing was a necessity in order to feed my family. I felt no guilt at all about stealing. The emotional block was centered on my guilt about the *ramifications* my theft had upon the ones from whom I stole—the negative effect or the consequences my stealing had upon their lives.

By the end of that lifetime as a thief, I deeply regretted the ramifications of my actions and carried this feeling forward as a subconscious emotional block into my current lifetime. This subconscious emotional block translated into a belief, in my current lifetime, that "if I had something, then it meant that someone else was going without." This significantly impacted my ability in this lifetime to not only receive but also to manifest, as there was a subconscious emotional feeling of guilt surrounding the acceptance of abundance because I subconsciously linked "my having abundance" to "someone else going without."

It is very powerful when we recognize a truth in our life. This session helped me to realize that we have lived many times previously and stored away experiences and emotional themes that we use as lights to guide us, energies to balance, or most importantly, tools to awaken us.

Eventually, as I continued my spiritual unfoldment, I came to think of myself as a spiritual being centered in Universe reflecting through self. This seemed to sum up my concept of being on earth. Basically, I never related to why I was on earth, as my heart and mind were much more centered on divinity and spiritual things.

I spent a lot of time reflecting on why I was on earth, and I just could not fully embrace the concept that earth is an academy of learning. Something about the concept seemed inaccurate. Finally, I realized the error in the earth-is-where-we-attend-school-to-become-perfected concept.

It was this: If nothing exists outside of divinity and divinity is perfect, then how can we be anything less than perfect—ever? If we were less than perfect, then it would mean that divinity isn't perfect, which is impossible. And if we are already perfect, then why would we need to attend earth-plane school to gain something we already possess? We wouldn't.

So, why are we really here experiencing life? What is our real purpose? There are many concepts. We are trying to gain enlightenment so we, as a part, will merge back into the wholeness of divinity. Or we are trying to become oneness where nothing other than one consciousness exists.

To me a concept involving "nothing" sounds as though nothing of my individual consciousness will remain after oneness; my identity, my unique essence, would be lost in the state of blissful oneness. In this state I would become absolute peace, peace so fulfilling it would be as though I was deeply asleep, with no thought of myself—snoring away, content beyond reason ... I don't think so. In all honesty, a place of oneness where nothing of me exists is personally very terrifying.

Did I really go through trying to awaken only to end up in eternal, unconscious sleep? That seems illogical and personally unsettling. It's difficult enough to view my search for enlightenment as an endless wheel. (I die, re-evaluate my missteps, reincarnate to try again, and experience immediate amnesia where my intention is difficult to perceive, only to die and repeat the same process over and over again.)

My dream: To be in a perfectly blissful state of being, remembering everything, feeling joy at being reunited with all that I love ... forever.

My fear: Nothing of me exists in oneness. Divinity is there—beautiful, peaceful oneness, without individual identity ... forever.

In thinking about which of these concepts was more real, the pondering of years before popped into my mind: "If everything is relative and relativity is a void, where does that leave us?"

There are two vastly different ways to interpret this higher conscious thought. One way is that there is no ultimate point to anything. Energy exists to grow and change, disintegrate, and grow and change—a never-ending cycle. We are just ever-changing energy, with no ultimate purpose, at our center. Wow, that's a bleak thought I just can't accept. Earthly experiences seem too organized, interconnected, and synchronistic for that to be true.

The second way to interpret this thought was that nothing is real in the sense we mean or in a way we understand, yet something unreal springs from within the eternal void in a profound enough manner that we feel it is real. So there must be something phenomenal at the center of all of this that makes it real and unreal simultaneously.

Though the second thought was certainly more confounding, I sensed it was closer to the truth.

All I knew was that we seem to be spiritual in nature, expressing in human form, and when we physically die, our soul consciousness leaves our body and continues to exist somewhere else. There seem to be many other dimensions or planes of consciousness in which other entities, spirits, or angels exist that can sometimes overlap this dimensional reality. Dreams, intuition, and precognition are just as real as any conventional reality. And there is a higher power assisting and protecting us.

So … *why am I here?*

It can't possibly be true that I'll be forever chained to a cycle of pain and suffering and endless lessons with no diploma—no graduation celebration.

In all the thoughts and all my experiences, the only thing I perceived as being present in any and all realities, whether human or spiritual, in this dimension or others, was consciousness. The fiber that wove everything together—that was connected to everything—was consciousness. And that fiber—consciousness—can appear both real and unreal.

Consciousness feels like the only thing connected to "Why am I here?" as it was the only concept that I couldn't perceive with holes. So, if consciousness is at the center, then what can be our purpose for being in earthly expression?

The answer did not begin to unfold in my waking consciousness until a couple of years ago through a process where I began to release subconscious blocks. This process was the catalyst for a phenomenal experience involving all aspects of my consciousness (subconscious, waking conscious, higher conscious) wherein the knowing I experienced as a child, held dormant within me until I could consciously understand, began to unfold. And with the unfolding of that knowing came answers to the questions I and many of us ponder: *"Who am I? Why am I here? What is my purpose for being on earth? What am I, really? Where is my home? Does consciousness continue after death?"*

There were extraordinary concepts about consciousness, creation, and us that unfolded in my waking awareness. Higher conscious insights were continuously perceived as I went about my daily life as well as conveyed through meditations, dreams, and visions. These insights— these truths—answered my innermost questions in a way that brought awareness to my mind, love to my heart, and peace to my life.

Why am I here?

We are here to awaken and remember our all-at-once divine nature. Individual human consciousness is the *bridge* between known and unknown, conscious and unconscious, and manifested and unmanifested. It is a conscious link between past, present, and future—between everything.

Part of our awakening is to consciously recognize that we have based our beliefs, experiences, and expressions on an inaccurate perception of our true essence. Once we embrace the truth of our divine beingness, our consciousness shifts, allowing us to experience our lives with a peaceful center and a new perspective of our self, our world, and the true nature of everything.

No longer will we need to journey as Avatars of Consciousness seeking or yearning for something that we misperceived to be outside of us because we will now consciously know the truth. Truth has been with us always, but our misperception shifted us from our own knowing.

We are extraordinary divine beings, and perceiving the truth of our nature shatters our original misperception while shifting our consciousness, allowing us to energetically embrace our all-at-once divine essence. We are here, even now, awakening.

Are you ready to place the fourth piece of your puzzle? You should be ready. We have been preparing for this moment since the beginning of collective human consciousness.

So let's go ahead and label this puzzle piece, *"Why am I here?"* and imagine the following words on this piece of your puzzle:

Why am I here?

I am here to awaken the remembrance of my all-at-once divine essence. My human consciousness is the divinely designed bridge of awareness between unconscious and conscious that will trigger my awakening and bring forth conscious remembrance of my divine beingness.

Remembering can be a spontaneous awakening, or your eyes may be fluttering open. No matter. The most important part of a shift in consciousness is that we have a clear moment—that "aha" moment—of awareness where we realize our truth. Once that happens, knowingness begins to flow through us, awakening our body, mind, and spirit. And as we continue our awakening, we are more cognizant of feelings, thoughts, or impressions that previously would have slipped through our awareness.

Intend that you are awakening and that you will be more consciously aware of your true self—the true nature of you. But never doubt that you are even now awakening. And you are not alone in your awakening. All of divine consciousness is supporting you.

Most importantly, we are already perfect. We don't have to worry about that concept ever again. We are not outside of that cottage door at all. Never again should we think of ourselves as being outside of that cottage door, outside of perfection. It was only a misperception. We need not search any longer to attain something we already possess. We need only continue awakening, unfolding the remembrance of our true state of beingness for our spiritual amnesia to lift. Then we must continue to shake ourselves awake through seeking to unfold our higher conscious awareness in our waking conscious state of beingness.

Just knowing the truth of our nature will shift our conscious perception, but we must still place our attention and intention on awakening in order to activate, engage, and express our all-at-once divine beingness more consciously in our lives.

I could go on forever about this piece of our puzzle, as it is so intriguing, but, it's time to embrace the gift of, "*Why am I here?*"

As you add the phrase, "*The gift of why I am here*" to your fourth puzzle piece, take a moment to consciously intend your awakening, your remembrance, as you write these words:

The Gift of Why I Am Here

I am already home in my divine perfection, and as my awakening continues, I consciously know that no separation from my divine essence is ever possible. My awakening is the benevolent promise of divinity's intention fulfilled.

Remember, you are here even now expressing as Avatars of Consciousness, awakening and remembering your all-at-once divine perfection.

Chapter 41

Puzzle Piece Five— What Is My Destiny?

Rather than list a zillion possibilities, the truest answer to the question, *"What is my destiny?"* is this: Your ultimate destiny is anything and everything imaginable—even the perceived impossible. You are going everywhere consciousness can flow. There is no limit to the wonderment, the love, the joy, and the bliss we will experience as avatars of all-at-once divine conscious love.

Even now, while in our current lifetimes, we are in the process of awakening to our divine nature. Remember, it's not about identifying with our divine nature but rather engaging in just being that nature. Keeping this intent at the forefront of our consciousness will prevent us from falling victim to the ego attachment of identifying ourselves *as* divinity. Rather, we must always consciously intend to just *be*.

Envision the lightness of your essence coming forth through your conscious intention. It is not a race. There is no clock. There is no opponent and no competition. It is just you remembering you. Be more conscious of your thoughts, your feelings, and the patterns you are attracting and begin focusing your attention, intention, reflection, and perception on the moments you are experiencing and expressing in your lifetime. Especially begin listening for the sounds of your own subconscious and higher conscious awareness so you will be able to pull these intuitive thoughts and feelings into your waking conscious mind. In this way, you will develop conscious awareness of cause and effect, thereby learning to interact and eventually trust the heart-thoughts of your higher self so you will become the energetic conscious bridge of your own divinely intended awakening.

The purpose of awakening is not to begin putting pressure on yourself to instantly "be" but rather to just consciously embrace the truth of your nature so that you know *who you are* as a divine beingness, *what you are* as an Avatar of Consciousness, and *why you are here* journeying through lifetime expressions to awaken to your remembrance.

First, we must awaken to the truth of our divine nature, which consciously shifts us out of misperception. Then, when we pull the knowing of our true essence through us, we will consciously realize that we are not now separated nor have we ever been separated from our perfection (home), each other, or divinity. It is impossible, because we are eternally one divine beingness, limitless in expression, and indivisible and inseparable in nature.

As that realization becomes stronger and stronger in our consciousness, the foundation of our knowing will grow more defined within our beingness, and once that occurs, our own consciousness will assist us in our awakening.

Our awakening is a journey to be enjoyed. I know it may be a natural reaction to assign it as a task and become our own task master, but we will miss the most profound part of our awakening if we do not allow it to come forth naturally without either sour thoughts about how long it is taking or confusing emotions about what we will leave behind. First of all, we don't leave anything behind; we merely allow things to move to a place in our heart or our mind that is more true or appropriate. And second, if we are thinking about how long it is taking, we have shifted our focus to fear or worry instead of love and knowing.

Everything we experience along our predestined paths while journeying through our current lifetimes is important; it is a part of our ultimate destination. No moment is more important than another because they all lead to our remembrance. Enjoy the moments of your lives and learn to live more consciously, without fear, identification, or doubt.

We are nearly consciously home! Never again will we experience longing for perfection, as it is already our essence, and it cannot leave us as we cannot leave it. To fully enjoy and express our essence, we must allow it to come forth. And come forth it will; of that there is no doubt.

We are destined to be as we always have been but momentarily forgot. We are destined to experience as Avatars of Consciousness awakened to our remembrance of our all-at-once divine beingness—experiencing as divinity experiences.

As you take out your fifth puzzle piece and label it, *"What is my destiny?"* imagine that there are no words written below the label at this time.

What is my destiny?

For right now, let's not define our destiny. Let's engage our limitless nature by not placing any boundaries on what we are destined to experience.

But I've already been given a sneak preview—and it is extraordinary. We will experience as divinity intended—as pure love ... as all-at-once divine conscious beings, eternally blissful in our remembrance of what we are, have been, and will eternally *be*.

It seems forever we have been seeking ... but it was only a moment ago.

We are not alone. We are not forsaken. We are not lost. We are not imperfect. We are not a fluke. We are well-intentioned divine conscious love, and we will live as that divine love eternally in our conscious knowing, trusting that full awakening and remembrance are occurring within all dimensions of our conscious beingness.

It is extraordinary to be here now, consciously aware of this moment—a moment many of us have sensed throughout our lives. For this is the moment where our consciousness forever shifts, and conscious awakening to our divine destiny and remembrance of our true nature has begun!

Imagine now that you are adding the words, *"The gift of my destiny"* to your puzzle piece and envision the following words:

The Gift of My Destiny

The gift of my destiny is that I will consciously awaken from my dream of misperception to the remembrance of my divine essence and experience the blissfulness of my limitless divine beingness for all eternity.

Chapter 42

The Ever-Unfolding You

Imagine the ever-unfolding you is an ongoing puzzle. The main pieces relating to *who you are* and *why you are here* are already fitted in, but there is lots of space around those pieces. This space represents what you are yet to write.

Take one of the blank pieces, and for a moment think about something you want to experience as an Avatar of Consciousness, as soul divinity, in your current lifetime.

Do you want peace? Do you want to fulfill your soul purpose for this lifetime? Do you want to be able to more consciously bring forth your higher conscious awareness as an Avatar of Consciousness? Do you want to clear all impediments to your consciousness in order to more fully realize your true nature now, in this lifetime? What do you intend?

The power of intention, love, and gratitude cannot be overstated. The energy of gratitude is very important to how we experience and express our lives. Every time we intend to experience anything, we should be expressing gratitude—not just when our desired prayer or intention manifests. Gratitude should be held as our constant conscious attitude toward our lives. Often we overlook the attitude of being grateful, but it is a cornerstone of our divine beingness. Embracing and expressing gratitude will not only hasten our awakening, but it will also positively influence how we view, experience, and manifest the moments we live.

Now, before reading on, hold your heart-felt intention in your mind with conscious clarity and in your heart with vibrational love and consciously and lovingly intend what you want to experience in your current life. (Your intention should be held in a conscious space of gratitude and love and worded as an affirmation, such as, "*I am consciously interacting with my higher self through intuitive thoughts and feelings.*") Then release your intention, trusting and knowing that the divine vibration of love will manifest that which is divinely intended for you to experience.

Imagine that this is your moment to impact the realities of your life, but always remember that consciously intending our realities does not guarantee they are divinely designed to manifest, only that we have merged our conscious intention with divine consciousness, trusting what is perfect for our awakening will unfold.

Please know that much can happen in your future, but it need not be rushed or pressure filled. Continue to consciously awaken in your own time and in your own way. That way may be to consciously process or ponder information presented in this book; it may be to set these concepts aside, feeling as though you are not yet ready to embrace them; it may be to take time to figure out how you want to continue your awakening; or it may be to immediately begin your more consciously intended awakening.

Do not worry. There is no set path. Don't think for one moment that you will miss the awakening train. It will not leave without you. It can't leave without you. Although consciously aligning can hasten your awakening, no one—not even you—can prevent your awakening as it has been divinely designed. Relax and let go of all fear, knowing that all happens when and as appropriate.

The most difficult part to realize is that knowing our truth—knowing our true divine nature—does not instantly zap us into another reality or alleviate all difficulties in our present lives. The experiences we live will always be present, because we will never be exempt from experiencing, but we can be consciously lifted above those experiences by our attitude and applying the tools of conscious intention to affect our realities—to affect how we live those experiences.

But be assured that the conscious knowing of our truth does forever change our misperception, consciously shifting us to a new foundation of awareness within our conscious beingness. *And that changes everything* because our conscious foundation affects all that we will perceive, experience, and express from that moment forward!

Although it may appear to be just a thought, just a concept, or just an awareness, it is the most important awareness we can hold in our consciousness. Why? Because once the truth of our divine nature strikes our consciousness, we have begun to remember what we already know deep within us ... we are an eternally perfect divine energy.

The most wonderful part is that even though we may have drifted into a deep sleep and awakened with amnesia, no matter how long we sleep or how long our amnesia lasts, we can never *unknow* what is already *known* within us.

We have always known the truth of our divine nature, even if not remembered, because even when asleep in our own awareness, we are still an all-knowing, all-at-once divine beingness. This is our truth—the extraordinary truth of all of us.

Why are we here? We are here to awaken ... and remember.

It is exciting to be me, to be you, to be us. We are *identical in divine essence*—no one greater or lesser than another—yet *unique in divine expression*!

Our divine beingness, even now, is reflected in the minds, the eyes, the thoughts, the hearts, the feelings, and the conscious embrace of each other.

Chapter 43

Be Your True Nature

There is no separation.
What happens as one,
happens as all.

We must always consciously intend to be our true nature. And what is our true nature? By now you realize that we are all only one essence in many expressions ... one divine beingness, one divine conscious vibration of love. There is no separation. What happens as one, happens as all.

This is why I perceived that my actions may let down my spiritual family. What was happening as one of them (me) was happening as all of them (my spiritual family).

We are Avatars of Consciousness in the process of awakening to our remembrance of our divine nature, and in our lives we express our unique beingness through our bodies, our minds, our hearts, and our spirits.

Our bodies are very much needed for journey questing as Avatars of Consciousness because we utilize physical form to perceive, experience and express consciousness.

Our minds are directly linked as divine All-at-Once Consciousness. And in order to allow higher (divine) consciousness to flow consciously through our minds, we must learn to utilize attention, intention, reflection, and perception because they are important to bridging awareness. As an Avatar of Consciousness, it's very important to have an open mind—not so open that any impression can take hold but open to possibilities. Also, it is very important to be honest at all times in our thinking process, especially in sorting through motivation and intent.

In addition, we must seek to keep our heart pure of ego or ulterior motives while learning to develop and trust our inner knowing.

Also, there is a very important aspect to the truths conveyed in this book that must be clarified so there can be no misinterpretation. Years ago, a woman I knew began constantly referring to herself by saying, "I am God." Every time she said this phrase, a wave of discord moved through me. Why? Because back then I was perceiving through the lens of separation—that divinity was above me to be adored and perfection outside of me to be gained. Now if she were to say, "I am God," I would be happy that she was perceiving her divine nature but I would sense discord within her if she did not consciously realize that she wasn't just divinity but also simultaneously herself as well as everything else (all-at-once divine energy).

We must be cautious of affirmations or statements that carry specific identification. For example, even the phrase, "I am God" carries identification, and that sense of identification will form a conscious or unconscious attachment, creating separation. Likewise, when you say, "I am Carol," you have still identified yourself *as* something.

Once we consciously accept that our true nature is the limitlessness of divine energy—without ego or identity—we realize that any form of conscious identification limits our limitless nature. Think of conscious identification as a form of focused singularity—the ego of "*limited I*" versus egoless, "*limitless all.*"

If our ultimate intention is to more consciously experience the limitlessness of our divine nature, we must learn to hold a consciousness without limit or ego identity.

We live in a world where we constantly have to claim or explain our identity—"My name is Carol. I am Carol"—so we might not be able to change that procedure. However, we can change how we perceive our self by simultaneously holding an *all* and *one* consciousness—not ever just a one *or* an all. That is the profundity of the "I am that I am" declaration. There is no identity at all in this mindset. So, if we consciously hold an *I am that I am* intention as we are saying anything, even "I am Carol," then identification does not form. Our conscious intention dominates, even if our words aren't always perfectly stated.

Divine energy just is, so we must remember that even though we are identical in essence to divinity, labeling ourselves in any manner is counterproductive to unfolding our true nature because it limits the limitlessness of our own divine beingness.

Trusting in your innate knowing while flowing with the unfolding of your awakening awareness is the realization and activation of consciously being an "I am that I am" expression, without ego or identification.

The truths in this book have not been given by divine consciousness so that we can just switch to a different misperception. They have been given to liberate us from that which binds us to our conscious state of separation. Anyone who reads this book and embraces these truths as knowing will realize that divine energy, perfection, truth, and love *just are*. And to consciously manifest our true divine nature, we need to begin consciously "being" rather than consciously "limiting our beingness" through ego, identity, and/or myopic perceptions.

It would be wise for us to choose affirmations that align us with our true nature, such as "I am divine energy expressing as the living vibration of love" or to hold the essence of our divine nature in a thought form while we are saying, "I am that I am."

Always we must be vigilant and try not to identify through ego attachment. This is not to say that ego is bad. It isn't. But ego limits us, and eventually we reach a wall in how far we consciously perceive.

Ego in the form of self-identification or self-realization was always necessary to trigger awakening, but we must remember not to stand in front of the mirror so long that we become entirely enamored with our reflected self. The point of the mirror wasn't to make us fall in love with ourselves to the exclusion of all. It was to make us aware that we are simultaneously *oneness*, *allness*, and all *onenesses*—an all-at-once divine beingness.

If you've identified too much with self, step away from the mirror and allow reflection to flow through you. If you have resisted embracing self, it is time to peer into the mirror and realize that perfection and the divine that you love and adore are identical to your own essence; embrace yourself as you embrace divinity.

Most importantly, love yourself as you love divinity. A key to alleviating misperception and awakening to our true nature is to recognize and love our self equally to all that we perceive to be love.

We must truly love the essence of divinity that is our own essence. Cease to think of yourself as a note and divinity as the music. Think of yourself as a concert of divine beingness, the notes, music, voice, and vibration—simultaneously expressing all-at-once.

Once someone shared a phenomenal lucid dream with me. In the dream, the person began spontaneously singing a song while feeling an intense vibration building in his solar plexus like a small seed of vibrating energy that was continuing to expand. Eventually, the vibration, person, and song merged, as though they had all become one. As the vibration continued to flow forth from him, he recognized the vibration as divinity and became aware that the song he was singing was divinity's song of love.

He became aware that the sound of the song was an energy that matched the essence of divinity's vibration of love because the sound was vibrating to the same frequency as the beingness of divinity. Then, as the intensity of the vibration of love continued to build and as the song unfolded in his conscious awareness, he was astonished to realize that the essence of the song was all about divinity loving divinity! There were no words, just the most beautiful, uplifting essence he had ever experienced conveyed through the tone and vibration reverberating inside his very own beingness. The essence was so pure that his entire beingness was awakened to the pure vibrational truth and magnitude of divinity's love for him as well as divinity's love for all of divinity. In that moment, he became consciously aware that there was no separation between him, as a child of God, and divinity. This person expressed to me that he felt as though he was experiencing divinity's song of love (the pure vibration of love) as the "oneness of his own beingness" as well as the "allness of divinity"—simultaneously *one* and *all*.

The person wasn't just experiencing love; he was being love in its purest vibration. Love just is. There is no separation between *what is love* and *what is expressing love*. Divinity singing about loving divinity is a profound reflection of divinity's love for all divinity. And when we can love ourselves and each other as divinity loves itself and all, then we will "be love" rather than perceiving love to be outside of us.

This book has been written with the vibration of love and with a conscious intention that the examples of my life will serve as triggers to your own remembrance of experiences, feelings, or thoughts in your life that you may have passed off as mind noise or coincidence. In this way, you will more deeply connect to the knowing that has always been moving through you, discerning your knowing from mere thoughts—and learning to trust that knowing if you don't already do so.

Also, divine consciousness imbued this book as I was writing it with a divine intention that as you read, your consciousness will shift and a more enlightened awareness will unfold with each reading. Divine consciousness simultaneously speaks on many frequencies, but we do not always hear until our awareness has reached a point of harmony. It is divinely designed that your consciousness will continue to shift the more you awaken and come into harmony with your true nature. Sometimes we immediately know it is our truth, and other times the knowing of that truth must unfold within us in stages. But once the fullness of the knowing unfolds, we are amazed to recognize that the knowing has always been standing right in front of us but we did not recognize it as such until our consciousness was ready.

Though it's amusing now, it was difficult to edit this book into final form because of that very intention. Each time I re-read a chapter for typos, my awareness shifted, and I sometimes ended up rewriting various sections. It is a profound and amazing aspect of this book and one that divine consciousness trusts you will not only benefit from but also enjoy experiencing!

One thing is certain. You'll realize that love and consciousness are the key. All of it—everything—is really about a loving state of consciousness, which you will more clearly remember as your awakening continues.

Chapter 44

The Vibration of Love
Thought and Feeling ... Identical in Knowing

Because we are in human embodiment, it is difficult for us to imagine that our true beingness has no parts or separation. As human beings, it's only natural for us to think of everything as part of something else and therefore separate. That's just how our conventional world appears to operate. Our brain and our heart are considered to be separate parts of our human embodiment. We associate thinking with our mind and feeling with our heart; we perceive thinking and feeling as two vastly different things.

But for explanation purposes, let's look at it another way—from the viewpoint of higher (divine) consciousness. Think of higher (divine) consciousness as the *all-knowing bridge* of divine energy, experienced as our own intuitive thoughts and feelings.

Think of intuitive, higher conscious thoughts as the divine vibration of love manifesting as thought form. And think of intuitive, higher conscious feelings as the vibration of love manifesting as feeling form.

Now hold the knowing in your conscious mind that there is no difference between intuitive thoughts or intuitive feelings. Why? Because divine energy is a broth of inseparable and indivisible beingness. There are no parts to divinity. Divine energy is indivisibly all knowing in any state of beingness or expression; therefore, a feeling expression of divine energy carries the identical knowing as a thought expression of divine energy. This can be a difficult concept for us to perceive because we assume "knowing" only relates to our mind, but it does not.

You may have experienced an intuitive, higher conscious knowing through the feeling side of your beingness but not realized what you were experiencing.

The following example is something that many of us have experienced. The phone rings, and immediately we have a hunch, a

313

feeling that the person on the other end of the line is someone we knew many years before. There was no prior knowledge that this person was going to call, yet we just know who it is. This intuitive reaction moves into our mind as a thought, and as we answer the phone, we realize we were right. How did we know? It is because feelings carry the identical knowing as thoughts, but we do not recognize intuitive feelings as easily as intuitive thoughts. Many times we will experience an intuitive feeling before any thought comes into our mind.

An example of this is something that happened one morning while I was sitting in my doctor's office. One of the office staff was interacting with me about a form to complete. As she was standing there, a feeling of new life came over me. It was a feeling of her being captured in a radiant springtime energy, bathed in beautiful diffused light. There was a feeling of flowers in her hair and birds chirping, announcing that new life was fully underway. The feeling was so strong that I could almost smell the flowers and hear the birds. There was an unmistakable energy of something brand new—a feeling of springtime in the air. I couldn't help myself. I had to ask her, "What's new in your life?" She responded, "Nothing … absolutely, nothing." As I was explaining what I was feeling, a thought then came into my mind and I asked her if she could be pregnant. She immediately said no but something in me said, "Yes, she is pregnant. That's the new life I'm feeling."

By this time our friendly exchange had moved us to the back of the office, and the doctor overheard the girl's response to me and good-naturedly asked us what was going on. We all enjoyed an easy rapport, so I shared my feelings and thoughts with the doctor. The doctor, who is very intuitive, replied to the girl, "I think you're pregnant too. Let's go have you take a test right now." (I loved it!)

While we were standing around waiting for the results of the test, the soul of the child this girl was carrying spoke with me though energetic thoughts, telling me that he was the little boy who had appeared to her in many dreams throughout her life, and she was very familiar with him. He said that they shared a special bond and that he was coming into her life as her son.

As I finished sharing this information with the girl, her eyes widened, and she exclaimed, "For years I've dreamed of a little boy who would be my son, but there is no way I am pregnant now. His words mean that he's coming some other time in the future."

My response was to tell her that this child, this soul, was already energetically here (conceived)—as he was very much communicating with me and he would be born the last of March. I then gave her the date that appeared in my mind through energetic knowing.

For a minute she was fully believing. Then, as the pregnancy test read negative, her energy shifted and she responded, "That's impossible. The pregnancy test is negative, and in order for this child to be born the date given, it can only mean that I'm pregnant right now."

I replied, "The pregnancy test isn't accurate. You are definitely pregnant now; your son is already energetically with you." Though she remained quiet, her gaze was unmistakably one of disbelief.

As I left the office, I was grateful to have experienced this new life bursting forth in such a vibrant and lovely energetic expression.

A few days later, I answered the phone, and both the doctor and her assistant were on the line. They were calling to tell me that the results of an ordered blood test were back and it confirmed that the girl was pregnant and that she had, in fact, been pregnant when I was in their office.

Though it didn't surprise me to learn she was pregnant, as I was certain her unborn child was energetically communicating with me, I still found it amazing that this entire experience began with impressions of intuitive feelings carried into waking awareness. Her son was born the last of March.

This story is a perfect example that higher conscious knowing is not limited to our thoughts. Don't think of love as limited to feelings and consciousness as limited to thoughts. Instead think of it as heart-thoughts and thought-feelings.

How can feelings carry the identical awareness as thoughts? It is because feelings and thoughts are not just expressions of a human heart and mind. They are the energetic essence of higher conscious knowing. And *knowingness just is*. Knowingness is not contingent upon anything occurring first. A thought or a feeling doesn't initiate knowing. Knowing is always present as our innate divine beingness, and a thought or a feeling only carries the knowing into our conscious awareness.

Think of intuitive thoughts and feelings as the expressions of divine energy always traveling the pathway of own higher consciousness. The more we learn to consciously engage in opening the pathways of higher conscious awareness, through our intuitive thoughts and feelings, the easier it will be for us to consciously recognize and access the divine all-knowing vibration of love that is our own benevolent essence.

No matter how we perceive divinity, the essence of divinity is never altered by its expression or by our perception. Divine beingness is always all-knowing whether that knowing is experienced (or expressed) as a thought or as a feeling.

This is why, when I was that little girl held in the stillness of Benevolence: "It was as though love itself carried all thoughts, for I was not only feeling absolute love, but I was also feeling absolute awareness."

That is also why, in my lifetime 1,001 lifetimes ago: "It was as if there was no difference between the pain I felt in my heart and the pain I felt in my mind—as though consciousness and love were both experiencing this loss to the same degree."

The reason that it felt as though "love itself carried all thoughts" and why "consciousness and love were both experiencing this loss to the same degree" is because there is no difference between a conscious thought or a conscious feeling when we are experiencing higher (divine) consciousness.

Consciously recognizing that feelings are not always just an emotional reaction is an important aspect of bridging higher (divine) consciousness in waking conscious awareness.

Once we recognize that our intuitive (higher conscious) feelings carry the identical all-knowingness as intuitive (higher conscious) thoughts, we can begin to more consciously access this profound bridge of divine all-knowing love that is always simultaneously flowing as our own higher self.

Chapter 45

Bridging Spirituality and Science
All-at-Once Consciousness ...
The Unifying Concept

Established principles of classical physics consistent with our physical world do not seem to apply to the subatomic (quantum) world. The subatomic world appears to operate according to a different set of principles that are inconsistent and "at odds" with our classical physics world.

One day while I was meditating, I perceived the quantum world and the classical world as one inseparable divine energy. Immediately, I realized that our divine nature of All-at-Once Consciousness answers why quantum particles appear the way they do—unbounded from the laws of classical physics. Although that's a bold statement, I believe it will be proven out as we continue to experience the new paradigm shift occurring in collective human consciousness.

The unusual phenomena being perceived in the subatomic world is really just a reflection of the basic nature of divine energy—*All-at-Once Consciousness*, and not really incongruent, inconsistent, or at odds with the *true* nature of our Universe and ourselves at all.

Forever science and spirituality were at odds, but no longer. Now is the time that science and spirituality will be bridged through understanding the true nature of ourselves and our perceived universe. Even now we are witness to the way in which science and spirituality are coming together in joint symposiums.

For all of us to better understand and experience our all-at-once divine conscious nature, we must learn to be both classical (one) and quantum (all) at the same time (all-at-once) and cease to identify ourselves as either one or the other. Remember, identification binds, and the purpose of All-at-Once Consciousness is to be unbounded from either a classical or quantum identity and just be our true nature (which is simultaneously both).

We should be moving as a divine conscious bridge, spanning both worlds, unbounded—expressing and being. But until we can hold the pure state of consciousness necessary to truly be unbounded, placing one foot in each world (quantum and classical) is symbolic of bridging consciousness. Think of it as though we are a living bridge between unconscious awareness (quantum, allness consciousness) and individual human consciousness (classical, onceness consciousness) in the process of remembering our divine All-at-Once Consciousness.

As humanity continues to consciously shift and awaken to their remembrance, the disparity between science and spirituality will fade. Eventually there will be no perceived difference at all, as we will consciously recognize the true nature of everything.

The quantum world perfectly reflects All-at-Once Consciousness. Particle (onceness) and wave (allness) simultaneously exist with no separation in the state of quantum allness.

Although we perceive particle as separate from wave, nothing is ever energetically separate or apart from anything else in our quantum world or even in our physical world—though it is difficult to perceive this truth while experiencing human consciousness in a matter-based reality.

The truth of All-at-Once Consciousness is that even in the perceived state of onceness (particle), allness (wave) is still 100 percent present, with no difference in *energetic* essence. Those individual expressions are not "parts" of one thing; they are one inseparable, indivisible energy expressing its entirety through focused intent (onceness/particle/soul consciousness)—in multiple places as identically the same one divine energy.

Theories about our quantum world are fascinating to learn about, as they imply so much more about us than is explainable by the boundaries of our known physical world or human embodiment. But the most fascinating aspect to me is that we are finally able to connect the dot of what is now visible in science to the dot of us—our true nature. And the synchronicity of these correlations is perfect for us to perceive our true nature through the lens of both the classical physics world as well as the quantum physics world.

The following are some of those connected dots. These correlations were the result of connecting thoughts about our quantum world—

overheard on the radio or shared in conversations with friends interested in physics—to my personal insights or experiences. As such, any references to the "quantum world" are not intended as a precise definition of anything scientific, but simply as a way to connect my perceptions of what is occurring in the subatomic world to All-at-Once Consciousness—*bridging* physical matter and energetic essence; science and spirituality; and classical and quantum science.

What are some of the examples of All-at-Once Consciousness being displayed in our subatomic, quantum world?

Correlation—Example 1

Quantum World: Experiments show that when one electron is separated away from another electron and relocated to another place, the separated electron instantly reacts to whatever the other electron experiences (and vice versa) even though the two electrons no longer share the same space. There are theories that this occurs because the two electrons are somehow still connected—what science refers to as *entanglement*.

All-at-Once Consciousness: The original and separated electron are not just connected (entangled). They are, in fact, identical to each other in essence, though appearing different in expression. Although science is now able to observe the connectedness of all things, everything is not just connected. We (and everything) are identically the same one thing. At the very basement level of our beingness, we are identically the same one divine essence in any perceived expression— sometimes even appearing to be identically the same one thing in two places at once.

This is because at the core of everything there is only one divine energy *simultaneously* projecting or reflecting as a single locale or as multiple locales—"allness" expressing through focused "onenesses."

Due to our original misperception of our own divine beingness, we are unable to consciously comprehend the true nature of what is occurring. Though the electron appears to be separated by space from the other electron, nothing is ever really energetically apart from anything else. It is impossible because everything is really the same one inseparable energy, an All-at-Once Consciousness that is nonlocal and simultaneously everywhere at once.

Energetic entanglement is not just occurring in the quantum, subatomic world. It is also occurring in our classical world, though we cannot always understand what we are experiencing or how it is even possible.

An example of one of these energetically entangled experiences happened one night while I was sleeping. During the night, I awakened to a sensation that something had just occurred behind one of my eyes and I instinctively placed my hand over the eye in protection. Simultaneous to experiencing this sensation, I had the energetic impression of my grandmother, Nana, holding her hand over the same eye.

Although it was late, I awakened my mother and shared the details of the experience and told her that we should check on Nana, as it felt as though she had just experienced something very serious.

It wasn't until later that afternoon that we learned that at the exact time that I had awakened to these energetic sensations, Nana was suffering a stroke behind one of her eyes, leaving her blind in that eye.

This experience perfectly exemplifies quantum entanglement experienced in our classical world. Just like the separated electron, when my grandmother was experiencing the stroke behind her eye, I was simultaneously experiencing the energetic "sensations" of this event as though no space existed between my grandmother and myself—as though I was personally experiencing the energy of the stroke.

Most importantly, I did not experience these simultaneous sensations because my grandmother and I were merely connected. I experienced them because even though it appears that we are separate beings, we are actually the same one indivisible divine energy, and what *one* experiences is instantly known (reflected) in *all*—even if not *consciously* realized.

Even though I did not experience a physical stroke, I did energetically experience the sensations of what was occurring in my grandmother's body as though it were occurring in my own body. And although I experienced these sensations while sleeping, it did not carry the same energetic feeling as a dream. In a dream, we are aware of what is happening to someone else, but we do not feel it energetically as if it were happening to us. But when we consciously experience quantum entanglement with another person, we personally experience the sensations of what is happening to them through our own senses (taste, smell, touch, sight, hearing, knowing), and it feels as though it is happening to us. For instance, if someone very close to you is hiking in the mountains and they fall and break their leg, you would feel pain in your own leg for a brief instant as their leg breaks. This experience puzzles you, as there was nothing going on in your life to cause the sharp pain you felt, but you realize that you momentarily thought of your husband as the pain was occurring. Later that day you learn your husband's leg was broken at the exact time and in the exact physical spot that you energetically felt the pain.

Although I originally viewed this event energetically shared with my grandmother as just one more inexplicable paranormal experience, I now realize that it is really energetic verification of the *truth of our nature*—a nature that is not readily apparent in our classical, physical world.

What is the truth of our nature? It is that everything is one indivisible, inseparable divine energy, simultaneously everywhere at once (All-at-Once Consciousness)—one divine essence (quantum possibility) simultaneously expressing as multiple things (classical reality).

Energetic entanglement is not just a connectedness, it is visible verification of our true nature, as seen through the lens of our quantum world.

We must never again think of ourselves as either alone or merely connected, because we are so much more than what we can even now perceive ourselves to be … we are one divine energy, indivisible and eternal.

Correlation—Example 2

Quantum World: Experiments show that unobserved electrons move as wave (unlimited possibility, simultaneously in all locations at once), whereas observed electrons appear to collapse into a single object in one position. It appears that the act of observation causes the unlimited potential to manifest into a single object.

All-at-Once Consciousness: Energy in its unobserved state (potential, static) appears as both particle and wave. Energy in its observed state (manifested, kinetic) appears as particle. And although it is difficult for us to comprehend that wave (*all*ness) and particle (*one*ness) are identical in energetic nature, it is absolutely true.

The concept that observation (consciousness) manifests something into reality is only part of what is occurring because even in that manifested oneness expression, wave is still 100 percent fully present (no true separation ever occurs).

In one very unusual session with Angela where the affirmation was about manifesting true state of beingness, the *emotion* was *anguish*, and higher conscious thoughts revealed that the *role* was *simultaneously* both *particle* and *wave*. (At the time of this session, I was unfamiliar with the meaning of these terms in relation to physics.)

The *original emotional theme* revealed through higher (divine) consciousness and tested as congruent was that, "wave felt anguish about losing consciousness (all-knowingness); and particle felt anguish about losing identity (self). Wave is consciously aware of *both* particle and wave, but particle is only aware of itself."

Although at the time of this session none of us consciously grasped the full meaning of what was being conveyed in this original emotional theme, we all found this information intriguing because we recognized that two expressions (particle and wave) were *simultaneously* existing, yet only one expression (wave) was consciously aware of both expressions.

Later, as the concept of All-at-Once Consciousness unfolded in my conscious awareness, I realized the profundity of what had been revealed in this particular session. This session was energetic corroboration of our true all-at-once nature in that we *simultaneously* hold both particle (oneness) and wave (allness) consciousness—even when we are only consciously aware of just one!

In this session, particle (oneness expression) was only *consciously aware of itself*. Particle did not consciously recognize that wave was *simultaneously fully present* at that particle expression. Conscious awareness of being *both* wave and particle was not known when in particle (oneness) expression, and particle felt like its self identity would be "lost" in wave (allness). And even though the entirety of allness (wave) was *fully present* at that oneness (particle) expression, wave felt like its all-knowingness would be "lost" in particle (oneness) expression.

Even though wave was consciously aware that both it and particle simultaneously existed, wave did not consciously view itself as identical in energetic essence to particle; and particle did not view itself as identical in energetic essence to wave.

Both wave and particle viewed themselves as separate entities, each with subconscious emotional blocks about their simultaneous (all-at-once) state of being. Wave was in a state of all-knowing consciousness and felt anguish that its state of consciousness would be lost in particle expression. Particle was in a state of individual consciousness and felt anguish about losing self identity in wave consciousness. Although these two "roles" simultaneously existed, neither role recognized themselves as an All-at-Once Consciousness, even though the "all" (wave) and the "once" (particle) were simultaneously present.

This session is energetic validation that our conscious misperception of our true nature (divine All-at-Once Consciousness) is present in various lifetime expressions, even when we are expressing in roles other than human beings. This misperception occurred at the Creation of collective human consciousness and has been carried forward through all conscious expressions (lifetimes) into the present time.

This experience reflects the profound truth that *everything* is simultaneously both particle and wave (All-at-Once Consciousness), even when appearing to be just one (whether expressed as particle or as wave). It is our misperception about our true nature that causes us to perceive ourselves and everything as *either* one *or* all, and not all-at-once divine energy.

Our original misperception causes us to view our classical physical world and our quantum essence world as disparate. We perceive physical matter through the lens of a oneness (particle) perception, and we perceive quantum essence through the lens of an allness (wave) perception. Once we are able to view both states of being (particle and wave, classical and quantum, oneness and allness) as being expressions of the same one divine energy, we will no longer perceive that any disparity exists. There will be only one unified bridge of conscious awareness between all perceptions and reflections of divine energy.

Expressing as human beings, we are simultaneously a "one" and an "all." But the one (our individual human consciousness) is not aware of the all (our collective unconscious all-knowing divine beingness), until it is awakened in our human conscious awareness. We are similar to that particle in that we are not aware that our allness exists; yet both one (*classical* particle) and all (*quantum* wave) are always simultaneously, fully present.

Even now we are not just a onceness. We are simultaneously co-existing as the "onceness" and the "allness" of one indivisible divine energy—though unperceived as such by us until we are awakened to the truth of our beingness. Amazing, isn't it?

Experiments involving wave collapsing into a single object are verification that conscious intent (observation) collapses the quantumness of our unlimited potentiality into classical manifested reality. But it is important to understand that when wave collapses into singularity, no quantum allness is lost in classical onceness expression. Although we may perceive this collapse as though unlimited allness is lost in that limited onceness, quantum allness is still energetically fully present at that singularity expression. There is no difference in essence between quantum wave potential or classical particle expression—only the appearance of change through our conscious perception.

Most importantly, these examples of the quantum and classical nature of our divine energetic essence reflect that consciousness affects all states of being—classical, manifested reality as well as quantum, unmanifested potentiality.

This can only mean that we, as *conscious* beings, have the ability to affect our state of beingness, our "reality."

Correlation—Example 3

Quantum World: There is a term in quantum science called *superposition*. Superposition is when an object is in all possible locations at the same time as long as it isn't being measured or observed. The act of observation causes the object to collapse into a definite single object in one location.

All-at-Once Consciousness: Everything does exist in all possible states simultaneously, because all objects are really only one inseparable divine energy—simultaneously existing as unmanifested nothingness, manifested onceness (a single thing), and manifested allness (everything). And although the act of observation causes an object to appear to manifest (collapse) into a single, limited expression, we must always remember this is a perception only because quantum allness is never limited in essence, only in "appearance."

Imagine that our allness is exemplified by a quantum (unlimited) nature while our onceness is more classical (limited). The act of conscious observation focuses the quantum energy (wave and particle) into a classical expression (particle), but that is a perception only because no separation between particle and wave has actually occurred. It is impossible due to the inseparable nature of divine energy.

We perceive separation because we are a quantum (unlimited) divine beingness perceiving, experiencing, and expressing in a classical (limited) dimension.

Correlation—Example 4

Quantum World: There is also something being viewed in quantum science called *single wave function*, which is when an observed particle is simultaneously the identical same one thing in multiple locations at once. This sounds like the same thing as superposition, but it is not. Superposition is the quantum state of simultaneously being in unlimited *potentiality* of multiple locations *before* observation. The phenomenon of single wave function (of simultaneously being the identical same one thing in multiple locations at once) occurs *after* observation, which is an impossibility in our classical world because something cannot simultaneously exist as the identical same one thing in multiple places at the same time. Yet scientists are viewing this "impossibility."

All-at-Once Consciousness: The reason that science is seeing the identical same one thing in multiple locations at once is because they are witnessing the very fabric of our beingness. Everything is simultaneously existing as the same one thing in multiple locations at once, because we are only ever one inseparable, indivisible divine energy in any expression or appearance.

The most difficult part about understanding the multiple appearances of a single wave function is that they are not "parts" of one thing. They are identically the same one thing, appearing to simultaneously exist in multiple places at the same time.

Think about it a minute. This would be like you appearing as multiple clones of yourself *except* those appearances are not duplications of you. Rather, they are the identical "one" you simultaneously existing in multiple locations at the same time. Everyone can wrap their head around the concept that something is a duplicated part of something else, but it is a lot more difficult (and extraordinary) to grasp that the same one thing is simultaneously existing in multiple places at the same time. Even in the phenomenon of simultaneous, multi-state existence, there are no parts and no duplications, ever. There is just one inseparable divine energy (All-at-Once Consciousness), appearing as separate manifested objects because of our conscious perception.

And even though I have no specific knowledge that this is being viewed in scientific experiments, something is both in singularity (particle) as well as allness (wave and particle) at the same time, and they are identically the same energetic essence in any and all forms and in any and all locations. The viewing of it may appear to be in line with classical physics, but the underlying subatomic fabric would reflect the simultaneous phenomenon of allness still being fully present even at a onceness expression. Wave could even behave as particle and particle could behave as wave because allness (wave and particle) is always 100 percent present at each and every onceness (particle) expression. It cannot be any other way, due to the intrinsic nature of our all-at-once divine conscious beingness—no matter how it may appear to be otherwise.

As in "Correlation—Example 1," entanglement is viewed as being energetically connected. In truth, everything is not just connected ... ***everything*** is identically the same one divine energy in any expression.

The very essence of our beingness is simultaneously both particle and wave; conscious and unconscious; real and unreal; classical and quantum. We are always existing as a quantum "potential" state everywhere at once (All-at-Once Consciousness). It is consciousness that determines "expression" and "perception."

This concept is very difficult for us to comprehend because it is not the way in which we typically perceive our reality, but it is absolutely true. Even in relation to us, when one energy (one soul consciousness) is affected, all energy (other soul consciousnesses) experience/react, whether they consciously perceive that they are inseparably, indivisibly one divine consciousness or not. Everything (all-knowingness) is always being broadcast throughout the entirety of collective human consciousness, even if it is not *consciously* perceived by anyone. This is why awareness may be mirrored (duplicated) in individuals, groups, or cultures separated by great distance (space) and time (years or even generations). And most importantly, when awareness shifts in one consciousness, the *entire* collective is affected whether consciously known or not, as consciousness is not limited to a location or any single individual, even though consciousness appears to be localized.

Always we must be mindful that our quantum-like experiences (experiential reality) may not yet be consciously understood by others nor recognized by science, yet these experiences are glimpses of what is at the very foundation of our beingness—the essence of our extraordinary nature.

Although we can experience states of conscious beingness that appear as both real (physical) and unreal (etheric), nothing is real in the sense we have come to define as real, but everything is made real through divine consciousness.

At first the concept that nothing is real created a sense of panic in me because I perceived the concept to mean "nothingness" and that nothing would remain. Then I realized that my perception was created from a state of fear. In reality, the concept of *not real* means anything and everything possible—limitless unmanifested possibility (quantum potentiality).

Why? It is because we, as *pure divine consciousness*, can never end. We are an energetic vibration, and energy is never extinguished. We can go anywhere, because consciousness is nonlocal—not bound by space or time. We are capable of manifesting wonderful experiences of any type for as long as we intend, because we are divine conscious co-creators of our own realities. And we, as pure divine consciousness, can remember all of who we have been as Avatars of Consciousness as well as everything that every other Avatar of Consciousness has ever been, because we are eternally one divine conscious energy.

If that isn't exciting, I don't know what is!

That is our truth, and it has always been our truth. We have just momentarily forgotten.

Although many of us, especially scientists, seek to understand the origins of the seen universe, that origin does not exist as matter in a specific location. All lifetimes, all experiences, and all aspects of matter that we perceive as a seen universe outside of us—reaching into the vastness of space—are in actuality a reflection from within the limitlessness of divine conscious energy. There is no outside place. Everything is one inseparable consciousness.

Is it possible that science may eventually be able to explain consciousness? Hmm ... I can't imagine how that can happen, due to the nature of reality (a reflection of divine consciousness), but it is fascinating to ponder. Scientists are phenomenal beings, great conscious ponderers, so, I'm going to imagine that it will be so!

Remember, Avatars of Consciousness, even though we appear to be expressing as a "onceness" while simultaneously experiencing two different vibrational realities (classical and quantum), we are always identically the same one inseparable divine energy in any appearance. Think of our human conscious mind as the *one*, more classical in nature, and our higher (divine) consciousness as the *all*, more quantum in nature. We are simultaneously both classical and quantum, human consciousness and higher consciousness, and one and all. Thus, we are a living, human expression of All-at-Once Consciousness.

Our perception—that we are either losing our allness when in individual self expression or we are losing our self when in collective allness is reflected in not only our spiritual concepts but also in the way in which we perceive our world. We fear losing our all-knowing consciousness through collapsing into individual expression; and we fear losing our self identity through merging back with collective allness. In reality, even though it appears that something is lost in either onceness or allness, nothing of us is ever lost or diminished in any conscious expression. The higher conscious thought, *All is not lost; nothing is gained* perfectly illustrates our truth, as nothing can ever be lost or gained when only one pure energy exists.

If we view our universe through the lens that everything is only one indivisible divine energy, then the classical world we embody as physical human beings is unified to the quantum world of our higher (divine) consciousness through the concept of All-at-Once Consciousness—a unifying concept that applies to everything:

- The essence of our divine beingness is unified to physical matter we perceive.
- Spirituality is unified/bridged with science.
- Science is unified with itself (classical and quantum physics).

The formula for bridging disparity in us as well as in science is to understand that the true nature of everything, seen and unseen, is the All-at-Once Consciousness of one indivisible divine energy.

Then, by shifting our perception, we will better understand ourselves and our seen and unseen world—and hopefully, we will be able to eventually know everything as *it is* rather than as ***how it appears***.

Epilogue

As I am standing at my kitchen sink, rinsing dishes and thinking about all of the profound experiences of my life and my interaction with higher consciousness (Benevolence), vision-like scenes begin clicking off in my mind as though I am being shown relevant snapshots of consciousness experienced throughout my current lifetime.

Snapshot 1

I am nine years old, and it is a short time after my profound experience with divinity while watching clouds in my front yard.

It is the first day of the new school year, and I have found myself just standing in the drizzling rain in front of the school. I was standing where the buses pull in to load and unload students, completely unaware of how or when I had even arrived at where I was standing. It felt as though I had just awakened from sleepwalking. I knew who I was, of course, and where I lived, but it was as though the memory of that day was not accessible to me at the moment. I felt very strange, the same as I had after my transcendent experience with Benevolence where I found myself just walking down the street away from my house, as though I was going home.

Buses were pulling into the curved area of the drive in front of the school, and as they filled with students and pulled away, I remained still, focusing on trying to remember anything of the day. It was all gone—as if it never happened. I lived on the street right next to the school, and all I had to do was turn to my left, walk around the school, and head through the woods and I would be home.

Still, I could not move. It was as though something wanted me to be aware of this very moment. I realized I was still a little girl, but I no longer felt only aware of just my little girl world. I was fully aware of my energetic connection to a benevolent presence within me—but it was more than just a connection. It was as though the presence and I were of the same mind, of the same energy.

Looking out through my eyes into the world before me, I sensed vastness in front of me and behind me, as though there was limitlessness all around the embodiment of my physical beingness.

My eyes felt full of love and knowing, as though the vibration of love and awareness was flowing from an eternal wave behind me, moving all the way through me, and then pouring out of my eyes into the world before me. My energy field felt as though I was enlivened by the kinetic power of that pure vibration of love and all-knowing awareness flowing through me. It felt as though I had just arrived at the threshold of a new world and was about to take my first step.

A wave of absolute peace enfolded me, and all the struggles of my mind and my fear abated. Now there was only the peace, the wave of love, and a feeling as though a robe of pristine white light had enveloped me.

The world before me seemed to be shimmering, as though the pure reflection of that light was welcoming me. I felt alive, filled with love, and there was a sense of purpose, as though I was gathering myself before embarking on a voyage that I knew would take me far and deep into the realm before me—the world that shimmered with promise. I felt such deep connectedness that there was no fear, no worry … nothing except absolute love. It was as though love was standing as me and I was standing as love. Movement was not even considered as expanding awareness surged through all cells of my body and all feelings and thoughts merged with this benevolent presence.

For a moment I wondered if the feeling of this presence would leave me when normal sensation returned. But then my thoughts traveled to the people, the children and the adults, around me, and I wondered if they too were experiencing this extraordinary moment. And my knowing gave me the answer. No, they were preoccupied with movement and activity. I alone was encapsulated in absolute stillness.

My heart kept hoping that Benevolence would lift me back up to that place of profound bliss previously experienced. Yet knowing told me that benevolent place of peace and all-knowing love was right there with me even now. I felt whole, well, happy, strong, purposeful, and full of knowing. Love was carrying all these thoughts from my heart to my mind.

I had no sensation of being soaked by the rain. All I felt was warm, brilliant light and cool, peaceful knowing. *It was extraordinary.*

Then in the space of a breath, I was instantly aware of how cold and wet I felt. And although I wasn't afraid of the benevolent presence that I still sensed, I was now afraid of why I couldn't remember even getting dressed that morning or eating breakfast. Why couldn't I remember? Did I fall? Was I hurt? I didn't feel hurt. I felt like this moment was significant somehow—but why, exactly, was unclear. While little girl thoughts flooded my mind, I simultaneously felt otherworldly, as though I was still the very same benevolent presence I was only a moment ago.

Over the years, I thought about this experience, wondering at the significance of it, for there was no doubt that this benevolent presence wanted me to remember and connect to that moment.

Then, quite surprisingly, the significance of this experience was revealed in one of my sessions with Angela, triggered by an affirmation about recognizing the allness of my being. Amazingly, the *emotion* was *self-conscious*, the *origin* was *age 9* when I was standing in front of my school, and the *original emotional theme* related to "the consciousness of all through the self."

In this extraordinary session, I learned my experience at age nine was related to, "the conscious activation of *all* and *one* simultaneously moving through my waking conscious awareness."

As I'm standing in stillness at my kitchen sink, encapsulated by all the pictures and thoughts and memories flooding my consciousness, knowing awakens and I realize that the *allness* of divine Benevolence and the *oneness* of my being were consciously bridged in my individual human consciousness when I was that little girl of nine, standing in the rain struggling with remembrance.

Tears of love and joy begin to flow from my eyes, as I feel the absoluteness of that benevolent presence with me even now—a presence that has been in all the moments of my life, even the ones not consciously recognized.

And in a moment of pure conscious clarity never before experienced, I realize that everything in my life has been experienced to awaken this very knowing. My life has not been experienced to "return" to oneness or to perfect my imperfections, but to consciously awaken to the remembrance of my own all-at-once divine beingness— an *awakening* that occurred when I was nine years old.

The entire purpose of my life experiences is for that benevolent truth, that knowing, to come forth in waking conscious awareness. And the divine purpose of sharing this awakening and remembrance through this book is to help others consciously remember that what they seek is not lost or in some other place, but is right now simultaneously existing as the beingness of their divine perfection in human conscious expression.

For many minutes I am unable to process anything except the pure bliss of this unexpected moment, as I realize that I am no longer seeking anything other than to allow my remembrance to continue to unfold through all the moments I will live from this day forward.

It is an extraordinary moment where I realize the shimmering light beckoning before me was the light of my own benevolent oneness calling me to come forth and awaken from the dream of misperception.

Memories of moments of my life continue pouring through me, and I realize that my life has been a voyage that I consciously embarked upon that day at age nine when I was standing in the rain, newly awakened to my own divine consciousness. I have always been the onceness of Carol, but now I am able to consciously recognize the simultaneous allness of divinity that is my constant conscious "companion."

My heart is no longer filled with longing. I am at peace. My spiritual voyage has taken me to ports in this dimension and others— across the vastness of Universe—and I now know that it was a divinely designed, purpose-filled voyage. It was one where I would awaken to the knowing always carried within me through the experiences unfolding along the way.

Love begins moving through me as I realize that this book is a log of the truth that was discovered, and sharing that truth has been divinely intended since the day I first consciously experienced Benevolence as a little girl. Why? Because it is a truth that must be shared with everyone because it is not a voyage that only I am making. We may visit different ports, take different routes, or choose different companions or vessels, but all of us share this voyage of conscious awakening.

I am smiling in wonder and amazement as I realize how perfectly the moments of our paths are orchestrated. We can be aware or unaware, but the moments are still always occurring, and they are perfect.

Snapshot 2

In another flash, I am reliving an encounter with an angel in my childhood. The angel is speaking with me about the *reconciliation of mankind*. I was puzzled by these words and told the angel I didn't understand. The angel only smiled and told me not to worry and that I would understand in the proper time.

Although I did not understand this message as a child, I carried the words within me from that day forward. Years later as my vocabulary increased, the definition of the words reconciliation and mankind were known to me. Yet the exact meaning of the angel's message still eluded me.

The vision fades, and I am once more in present-time reality in my kitchen.

As I'm standing there, memories of other messages spoken of by angels in my childhood begin flowing through me. There were many messages given to me of things to come in future years, some of which have already happened. Others yet to be.

And in a moment of lucid consciousness, I realize that we are presently living the message of which this angel spoke, the reconciliation of mankind. Change is upon us; our consciousness is shifting. But these changes are not to be feared, because they will assist us in our awakening. These planetary, economic, energetic changes are catalysts for the new paradigm shift divinely designed to awaken all collective human consciousness.

It is important to realize that the divine intention of experiencing human consciousness is to bridge awareness between our perceived nature and our true nature, consciously shift our misperception, and awaken remembrance of our extraordinary divine beingness.

Throughout the ages, there have been mystics, sages, and spiritual beings that have foreseen tremendous changes that will occur on our planet as humanity transforms to a loving and peaceful people. And though we are approaching one of the most significant of times for mankind, as spoken of by an angel in my childhood, it is very important to realize that anything can be altered by the conscious intention of love.

Rather than focus on the negatives of what could transpire, it is much more powerful and beneficial for us to hold the conscious vibration of love as our intention. Not only will this affect the individual realities we live, but through the joint effort of all of us holding love as our conscious center, we will also affect the realities the entire collective experiences.

At first, when we consciously hold the vibration of love, it may not appear that much has changed, but as the shift in consciousness continues, we will get traction and begin to consciously affect ourselves, each other, and our planet—everything. Then once we are more awakened as a collective, disruptive natural, economic, and physical experiences will no longer be necessary to get our attention. These experiences only exist as a reflection of what is incongruent and needs to be reconciled between ourselves as mankind and our true nature as divine energy.

We as mankind will then be in the process of remembering, and what is disharmonious will continue to fall away as our remembrance comes forth. Eventually, all will come into alignment. The *conscious I* and *our divine nature* will be reconciled as one divine beingness. And we will be consciously living as our divine essence. The incongruency between mankind's perceived nature and true divine nature will be *reconciled*. Can you imagine it? I can. I've seen it. It is the divine destiny shown to me by the angel of my childhood.

Snapshot 3

A snapshot of a higher conscious moment from years before pours through my mind. In this snapshot, I am interacting with a familiar spiritual energy as the following higher (conscious) thought flows through my mind, *"The dimensions are collapsing."*

Over the years, I had pondered the meaning of these words. Now, as I'm standing transfixed in my kitchen, the meaning of this message is clarified through higher (divine) conscious thoughts.

The dimensions of collective human consciousness are collapsing back into themselves, as this *venue*, created by divinity for our

336

awakening, will no longer be necessary. Even now we should be heartened by the quickening that is occurring—the accelerating collapse of the dimensions—because it heralds that our full remembrance is nearly awakened within all of us.

The signs of the collapsing dimensions are why time seems to fly by faster and faster each year. One day it is New Year's Eve, and only a short time later, it is June. Never before has time seemed to fly by so fast. Time appears to be accelerating because as the dimensions continue to collapse, we will feel the momentum of the collapse and the overlap of the dimensions through our own waking consciousness, creating an illusion that slower-paced time seems to have all but disappeared.

Time is not really disappearing but rather *perceived* space in consciousness is collapsing, causing our conscious perception of time to shift. Time and space are inseparably entwined as part of the venue of collective human consciousness (the divine blueprint of our awakening), created by divinity as a tool to assist us in remembering our true essence. Time only *exists* to afford us space in our consciousness to experience, express, reflect, and perceive. There is no true time or space in divine energy ... divine energy exists all-at-once.

Time and space are an illusion created by the mirroring of divine energy as part of the original act of Creation. Without time and space we would be unable to consciously perceive the depth of our true essence. Think of it as though we are fully encapsulated, fully immersed, in our beingness as a one-dimensional divine energy—a beingness that is an All-at-Once Consciousness. In order to help us awaken to the truth of our nature, divinity created a playground, a venue, of awakening. This venue would be a multi-dimensional state of consciousness (collective human consciousness) that would include time and space as a way for us to be able to *consciously* step off to the side of our divine self—our all-at-once nature—in order to gain perspective and comprehend all the nuances of our beingness. Think of it as though we were unable to perceive our true essence while in our one-dimensional state of divine beingness because we have fallen asleep to our divine self and are experiencing a state of divine amnesia while in the dream of misperception.

Think of time and space as a *consciousness air bubble* in divine energy. And although this air bubble is important to help facilitate our awakening, it is also a reflection of our conscious perception of separation. When we no longer perceive ourselves as separate, time and space will cease to exist. Thus, time and space is a reflection of our conscious misperception of separation—a reflection of what is incongruent in our consciousness. Once we are *fully awakened* to the remembrance of our eternal, limitless divine energy, there will no longer be the *reflection* of time and space because our perceived sense of separation will no longer exist ... There will no longer be anything to cast the reflection of misperception, as we will be fully reconciled to our true divine nature.

As space continues to collapse, overlapping dimensions will result in conscious access to subtler planes of consciousness. More and more people will be experiencing quantum (paranormal) phenomena than ever before.

Think once more of the accordion as representing the venue of collective human consciousness. This fully extended accordion is now in the process of the pleats (dimensions) collapsing back into a flattened, one-dimensional state. Once all dimensions, all realms, and all realities are collapsed back into one dimension, it will be as it was prior to the original act of Creation, with one extraordinary difference. Now, we will be fully awakened from the dream of misperception to the absolute bliss of our all-at-once divine beingness.

The collapsing dimensions are a beautiful sign that we are nearly fully awakened to our remembrance and our venue for awakening will no longer be necessary. Think of it as a tremendous opportunity to consciously experience simultaneous, multi-state consciousness—lucid dreaming, higher conscious events, interaction with angels and other spiritual beings, and more conscious perception of our higher self. It is an extraordinary time for humanity.

Once we as Divine QUA are fully awakened to our remembrance, the divine purpose for the original act of Creation will be fulfilled, and we will consciously experience beyond what can even be imagined in our present state of human consciousness!

Although we may not consciously realize it, the foundation is already set within us for the magnificence of our beingness to come forth in conscious expression. Even now we are beginning to experience glimmers of our radiant beingness breaking through our perceived barriers of human awareness.

As I'm standing in the stillness of my kitchen, pure joy fills my heart as I realize that no one will be left out or fall short—absolutely no one.

When I was a little girl, my knowing of Benevolence (divinity) did not match religious concepts being taught to me. One concept was about hell being an eternal place for those who didn't believe. My knowing told me it couldn't be true. If divinity is in everything (every blade of grass, every soul, every energetic expression), then how could divinity abandon even one blade of grass, let alone one soul? It would essentially mean divinity was abandoning divinity. Impossible. No soul can be lost forever because no energy is ever truly lost. To me this sounded like a manmade concept to scare people into believing there are time limits being given by an impatient divinity. Absurd. We are divinity as divinity is us; nothing of us can ever be lost.

Our story is about all of us. It is not a truth that discriminates or restricts anyone. I especially love that part. While it is true that some may come to the awareness more quickly, it is not true that there is a hierarchy in divine energy. If we are all identically the same one thing, how can there be levels or hierarchy? It would be like saying divinity is more divine than divinity or perfection is more perfect than perfection.

I absolutely love that no one is left out. No one needs worry about getting kicked off the team for being too slow, too aggressive, too nerdy, or too skeptical. We are one team—actually, we are a one-member team wearing different hats.

I thought about all the things I could share with you as far as concepts to help you more consciously awaken, and I've come to a suggestion that I think is perfect for wherever you are in your conscious unfoldment.

When we sleep, we are experiencing simultaneous, multi-state consciousness. By placing a piece of paper with the name of this book (or a copy of the book) underneath your pillow, the vibrational message of *"The Extraordinary Truth About Consciousness, Creation & Us"* will flow into your subconscious. Then, as is appropriate to your individual awakening, knowing will unfold in your conscious awareness.

We must always intend to hold love within our conscious mind and our expressing heart. The more we love, the more we awaken to our true self and the entire collective.

Throughout my life, interactions with higher consciousness have helped me tremendously in being able to understand spiritual truths. A specific, beautiful thought from my higher consciousness, conveyed many years ago, helped me to realize the nature of truth:

"Truth stands as its own light.
What you believe doesn't make
truth any more or any less true."

Truth just is. No opinion we hold of truth, one way or the other, alters the weight or veracity of truth.

The beauty of truth is that it stands as its own light, and when we are able to stand as our own light, unaffected by circumstances, opinions, or experiences, just being light, love, and truth, we will awaken conscious awareness of the allness of our beingness in the moments we are living.

Always, seek truth and light will come; seek light and love will come; and seek love purely for the essence of love, and **all** will come … it can be no other way, for love is the essence of our true divine nature.

Avatars of Consciousness, Awaken to Your Divine Destiny…

Your reality is even more profound than any dream imagined.
Come forth and embrace yourselves,
each other, and all … in love.

Afterword

As I am anticipating your *awakening to your divine destiny,* I am reminded of the higher conscious insight, "You are divinity's living experience. As you experience, divinity experiences." I love this thought. It is so true. We are all simultaneously experiencing not only our self but also each other and all of divine consciousness.

Remember: Do not strip away your identity in order to try and conform. We are not divinely designed to be *identical in expression*—only *identical in essence.* We were divinely designed as creative consciousness. Be creative! Enjoy yourself! Enjoy others! I think we've done a terrific job at all of this (considering that we've had a very severe case of spiritual amnesia).

Less than three years ago, my true essence had been eroded to the point that my joy was stifled and my enthusiasm had definitely waned. But now, I am enlivened and invigorated with the possibilities ahead. One extraordinary moment leads to another. No matter how you have perceived yourself in the past, now know the truth: You are perfection—always. You are love—always. You are divine energy—always. Don't ever give up. You are not alone, and you matter. We all matter. You are love itself, and love is all that matters. Be kind to yourselves and others, for we are all experiencing the most extraordinary manifestation of our beingness in individual human consciousness but we are not always consciously aware of the true magnificence we embody ... divine All-at-Once Consciousness.

And if, by chance, you should ever have the misperception that another's light is brighter than your own, *remember:*

"Light does not shine to point out darkness, but rather light shines
to trigger remembrance in all of us so we may awaken to our
knowing that we are eternally one vibration of love
... divine consciousness itself."

Beloved ones, you are loved beyond your comprehension ... now and always.

Acknowledgments

First, I would like to thank all those wonderful benevolent energies that have guided, protected, and uplifted me throughout my life. I would like to thank them not only for the major things, such as saving my life on several occasions, but also for all of the conscious interaction related to simple things, such as available parking spaces, and profound things involving inspirational concepts and spiritual insights.

I'm so very grateful for the companionship that is always with me and years spent engaging and interacting has taught me that this divine presence (Benevolence) is with everyone. It is my hope that my experiences will help others to recognize what is already present in their own lives.

When I was a young child, there were memories of other places, other lifetimes, but the most sacred memory was of a benevolent presence I can only describe as divinity and a place of love and perfection that can only be called home. For years I thought the reason I remembered was just so that I could remain close to these vibrations while experiencing human incarnation.

Now I realize it is because I was intended to live the contents of my life as an example of what we all embody as well as what we all long to awaken.

Many thanks to Louise L. Hay for creating the vehicle (Balboa Press) through which I am able to share this book with humanity on behalf of the divine conscious vibration of love that is our very own nature—a divine nature that can heal any and all emotional, mental, physical, or spiritual incongruencies that prevent us from living and expressing our most profound self. Ms. Hay, you are a loving, inspirational light; a true trailblazer; and a spiritual blessing to humanity.

I also extend immeasurable appreciation to everyone at Balboa Press that worked on bringing this book into the world. Heartfelt prayers go out to all of you for your personal well-being and continuing success.

There are many people who have shown me love and friendship in this life but none more profoundly when working on this book than Ellen Barber, my friend and spiritual sister who made any difficulty easier by your calm nature and gifts of intuition and faith. In any situation, your steadfast friendship has never wavered. You are loyal, loving, and selfless, Ellen, and the quiet way in which you conduct yourself and live your life is inspirational. You are very much appreciated by someone who recognizes the beautiful essence within you that illuminates our friendship.

To John Briggs, a truly wonderful and supportive friend. Thank you for not only being an interesting and entertaining conversationalist, able to deliver wit, humor, and insight through your words, but also for your generous heart and gracious spirit that provides comfort and support to those of us fortunate enough to know you as friend. I'm very grateful to you, John, not just for making the publication of this book possible but also for the swift, benevolent, and trusting manner in which you stepped forward to help. May you be forever blessed for the part you played in making this message known.

Loving thoughts also to Raoul Cohen for being the most naturally optimistic, fun-loving, and joy-filled person I've ever known. Thank you for all the kindness, love, and support you have shown me throughout my life. Most of all, Raoul, I am forever in your debt for awakening my awareness to how wonderful and magical life can be. I give you heartfelt gratitude for all the shared joy and for teaching me so many things about how to live life. Attitude is everything, as you well demonstrate, and a sense of wonderment is not just for children! I am forever blessed by knowing you and calling you true friend. Je t'aime, Monsieur Tortue.

Though he would want no mention, my deepest love and appreciation to my husband for recognizing my true essence and giving it flight in this world and others through his love, support, and encouragement of my unusual abilities and expressions. Our many profound conversations reflect the deeply insightful and wise spirit that resides within you, though your love of divinity and spiritual truth touches my heart beyond all others. Although you never would claim it, you are the kindest of hearts, the strongest of spirit, and the most inquisitive of nature that I will ever be blessed to know. Forever and ever and three days may not be enough to thank you, sweetheart, for your spiritual companionship and for always making me feel safe and loved no matter how unusual, difficult, or profound the experience.

And of course, special thanks to Angela King, AP, DOM (Acupuncture Physician, Doctor of Oriental Medicine). Thank you, Angela, for your assistance in helping these profound glimpses of enlightened awareness to so purely unfold while my higher consciousness and subconscious spoke of things experienced throughout my soul divinity's journey as an Avatar of Consciousness from the very beginning of collective human consciousness. Heartfelt blessings to you, Angela, for helping me to bring forth and fulfill my soul's purpose in a space where I felt supported, comfortable, and understood even when the information revealed stretched the boundaries of human conscious awareness. Although your role in my life was revealed to me many years ago by higher (divine) consciousness, it manifested in a way that was more profound and inspirational than I ever could have dreamed. I am forever grateful to you for helping this knowing to consciously awaken—a knowing held dormant in my consciousness since childhood—for I now know it was always divinely designed to happen in just this manner. May you always know that you are loved and respected as a person, a professional practitioner, and a soul divinity by someone who recognizes a light and love in you capable of releasing those desiring to be set free of all that has bound them from experiencing peaceful and happy lives; embracing their life purpose; or even fulfilling their soul's destiny—thank you, Angela.

Most importantly, always and forever I am grateful to have a conscious relationship with divinity. No more needs be said in words, for my heart, my mind, and the love I feel for divinity and humanity is well known within divine Benevolence.

I am grateful, so very, very grateful, for the life I am blessed to be living and to be so consciously experiencing the grace of benevolent love that is eternally ours ...

—*Carol Romine*

About the Author

Carol considers Florida her truest home on earth, for it is the place where the bliss of spiritual awakening unfolded through the inner path of a mystic and spiritual teacher. In this place so near the ocean, while interacting with kindred spirits—many of whom she has been blessed to know as friends—the profound promise of her childhood was fulfilled.

Carol shares her spirit through writing, teaching, and lecturing to help others understand universal truth and connect with their own inner knowing to consciously awaken, clear misperception, and live their truest life.

Carol welcomes you to visit her at Facebook or her websites to view upcoming events; to learn more about group workshops and private sessions; and to download tools and materials intended to awaken consciousness, engage and interact with higher consciousness through intuition, and bridge awareness of our true nature of divine All-at-Once Consciousness.

Websites: www.carolromine.com
               www.avatars-awaken.com

Facebook: www.facebook.com/carolromine.avatar